Casseroles
COOKBOOK

Dear Homemaker,

The creative preparation of delicious casseroles is another of the invaluable books included in the Favorite Recipes of Home Economics Teachers Cookbooks series. America's home economics teachers graciously share their favorite recipes with you and demonstrate their remarkable versatility with casseroles of all kinds. A wide variety of exciting new ideas will teach you marvelous techniques to spark your menus with new interest and best of all, utilize leftovers with imagination and good taste!

We gratefully acknowledge the contributions of those teachers who sent us their home-tested recipes for inclusion in this volume. The compilation of this cookbook would not be possible without their enthusiastic willingness to share their cooking ingenuity.

Thank you for your interest and confidence in the Favorite Recipes of Home Economics Teachers Cookbooks. We are certain that the many reliable and imaginative casserole recipes contained in this book will become your family favorites, too. Remember, by purchasing this volume, you are not only enriching your cookbook library, you are also supporting your school's home economics department. Thank you.

Sincerely yours,

Mary Anne Richards

Mary Anne Richards

© Favorite Recipes Press MCMLXXIII
P. O. Box 3396, Montgomery, Alabama 36109
Library of Congress Catalog Card No. 73-91836
ISBN 0-87197-059-7

Preface

The tantalizing aroma of meats and vegetables blending their flavors
. . . the mouth-watering sight of a bubbling hot meal-in-a-dish . . . the
sheer joy of popping your entire supper into the oven to bake . . .
welcome to the wonderful world of casseroles!

It *is* a wonderful world, for casseroles are among the most versatile
dishes known. Home Economics Teachers know how convenient and
well suited casseroles are to the menu plans of today's busy homemakers. Accordingly, they have submitted recipes in a wide variety
of categories that will satisfy every possible need. Just browse
through the pages. Beef and veal . . . ground beef . . . pork . . .
poultry . . . fish and shellfish . . . lamb and game . . . combination
meats . . . vegetables . . . cereals, pasta, egg and cheese . . . these are
the classifications of delicious casserole recipes you'll find in this
useful new cookbook.

And there's more! There is a General Information section that gives
many helpful hints about the fine art of casserole cookery. There is a
description of the many types of casserole dishes and how to choose
the right one(s) for your specific needs. In addition, there is an
informative section which tells how to use herbs and spices to the
best advantage when adding seasonings to your casserole recipes.
There are also some very helpful and time-saving hints on freezing
casseroles for later use.

This is a book for today's modern homemakers from Home Economics Teachers throughout the nation. The excellent recipes and helpful
hints contained within its covers are certain to make it an indispens-
able part of every cookbook library.

Cover Recipe

STEW BRASILIA

2 pork chops
1 lb. round steak
2 links pork sausage
1 lg. green pepper
1/4 c. Planters peanut oil
1/2 c. chopped onion
2 cloves of garlic, crushed
1 tbsp. (firmly packed) light
    brown sugar
1 1/2 tsp. salt
1/2 tsp. turmeric
1/4 tsp. cayenne pepper
1/4 tsp. oregano leaves
Generous dash of powdered saffron
1/2 c. water
1 tbsp. white vinegar
2 pimentos, cut into strips
3 c. hot cooked rice
1/2 c. Planters cocktail peanuts

Cut pork chops, steak and sausage into bite-sized cubes, reserving bones of pork chops. Cut green pepper into 1/2-inch thick strips. Heat oil in Dutch oven or large, heavy skillet. Add meats and pork bones, about 1/3 at a time; cook, stirring frequently, until well browned, removing meats from Dutch oven after each portion is browned. Add onion and garlic to Dutch oven and cook until golden, stirring frequently. Return meats to Dutch oven. Add brown sugar, salt, turmeric, cayenne pepper, oregano, saffron and green pepper; stir in water and vinegar. Cover; simmer for 45 minutes. Remove bones; stir in half the pimento strips. Place rice around outside of serving bowl; spoon meat mixture into center of bowl. Sprinkle with peanuts; garnish with remaining pimento strips. Serve with fresh vegetable salad, if desired. Yield: 4-6 servings.

Photograph for this recipe on cover.

Color Explanation

This edition of the HET Cookbook series contains hundreds of exciting casserole recipes chosen and submitted by the nation's home economics teachers. Beautiful full-color photographs, chosen by the editors of Favorite Recipes Press, expand the book into other food subject areas. We hope that the colorful photographs located throughout this volume will offer you menu ideas to add to your cooking enjoyment.

Contents

Casseroles –
Main Dish Magic

Casserole cookery began over 200 years ago in France. The term *casserole* developed about 1725 from the word *casse*, a utensil used by European cooks for cooking stews and other large amounts of food. The *casse* was and still is a squat-type container with bulging sides, easily grasped round handles and a slightly arched lid.

Even today in France the term *casserole* refers to a cooking vessel made of metal or pottery. However, we Americans, sometime around the 19th century, began to refer to the *contents* of the cooking vessel as a casserole. And today the term *casserole* is sometimes confusing because we use both meanings.

There are many terms to describe casseroles — delicious, filling, nutritious — but the most frequent term used by modern homemakers is *easy*. Casseroles are a simple yet delicious way to bring together main course foods in one dish. Such a wonderful advantage allows today's housewife to add bread, salad and a beverage and serve a filling meal with minimal time and effort.

Another descriptive term for casseroles is *economical*. They present a wonderful way to serve leftovers. Tidbits of leftover meat and vegetables take on a delightfully different flavor when combined with sauces or consommes and served as a bubbly hot casserole. Less tender cuts of meat, which are likewise less expensive, are perfectly adapted because they demand long cooking at low temperatures, as most casseroles do.

Just because casseroles are simple to prepare and economical to serve doesn't mean they aren't suitable for the most formal dinner party. They can be as elaborate as you wish to make them. And for this reason, homemakers are particularly pleased that the preparation of casseroles doesn't demand constant attention. In fact, many casseroles can be made a day ahead of time and kept covered in the refrigerator until ready to bake. Hostesses can relax and chat with guests right up until serving time.

Casseroles are fun to experiment with, too. Try new combinations of meats, vegetables, sauces, consommes, seasonings and spices. With a dash of this and a bit of that, you can create casserole masterpieces. Cut pastry toppings into unusual designs. Add vegetables or herbs you've never before included. Use a variety of canned creamed soups or jiffy gravy mixes. Experiment with a wide variety of seasonings — mashed garlic — lemon juice — mustard — catsup — chili sauce — salad dressing — tomato sauce — parsley — tomato paste — and many others. Take one of your old casserole recipes and substitute new ingredients for old ones. You'll be surprised what you can create with a little imagination.

Making
of a Casserole

Basically, casseroles are made in four ways: with meat, a combination of meat and vegetables, vegetables, or cereals and pastas. To these four bases, you can add any foods, flavorings and seasonings you want. Gravies or sauces add flavor to meat dishes. Canned creamed soups are convenient and add zest to most casseroles. Cooked rice, spaghetti, noodles and macaroni are economical and make leftovers go further.

Even without a definite recipe, you can conjure up a taste-tempting casserole. Just prepare two cups of chopped meat, fish, poultry or vegetables (leftovers are perfectly suitable). Combine with two cups of sauce or gravy. Place the mixture in a 1 1/2-quart casserole. Top with bread crumbs flaked with butter and bake.

Of course, you may add any selection of ingredients you wish, and as many as you like. You may choose also from a wide variety of delicious toppings: bread crumbs, cracker crumbs, cereals, potato chips, corn chips, biscuits, cheese . . . the list is limited only by your imagination.

Actually toppings have a double advantage. They not only provide additional flavor, but they also serve to protect the surface of the casserole and prevent the ingredients from drying out.

Most toppings are added in the last few minutes of baking so that they may be delicately browned in the oven just before serving. Follow recipes and cooking instructions closely in order to insure that the topping will be properly cooked.

As previously mentioned, a good way to begin creating your own casseroles is by taking an old casserole recipe and substituting new ingredients. You will not only come up with a brilliant new concoction, but you will also have lots of fun.

In casserole recipes, you will find some instructional terms mentioned repeatedly. The following list presents most of these terms and defines them for you.

Au gratin — To top with bread crumbs or cheese
Bake — To cook foods in the oven
Bind — To hold foods together with a sauce
Blend — To thoroughly mix two or more ingredients
Chop — To cut into pieces with a sharp knife
Dice — To cut into small cubes
Dot — To scatter small pieces of butter or other fat over the top of foods
Dredge — To coat with flour or crumbs
Flake — To break into small pieces with a fork
Garnish — To decorate foods, usually with other foods
Grate — To cut food into minute particles by rubbing on a grater
Julienne — To cut or chop into long, thin strips
Mince — To cut or chop into very small pieces
Mix — To combine ingredients in any way that evenly distributes them
Saute — To cook quickly in a small amount of fat
Scallop — To bake food in layers with a sauce
Shred — To cut finely with a knife or sharp instrument
Sliver — To slice into long, thin strips
Stir — To mix foods with a circular motion for the purpose of blending or securing uniform consistency

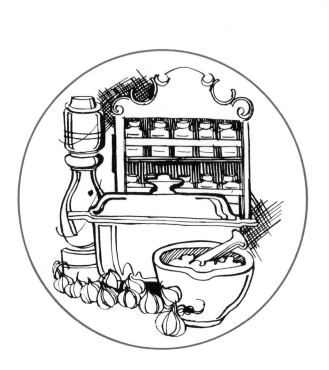

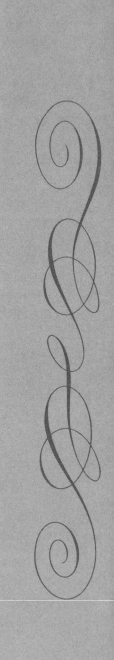

Herbs
and Spices
for Casseroles

In the process of creating new casseroles, don't forget to
try many different spices and herbs. They, too, add
remarkable flavor to casseroles. Enjoy experimenting
with different ones. If you are unfamiliar with flavors of
some herbs and spices, use the chart on the following
page as a guide.

Herbs and Spices for Casseroles

BASIL — a slight peppery, clove-like flavor

Beef, pork, lamb, veal dishes; poultry, seafood; cheese souffles.

BAY LEAF — aromatic, slightly bitter taste

Lamb, veal, beef, poultry and fish.

CARAWAY SEED — pleasantly spicy, warm taste

Cabbage, turnips, cauliflower.

CHILI POWDER — hot or sweet, biting

Ground beef, poultry, vegetables, sauces.

CINNAMON — slightly sweet

Baked beans, sweet potatoes, squash; ham, lamb.

CURRY POWDER — several ground spices

Fish, seafood, poultry, rice.

GINGER — pungent taste

Chopped beef, lamb, veal.

MARJORAM — sweet, fragrant

Creamed veal, beef, lamb, fish; mixed greens; green vegetables.

MUSTARD — biting, pungent

Baked beans, lima beans; most casseroles.

OREGANO — strong, pungent flavor

Spanish, Mexican, Italian casseroles; barbecue sauce; green bean casserole.

PAPRIKA — mildly pungent

Vegetable; fish, poultry.

PEPPER — biting, pungent

Meat, egg, seafood, vegetables, cheese dishes; sauces, gravies.

ROSEMARY — sweet, delicate flavor

Egg; beef, veal, pork, lamb.

SAFFRON — aromatic, pungent

Curries; poultry, rice.

SAGE — bitterish, astringent taste

Butter and meat sauces; pork, poultry, fish.

SAVORY — agreeably piquant taste

Egg, beef, ham; mixed greens; green vegetables.

TARRAGON — tangy, spicy flavor

Fish, squab, chicken, duck, steak.

THYME — pungent flavor

Tomato dishes, eggplant, mushroom, beets.

Containers for Casseroles

To American homemakers, a casserole is a one-dish main course, or a complete meal in a dish. But to their French counterparts, a casserole is the special kind of dish for oven or top-of-the-stove cooking in which these recipes are prepared. These dishes come in many sizes, shapes and materials.

Covered baking dishes may be round, oblong, square or oval. Many have handles. The most popular sizes are 1, 1 1/2 and 2-quart sizes.

Shallow rectangular baking dishes are sometimes divided with partitions so that two casseroles may be baked at once. The most common sizes are the 1 1/2-quart (10 x 6 x 1 1/2), the 2-quart (11 1/2 x 7 1/2 x 1 1/2), and the 3-quart (13 x 9 x 2).

Shallow, round, open baking pans are excellent values because they double as cake pans. They are recommended as a suitable substitute for a **gratin** dish.

Individual casseroles are available in either earthenware or other ovenproof materials. The usual size for an individual serving is one cup. Therefore, a recipe for one quart of a casserole mixture will fill four individual dishes.

Nice-to-have dishes include porcelain souffle dishes which are straight-sided and ramekins, a kind of individual souffle dish. Either type may be adapted for any kind of casserole cookery, not just souffles.

What are today's casserole dishes made of? Just about every material imaginable, ranging from the earthenware used in a Swiss fondue pot (which serves as an excellent casserole dish) to the freezer-to-oven dishes so popular with American homemakers. One of the best and most attractive materials is enamel-covered cast iron. It is sturdy, colorful and will keep food warm for some time after it is removed from the oven. There are ovenproof glass casseroles of the Pyrex type which may be "dressed up" by placing them in a wicker or metal casserole holder, available wherever cooking utensils are sold. Bright and beautiful casserole dishes are available in California clay, too. Chip resistant and flameproof, these gaily colored casserole dishes are made from thick pottery, glazed on the rims, the inside and the cover. The body is unglazed, natural terra cotta. These warm earth colors bring lovely accents to your dinner table. Finally, there are the tin-lined copper casserole pans, often referred to as **gratin** dishes. These are among the very finest dishes available and, like other fine things, they require special care. Copper is very soft and needs careful handling. A wooden spoon is a "must" for stirring, because wood will not scratch the delicate copper or its tin lining. The lining may wear off and need replacing. So, in spite of their elegant appearance and efficient heat-conducting properties, a copper casserole pan may not be the most practical investment for a young and active family.

In addition to casserole dishes, there are many other pots and pans which are helpful to have for casserole preparation. A **double-boiler** is great for cheese sauces and egg dishes which must be cooked over indirect heat. The **single-pan chafing dish** and its deeper cousin, the **fondue pot**, are nice to have. The food is cooked over direct heat supplied by an alcohol or canned heat burner or electricity.

The **Bain-marie** (from the French word for water bath) chafing dishes combine the virtues of single pan dishes with those of a double-boiler. This dish has two pans — one for cooking over direct heat, the other for cooking over water — and can also serve as a warmer for cooked foods. This dish is an excellent investment and comes in a wide range of colors, materials and sizes.

Freezing Casseroles

Smart homemakers are always aware of the number of times unexpected guests drop in when there is no time to grocery shop or linger in the kitchen searching for needed ingredients. They know that casseroles in the freezer are insurance that a delicious meal may be cooked in the oven while casually chatting with guests.

The most convenient time to prepare casseroles for the freezer is while preparing the family meal. Make two instead of one. Then serve one and freeze one.

If you feel you can't spare a dish for the freezer and out of daily circulation, just line the casserole with heavy duty aluminum foil. Be sure the edges of the foil extend enough on all sides of the casserole. Pour the food mixture into the foil-lined dish. Freeze solid. After the food is frozen, carefully remove from the dish the foil containing the block of food. Peel off foil and place the block of food on a sheet of freezer wrapping material about 1 1/2 times as long as would be required to go once around the food being wrapped. Wrap the casserole so that paper is tight against the food, making pointed end folds. Press paper close to end surfaces of the food to avoid air pockets. Turn end folds under package and seal with freezer tape. Label package with contents, date and return to freezer.

Casseroles may be thawed in the refrigerator and then heated thoroughly before serving. However, a quicker method is to heat the frozen dish in the oven, at the cooking temperature called for in the original recipe. Should you use the freezer-to-oven method of thawing, be sure to allow longer than the original cooking time. Even though most casseroles are cooked before they are frozen, these directions should still be followed. This method works well with all but very large casseroles. To prevent singed edges and a still-frozen center, it is better to plan to thaw large casseroles in the refrigerator, then heat thoroughly in the oven just prior to serving.

If you are in doubt about freezing certain foods or skeptical about the effect freezing will have on certain combinations of foods, use the following ten tips on freezing as a guide.

1. The smaller the pieces of meat frozen, the more they will dry out in the freezer.
2. Most fried foods will lose their crispness when frozen.
3. Monosodium glutamate can be added to precooked foods during reheating to bring out the flavor of meats and vegetables.
4. A topping for a casserole should be added just before reheating.
5. Use only the best ingredients. You cannot expect a delicious casserole to develop from poor quality ingredients.
6. Do not completely cook the food in the casserole as it may become soft when reheated.
7. Add only small amounts of fat to food which will be frozen. It becomes rancid after about two months.
8. Garlic, cloves, pimento and green pepper become strong after frozen. It is best to underseason casseroles with these. Onions tend to lose flavor.
9. Salad greens and other raw vegetables lose crispness when frozen.
10. Diced potatoes should be added just before reheating casseroles as they will crumble when frozen with other ingredients.

Quick Shepherd's Pie

Ground Beef Favorites

Ground beef is a boon to every homemaker! With it she can balance her budget while preparing quick and easy family-pleasing dishes. And with it she can transform vegetables and pasta into marvelous casseroles. In the following section, you'll find an unusual selection of recipes from the kitchens of America's Home Economic Teachers.

There is a quick and easy Beefy-Cheesy Biscuit Casserole which is a delicious meat pie using canned biscuits for the crust — it's so convenient and economical! The Egg-plant Lasagna is a wonderful and savory variation of the famous Italian dish — instead of the traditional wide noodles, you substitute broad, flat slices of peeled egg-plant to layer with the meat sauce — it's fantastically good! The Hungarian Goulash combines the rich flavors of Cheddar cheese, corn, green pepper, ground beef and macaroni in a rich tomato sauce. Your family will be delighted with this hearty and satisfying taste treat — they're certain to ask for it again and again.

Ground beef with vegetables . . . pasta . . . rice . . . recipes for all these combinations and more are found in the following section. Every recipe has been perfected by a Home Economics Teacher. These creative cooks share their recipes with you, hoping that you will take as much pleasure in serving these dishes as they have in developing them.

17

HAMBURGER-BEAN CASSEROLE

1 onion, chopped
1/3 lb. bacon, diced
1 lb. hamburger
1 lg. can pork and beans
1 can tomato soup

Saute onion, bacon and hamburger until browned; drain off fat. Combine hamburger mixture with beans and soup; pour into casserole. Bake in preheated 350-degree oven for 1 hour. Yield: 6 servings.

Nona Verloo
Bureau of Homemaking Ed., State Dept. of Ed.
Sacramento, California

CONFETTI CASSEROLE

2 lb. ground beef
1/2 c. chopped onion
2 tsp. salt
1/4 tsp. pepper
1/2 tsp. dry mustard
2 tbsp. brown sugar
1 8-oz. package cream cheese
2 8-oz. cans tomato sauce
2 10-oz. packages frozen mixed
*   vegetables, thawed*
Crushed corn chips

Brown ground beef in skillet. Add onion and cook until tender. Add seasonings, sugar and cream cheese; stir until cream cheese melts. Add tomato sauce and vegetables. Turn into a 3-quart casserole. Sprinkle corn chips over the top; cover. Bake in preheated 375-degree oven for 40 minutes. Uncover and bake for 10 minutes longer. Yield: 10-12 servings.

Mrs. Dorothy M. Ham
Brantley Co. H.S., Nahunta, Georgia

CHOW MEIN WITH GROUND BEEF CASSEROLE

1 lb. ground beef
1 c. chopped celery
1 can cream of chicken soup
1 can chicken with rice soup
1 can mixed vegetables
1 can mushrooms
3 tbsp. soy sauce
2 c. chow mein noodles

Cook ground beef in skillet until brown. Add celery; cook until limp. Add soups, vegetables,

mushrooms and soy sauce. Combine ground beef mixture with noodles; spoon into casserole. Top with additional noodles. Bake in preheated 325-degree oven for 45 minutes.

Mrs. Don Bauer
Harvey H.S., Harvey, North Dakota

CORN CHIP CHILI

3 15-oz. cans red kidney beans,
*   drained*
2 10-oz. cans enchilada sauce
2 c. shredded Cheddar cheese
1 1/2 tbsp. chili powder
1 6-oz. package corn chips
1 1/2 lb. ground beef
1 1/2 c. chopped onions
1 clove of garlic, minced
1 c. sour cream

Combine beans, enchilada sauce, Cheddar cheese, chili powder and corn chips. Cook ground beef with onions and garlic until beef is brown and onions are tender. Combine bean mixture and ground beef mixture. Spoon into a 3-quart casserole or baking dish. Bake, uncovered, in preheated 350-degree oven for 30 minutes. Remove from oven; top with dollops of sour cream. Return to oven; bake for 5 minutes longer. Yield: 8-10 servings.

Mrs. Doris Malo
Mountain View H.S., Mountain View, California

BEEF-EGGPLANT CASSEROLE

1/4 c. salad oil
1 clove of garlic, crushed
3/4 c. chopped onion
1/3 c. chopped green pepper
2 1/2 lb. ground beef
1 1/2 c. tomato paste
4 c. tomato juice
1 tsp. salt
3/4 tsp. celery seed
1/2 tsp. sugar
3/4 tsp. Worcestershire sauce
1/8 tsp. pepper
1/2 c. red wine
1 eggplant
3 tbsp. Parmesan cheese

Heat oil in large kettle; add garlic, onion and green pepper. Cook over low heat for 5 minutes. Add ground beef; stir well. Brown over high heat. Add tomato paste, juice and seasonings. Simmer for 1 hour, then add wine. Cook for 1 hour longer or until thick. Peel, then cut eggplant into 1/2-inch slices. Alternate slices of eggplant with meat sauce and cheese in a 1 1/2-quart casserole. Bake in preheated 350-degree oven for 1 hour.

Jeanne Scheinuha
Valders H.S., Valders, Wisconsin

EGGPLANT LASAGNA

1 lb. ground beef
2 med.-sized onions, chopped
Salt
1/2 tsp. oregano
1 8-oz. can tomato sauce
1 10-oz. package frozen chopped
*   spinach*
1 lg. eggplant
2 eggs, beaten
1/4 c. (about) salad oil
1/4 lb. mozzarella cheese, thinly
*   sliced*

Cook ground beef and onions in a frying pan until brown. Stir in 1 teaspoon salt, oregano and tomato sauce. Simmer for 10 minutes. Add frozen spinach and cook until spinach is thawed. Skim fat from sauce, if necessary. Cut eggplant in lengthwise slices 3/8 inch thick. Sprinkle eggplant slices with salt and dip in egg. Heat enough oil in a frying pan to coat the bottom; add eggplant slices, a few pieces at a time, adding oil as needed. Cook until brown on both sides. Make a layer of 1/3 of the eggplant slices in a deep 2-quart casserole. Spoon in 1/3 of the ground beef mixture; top with alternating layers of eggplant and ground beef mixture. Cover surface with cheese slices. Bake in preheated 375-degree oven for 30 minutes. Casserole may be prepared ahead and refrigerated until baking time. Yield: 6 servings.

Mrs. Eileen B. Yeakley
Martinsville Jr. H.S., Martinsville, Indiana

EGGPLANT PARMESAN

1 lb. hamburger
1 7 3/4-oz. can mushroom sauce

1 7 3/4-oz. can marinara sauce
2 8-oz. cans tomato sauce
1 1/2 tsp. Italian seasoning
Salt and pepper to taste
1 lg. or 2 med. eggplant
1/2 c. (about) olive oil
2 c. bread crumbs
1/2 c. Parmesan cheese
1 tbsp. chopped parsley
1/2 lb. mozzarella cheese,
*   thinly sliced*

Cook hamburger in skillet until brown, then add the sauces and seasonings. Let simmer for 30 minutes to 1 hour for flavors to blend. Cut eggplant in 1/2-inch slices; soak in hot, salted water for 5 minutes. Dry thoroughly. Fry in hot olive oil for about 3 minutes on each side or until tender. Combine the bread crumbs, Parmesan cheese and parsley; toss until well mixed. Layer half the eggplant in a casserole; cover with half the crumb mixture. Spoon half the meat sauce over crumb mixture. Repeat layers; top with mozzarella cheese slices. Bake in preheated 350-degree oven for 30 minutes. Yield: 4-6 servings.

Cathy A. Mauch
Jackson H.S., Jackson, California

EGGPLANT CASSEROLE DELIGHT

1 lg. eggplant
Margarine
1 lb. (about) ground beef
1 med. onion, chopped
1/2 c. chopped celery
1 egg
2 c. cracker crumbs

Cut eggplant into 4 pieces and cook in salted water until tender. Peel eggplant; add 2 tablespoons margarine. Mash until smooth. Combine ground beef, onion and celery in frypan; cook, stirring, until lightly browned. Add 1/2 cup water and cover. Cook for several minutes longer. Stir in eggplant, then egg. Melt 1/4 cup margarine in a large casserole; add a thin layer of ground beef mixture. Top with half the cracker crumbs; add remaining ground beef mixture. Top with remaining crumbs. Dot with margarine. Bake in preheated 375-degree oven until crumbs are brown.

Connie Granato
Escobar Jr. H.S., San Antonio, Texas

19

Bonanza Casserole

BONANZA CASSEROLE

1 egg, slightly beaten
1/4 c. milk
1/4 c. fine dry bread crumbs
1 tsp. salt
1 lb. ground beef
1   5 1/2-oz. package French's
   au gratin potatoes
1 green pepper, chopped

Place egg, milk, bread crumbs and salt in large bowl; stir until mixed. Add ground beef; mix well. Shape into 16 small meatballs. Prepare potatoes according to package directions, using a 2-quart casserole. Stir in green pepper and about half the meatballs; arrange remaining meatballs on top. Bake in preheated 400-degree oven for 30 to 35 minutes or until potatoes are tender. Yield: 5-6 servings.

EASY LASAGNA

1 lg. jar Ragu spaghetti sauce
1 can tomato paste
1/2 lb. ground beef
1 can sliced mushrooms
1 pkg. lasagna

1 lb. cottage cheese
Parmesan cheese

Combine sauce and tomato paste in saucepan; add 1 cup water. Heat until bubbly. Break up ground beef into small pieces and stir into sauce. Add mushrooms; simmer until thick. Cook lasagna according to package directions. Spread a layer of sauce in a 13 x 9 x 2-inch baking pan. Add layer of lasagna, then sauce and cottage cheese. Continue layers until all ingredients are used, ending with sauce. Sprinkle with Parmesan cheese. Bake in preheated 350-degree oven until bubbly.

Susan J. Smith
Fall Mountain H.S., Langdon, New Hampshire

LASAGNA WITH MRS. B'S SAUCE

1 lb. ground beef
2 pt. Mrs. B's Tomato Sauce,
   thawed
9 lasagna noodles
2 c. ricotta cheese
1 lb. mozzarella cheese, thinly
   sliced

Brown ground beef in medium skillet over medium-high heat. Pour off drippings. Add tomato sauce and bring to a boil. Cook noodles according to package directions; drain.

Return to pan with a small amount of cold water to prevent sticking. Spread 1 cup sauce in 13 x 9-inch baking pan; place 3 well-drained noodles lengthwise in pan. Spread with 1 cup sauce, then 1/2 of the ricotta cheese. Arrange 1/4 of the cheese slices evenly on top. Repeat layers, topping with remaining 3 noodles, sauce and cheese. Bake in preheated 350-degree oven for 30 minutes. Let stand 10 minutes for easier serving.

Mrs. B's Tomato Sauce

    4 med. onions, chopped
    3 sm. garlic cloves
    3 tbsp. salad oil
    4 29-oz. cans tomato juice
    4 6-oz. cans tomato paste
    1 lb. mushrooms, sliced
    1 c. chopped parsley
    3 tbsp. sugar
    3 tbsp. salt
    4 tsp. oregano leaves
    2 bay leaves

Cook onions and garlic in oil in a large kettle until onions are limp. Discard garlic. Add remaining ingredients. Reduce heat to low; simmer, covered, for 2 hours. Discard bay leaves. Ladle sauce into 1-pint freezer containers, leaving 1 inch head space for expansion. Refrigerate until chilled; freeze. Yield: 1 gallon sauce.

Pauline K. Brown
Lone Wolf H.S., Lone Wolf, Oklahoma

EMERGENCY LASAGNA

    1 lb. ground beef
    1 clove of garlic, minced
    1 can stewed tomatoes
    1 can tomato sauce
    2 cans meatless spaghetti sauce
    Dash of seasoned salt
    1/2 box lasagna
    2/3 c. grated Parmesan cheese
    1 lb. sharp Cheddar cheese,
        sliced
    1 lb. mozzarella cheese

Brown beef in skillet; drain off excess fat. Add garlic, tomatoes, tomato sauce, spaghetti sauce and seasoned salt; simmer for 30 minutes. Cook lasagna according to package directions; drain. Arrange sauce, lasagna and cheeses in layers in baking dish. Bake in preheated 350-degree oven for 30 minutes. One can sliced mushrooms may be added to sauce, if desired.

Mrs. Nan Tate
Milton H.S., Alpharetta, Georgia

CLASSIC LASAGNA

    1 lb. ground beef
    2 tbsp. salad oil
    2 tsp. salt
    1 tsp. French's Italian seasoning
    1/4 tsp. French's black pepper
    1/4 tsp. French's crushed red pepper
    1/8 tsp. French's garlic powder
    2 6-oz. cans tomato paste
    1 1-lb. 11-oz. can tomatoes
    1 8-oz. package lasagna
    1/4 lb. mozzarella cheese slices
    1 c. cottage or ricotta cheese
    1/2 c. grated Parmesan cheese

Cook beef in oil in skillet over medium heat until brown; spoon off excess fat. Add seasonings, tomato paste and tomatoes to beef; mix well. Bring to a boil; reduce heat. Simmer for 10 minutes, stirring occasionally. Cook lasagna according to package directions while beef mixture is cooking; drain. Cover lasagna with cold water, then drain just before placing in baking dish. Line bottom of lightly oiled 11 1/2 x 7 1/2-inch baking dish with half the lasagna. Cover with 1/3 of the beef mixture, then 1/3 of the mozzarella cheese. Add half the cottage cheese, then half the Parmesan cheese. Repeat layers, ending with beef mixture, then mozzarella cheese. Bake in preheated 350-degree oven for 30 minutes. Let stand in warm place for 15 minutes before serving. Yield: 6-8 servings.

Classic Lasagna

BEEFY MACARONI AND CHEESE

2 c. elbow macaroni
3/4 lb. ground beef
1 sm. onion, finely chopped
1/2 c. cubed Cheddar cheese
1 tsp. parsley flakes
Salt
Dash of pepper
3 tbsp. butter or margarine
3 tbsp. flour
1 1/2 c. milk

Cook macaroni according to package directions; drain. Cook ground beef with onion
until beef is lightly browned. Drain off grease.
Mix macaroni, ground beef mixture, cheese,
parsley flakes, 1/2 teaspoon salt and pepper.
Place in a buttered and floured 2-quart casserole. Melt butter over low heat in saucepan.
Blend in flour and 1/2 teaspoon salt, stirring
until mixture is smooth and bubbly. Remove
from heat. Add milk gradually, stirring to
make a smooth paste. Return to heat. Bring to
a boil again, stirring constantly, until thickened. Pour white sauce over top; top with several strips of cheese, if desired. Bake, uncovered, at 350 degrees for 30 minutes. Yield: 6
servings.

Mrs. A. A. Luyben
Carroll H.S., Fort Wayne, Indiana

BUSY DAY BEEF CASSEROLE

1 tbsp. margarine or cooking oil
1 lb. ground beef
1 onion, diced
1 tsp. parsley flakes
1 can tomatoes, chopped
1 sm. box macaroni
1 can mushroom soup
1 c. buttermilk
Grated Parmesan cheese

Melt the margarine in a large frying pan; add
the ground beef, onion, parsley flakes and tomatoes. Cook, stirring, until beef is brown.
Prepare the macaroni according to package
directions. Combine beef mixture, macaroni,
soup and buttermilk; turn into well-greased
casserole. Sprinkle with Parmesan cheese.
Bake in preheated 350-degree oven until
bubbly.

Mrs. Geraldine Beveridge
East Carteret H.S., Beaufort, North Carolina

BLACK OLIVE-BEEF BAKE

1 pkg. macaroni-cheese dinner
1 lb. ground beef
1 med. onion, chopped
1/2 green pepper, chopped
1 can cream-style corn
1 can tomato soup
1/2 c. chopped black olives

Prepare the macaroni-cheese dinner according
to package directions. Cook ground beef with
onion and green pepper until beef is brown;
drain grease. Combine macaroni dinner,
ground beef mixture, corn, soup and olives;
mix well. Spoon into casserole. Bake in preheated 350-degree oven for 30 minutes. Yield:
6-8 servings.

Mrs. Cheryl Assenheimer
Troy Jr. H.S., Avon Lake, Ohio

CHEESE-IT-UP-BEEF

2 lb. hamburger
Salt and pepper to taste
1 med. onion, chopped
3 8-oz. cans tomato sauce
1 pkg. macaroni
1 recipe cheese sauce
Cheese slices

Season the hamburger with salt and pepper.
Cook the hamburger and onion in a skillet
until hamburger is brown. Add the tomato
sauce and simmer for 15 minutes. Prepare the
macaroni according to package directions.
Place macaroni in a casserole and add the
cheese sauce. Place the hamburger mixture on
top of the macaroni. Arrange cheese slices on
top. Bake in preheated 400-degree oven until
cheese is melted.

Jo Ann Been
Devine H.S., Devine, Texas

CRUSTY GROUND BEEF BAKE

1 to 1 1/2 lb. ground beef
2 med. onions, chopped or
*   2 tsp. onion powder*
1 15-oz. can tomato sauce
1 lb. elbow macaroni
1 can Cheddar cheese soup
1 tsp. salt
1/2 tsp. pepper
1/2 tsp. garlic powder

1/2 lb. sharp Cheddar cheese
   slices

Saute beef and onions in frypan until browned. Add tomato sauce; let simmer while cooking macaroni. Cook macaroni according to package directions, then drain. Combine macaroni and Cheddar cheese soup; mix well. Stir in beef mixture and seasonings; pour into 12 x 15-inch baking pan. Top with Cheddar cheese slices. Bake at 350 degrees for 30 minutes or until cheese is melted and top is crusty.

Mrs. Fred Yost
Cairo Central Sch., Cairo, New York

HAMBURGER AND MACARONI DELIGHT

1 lb. hamburger
2 c. cooked macaroni
2 c. green beans
2 c. tomato juice

Brown hamburger in frypan. Mix hamburger, macaroni, beans and tomato juice in greased casserole. Bake in preheated 350-degree oven for 40 minutes.

Shirley Rose
New Germany Rural H.S.
New Germany, Nova Scotia, Canada

MACARONI ROMA

1   8-oz. package elbow macaroni
1/4 c. butter
1 med. onion, diced
1 clove of garlic, pressed
1 lb. lean ground beef
1 1/2 tsp. salt
1 tsp. sugar
1/2 tsp. oregano
1/2 tsp. basil
1 1/2 tsp. chili powder
Dash of pepper
1 No. 2 1/2 can tomatoes
1   6-oz. can tomato paste
2 c. creamed cottage cheese
1/2 lb. sharp American process
   cheese, shredded
2 tbsp. melted butter
1/2 c. dry bread crumbs
1/4 c. grated Parmesan cheese

Cook macaroni according to package directions; drain. Rinse with cold water thoroughly; drain well. Melt butter in heavy sauce-

pan or deep skillet. Add onion and garlic; cook until onion is transparent, but not brown. Add beef; cook until beef loses red color. Add seasonings, tomatoes and tomato paste; simmer for 1 hour and 30 minutes to 2 hours, stirring occasionally. Combine cottage cheese and macaroni. Pour 1/4 of the beef sauce into buttered 2 1/2-quart casserole; top with 1/3 of the macaroni mixture, then 1/3 of the American cheese. Repeat layers, ending with beef sauce. Combine the melted butter, bread crumbs and Parmesan cheese; sprinkle over beef sauce. Bake in preheated 325-degree oven for 1 hour. Let stand for 10 minutes before serving. Yield: 6-8 servings.

HUNGARIAN GOULASH

1 med. onion, chopped
1/2 green pepper, chopped
1 lb. ground beef
1 c. cream-style corn
1 c. cooked macaroni
1 can tomato soup
1 c. grated Cheddar cheese

Cook onion and green pepper in oil in skillet until brown. Add ground beef; cook and stir until brown. Add corn; stir to mix well. Remove from heat. Place the macaroni in a greased casserole; add the ground beef mixture. Pour tomato soup over top. Sprinkle with grated cheese. Bake in preheated 375-degree oven for 20 minutes.

Martha Harless
Bayside Jr. H.S., Virginia Beach, Virginia

Macaroni Roma

MOTHER'S STEAK CASSEROLE

1 1/2 lb. ground steak
1/2 med. green pepper, chopped
1 med. onion, grated
Salt to taste
1 7-oz. box macaroni
1 1-lb. can stewed tomatoes
1 14-oz. can tomato sauce
8 oz. American cheese or
    Velveeta cheese, diced

Saute steak in frypan until brown, then drain.
Saute green pepper and onion until golden;
add to steak. Season with salt. Prepare macaroni according to package directions. Combine
macaroni, stewed tomatoes, tomato sauce,
beef mixture and cheese. Place in buttered
casserole. Bake, covered, in preheated 350-
degree oven for 1 hour.

Sister M. Magdalene
Our Lady of Mount Carmel, Wyandotte, Michigan

SAUCY MACARONI AND BEEF CASSEROLE

1 sm. onion, chopped
1 lb. ground beef
1 12-oz. package macaroni,
    cooked and drained
1 8-oz. can ranch-style beans
    and liquid
1 c. medium white sauce
1/2 c. grated American cheese

Saute onion in small amount of fat until
golden brown. Add ground beef; cook until
browned. Stir in macaroni, beans and white
sauce. Pour into casserole; sprinkle cheese on
top. Bake in preheated 375-degree oven for 15
minutes or until hot and bubbly.

Mrs. Carol Bowers
Whiteface H.S., Whiteface, Texas

MULLIGAN

1 8-oz. package elbow macaroni
1 lb. hamburger
1 med. onion, finely chopped
1 can tomato soup
3/4 c. milk
1 No. 2 can dark kidney beans
1 tsp. salt
1/2 tsp. pepper
1/2 c. crushed Ritz crackers

Cook macaroni in boiling salted water until
tender, then drain. Brown hamburger and
onion in skillet, breaking hamburger in small
bits with wooden spoon. Stir tomato soup and
milk together until blended. Add to hamburger mixture. Combine macaroni, hamburger mixture, kidney beans, salt and pepper.
Place in a 1 1/2-quart casserole. Sprinkle
crushed crackers over top. Bake in preheated
350-degree oven for 35 minutes or until bubbly. May be prepared the day before and
stored in refrigerator until baking time. Yield:
6 servings.

Mrs. M. Judelle Jones
Turlock H.S., Turlock, California

MOCK PIZZA CASSEROLE

1 lb. lean ground beef
1/2 c. milk
1/2 c. dry bread crumbs
1 tsp. salt
1/4 tsp. pepper
1 c. water
1 c. shredded Cheddar cheese
3/4 c. tomato paste
3/4 c. canned mushrooms with
    liquid.
1 tsp. leaf oregano
1 tbsp. grated onion or minced
    onion
1/3 c. grated Parmesan cheese

Combine ground beef, milk, bread crumbs,
salt, pepper and water in medium bowl; mix
well. Pat into a deep casserole. Combine remaining ingredients except Parmesan cheese in
bowl; mix well. Spoon over ground beef mixture. Sprinkle with Parmesan cheese. Garnish
with slices of cooked sausage, green pepper,
mushrooms and olives, if desired. Bake in preheated 350-degree oven for 30 to 40 minutes
or until beef is done. Yield: 4-6 servings.

Mrs. Helen M. Godwin
Northwest Sr. H.S., Greensboro, North Carolina

MEATBALL OVEN STEW

1 lb. hamburger
1 sm. onion, finely minced
1 sm. green pepper, chopped
1/4 c. cracker crumbs
Salt
1 1/2 tsp. dry mustard

1 tsp. chili powder
1 egg
1/2 c. milk
Flour
1 can tomato sauce
2 1/2 c. water
Pepper
3 carrots, peeled
3 potatoes, peeled
1 onion, thickly sliced

Combine hamburger, minced onion, green pepper, crumbs, 1 teaspoon salt, mustard and chili powder in a medium bowl; mix well. Beat egg and milk together; add to hamburger mixture. Form into meatballs; dredge in flour. Brown meatballs in small amount of hot oil in skillet; remove from skillet. Stir 2 tablespoons flour into drippings; cook until golden. Add tomato sauce, water and salt and pepper to taste. Bring to a boil. Cut the carrots and potatoes in half; place in a large casserole. Cover with onion slices. Arrange meatballs over onion; pour sauce over top, then cover. Bake in preheated 375-degree oven for 2 hours. Yield: 4 servings.

Eileen Silva
Escalon H.S., Escalon, California

AMERICAN CHOP SUEY CASSEROLE

1 lg. onion, minced
1 green pepper, diced
1 lb. hamburger
1 lg. can tomatoes
1 lg. can tomato sauce
1 sm. can tomato paste
1 tsp. salt
1/2 tsp. pepper
1/4 tsp. garlic powder
1 1/2 tbsp. Worcestershire sauce
6 to 8 c. cooked macaroni
1/2 lb. sharp Cheddar cheese,
* sliced*
1 stack pak Ritz crackers,
* crumbled*
2 tbsp. butter

Saute onion and pepper until tender. Add crumbled hamburger; cook until brown. Stir in tomatoes, tomato sauce, tomato paste, seasonings and Worcestershire sauce. Simmer for 15 minutes. Pour over macaroni and stir until coated. Pour mixture into greased 9 x 13 x 2-inch pan. Top with cheese slices. Sprinkle with crumbs. Dot with butter. Bake in pre-

heated 400-degree oven for 1 hour. Yield: 6 servings.

Mrs. Linda B. Wilbur
North Middle Sch., Westford, Massachusetts

BEEF-NOODLE DELIGHT

1 lb. ground beef
1/3 c. chopped onion
1 c. shredded Cheddar cheese
1   10 1/2-oz. can tomato soup
2 c. cooked noodles
1 c. cooked corn or green beans
1/4 c. water
1 tsp. prepared mustard
1 tsp. salt

Cook beef and onion in saucepan until browned, stirring to separate beef. Pour off fat. Stir in 3/4 cup cheese, soup, noodles, corn, water, mustard and salt. Pour into 1 1/2-quart casserole. Top with remaining cheese. Bake in preheated 350-degree oven for 30 minutes. Yield: 4 servings.

Mrs. Margery Creek
Francis Scott Key Jr. H.S.
Silver Spring, Maryland

BEEF-NOODLE SUPREME

1   8-oz. package fine egg noodles
1 1/2 lb. ground beef
1 tbsp. butter
2   8-oz. cans tomato sauce
Salt and pepper to taste
1/2 lb. cottage cheese
1   8-oz. package cream cheese
1/2 c. sour cream
1/3 c. scallions
1 tbsp. minced green pepper
2 tbsp. melted butter

Cook noodles according to package directions; drain. Saute beef in butter until brown. Add tomato sauce, salt and pepper. Remove from heat. Combine cottage cheese, cream cheese, sour cream, scallions and green pepper. Spread one-half the noodles in a square 2-quart casserole and cover with cottage cheese mixture. Add remaining noodles; pour melted butter over noodles. Spread ground beef mixture over top. Chill. Remove from refrigerator 20 minutes before baking. Bake in a preheated 350-degree oven for 45 minutes.

Arlyne Ehli
Penn Jr. H.S., Bloomington, Minnesota

HAMBURGER STROGANOFF

    1 6-oz. package noodles
    1 1/4 lb. ground beef
    3/4 c. sliced onions
    1/4 c. flour
    Dash of pepper
    3/4 tsp. salt
    1/4 c. catsup
    2 tsp. Worcestershire sauce
    1/4 c. mushroom bits and pieces
       with liquid
    1 1/3 c. buttermilk

Preheat oven to 350 degrees. Cook noodles according to package directions. Cook beef and onions in frying pan until brown, stirring to break up beef. Remove from heat; blend in flour, pepper and salt. Stir to mix well. Add catsup, Worcestershire sauce, mushrooms and buttermilk. Mix well. Arrange half the noodles in 9 x 13-inch pan. Spoon half the ground beef mixture over noodles. Place remaining noodles on top, then add remaining beef mixture. Stir until well mixed. Bake for 25 to 30 minutes. Yield: 8 servings.

Jolinda Willis
Northern Burlington Co. Regional H.S.
Columbus, New Jersey

HAMBURGER AND TOMATO CASSEROLE

    1 lb. hamburger
    1 onion, chopped
    1 green pepper, chopped
    1 c. chopped mushrooms
    2 c. tomatoes
    1 tsp. salt
    1 tsp. pepper
    1 1/2 tsp. basil
    1 tsp. thyme
    4 to 5 c. egg noodles
    Mozzarella cheese slices

Cook hamburger in skillet until brown. Add onion and green pepper; cook until tender. Add mushrooms, tomatoes and seasonings. Cook over medium heat until consistency of spaghetti sauce. Cook noodles according to package directions. Combine noodles and sauce in casserole. Top with cheese. Bake in preheated 350-degree oven for 45 minutes.

Joann Gardner
Pembroke H.S., Hampton, Virginia

HAMBURGER AND CORN CASSEROLE

    1 1/2 lb. lean ground beef
    1 med. onion, chopped
    1 12-oz. can whole kernel corn,
       drained
    1 can cream of chicken soup
    1 can cream of mushroom soup
    1 c. sour cream
    1/4 c. chopped pimento
    3/4 tsp. salt
    1/2 tsp. monosodium glutamate
    1/4 tsp. pepper
    3 c. cooked noodles, drained
    3 tbsp. melted butter
    1 c. soft bread crumbs

Cook ground beef until lightly browned. Add onion; cook until tender, but not brown. Add corn, soups, sour cream, pimento, salt, monosodium glutamate and pepper; mix well. Stir in noodles; taste and add seasonings as desired. Spoon into 2 1/2-quart casserole. Combine butter and crumbs; sprinkle over casserole. Bake in preheated 350-degree oven for 30 minutes. Yield: 10 servings.

Mrs. Margaret W. Lyles
Westminster H.S., Westminster, South Carolina

CRUNCHY NOODLE CASSEROLE

    2 lb. ground beef
    1 onion, chopped fine
    1 8-oz. package fine noodles
    1 can mushroom soup
    1 can evaporated milk
    1 med. bottle stuffed olives,
       sliced
    1 4-oz. can mushrooms
    1/2 lb. American cheese, grated
    1 sm. can grated Parmesan cheese
    1 can chow mein noodles
    1/4 lb. salted mixed nuts

Cook the ground beef and onion in skillet until brown. Cook noodles according to package directions. Stir soup and milk together until blended. Combine noodles, olives, soup mixture, mushrooms and ground beef mixture. Alternate layers of noodle mixture and cheeses until all ingredients are used. Bake, covered, in preheated 350-degree oven for 30 minutes. Spread chow mein noodles, then nuts on top and bake, uncovered, for 10 minutes longer.

Borghild Strom
Pattengill Jr. H.S., Lansing, Michigan

Beef-Stuffed Rigatoni

BEEF-STUFFED RIGATONI

1 12-oz. package rigatoni
1 9-oz. package frozen chopped
  spinach
1/3 c. chopped onion
1/3 c. chopped green pepper
1 clove of garlic, minced
1 tbsp. cooking oil
1 1/2 lb. ground beef chuck
1 1/2 tsp. salt
1 tsp. mixed Italian herbs
3/4 c. shredded Parmesan cheese
1 14 1/2-oz. can Italian tomatoes
1 8-oz. can tomato sauce
1 3-oz. can mushrooms
1 8-oz. package sliced mozzarella
  cheese

Cook rigatoni in 4 quarts boiling, salted water for about 8 minutes or until just tender. Do not overcook. Drain; cover with cold water. Cook spinach according to package directions; drain, pressing out all liquid so that spinach is dry and fluffy. Cook onion, green pepper and garlic in oil in skillet until soft, stirring frequently. Add beef, salt and herbs; cook, stirring, until beef is brown. Combine 2/3 of the beef mixture with spinach and 1/4 cup Parmesan cheese; reserve. Add tomatoes, tomato sauce and undrained mushrooms to remaining beef mixture in skillet; cook over low heat, stirring occasionally, while stuffing rigatoni. Drain rigatoni; stuff each piece with reserved beef mixture, using fingers. Arrange layers of sauce, stuffed rigatoni, mozzarella cheese and remaining Parmesan cheese in 8 or 9-inch casserole, ending with layers of sauce and cheeses. Bake in preheated 350-degree oven for 30 to 40 minutes or until hot and bubbly. Yield: 8 servings.

FAVORITE PIZZA CASSEROLE

1 lb. ground beef
1/3 c. chopped onion
1 clove of garlic, minced
1 tsp. oregano
1/2 tsp. salt
1 can tomato soup
1/3 c. water
2 c. cooked noodles
1/2 c. shredded cheese

Cook ground beef, onion and seasonings in skillet until beef is brown. Add soup, water and noodles. Spoon into greased casserole. Sprinkle cheese on top. Bake in preheated 350-degree oven for 30 minutes. One cup crushed cheese crackers may be sprinkled over the cheese before baking, if desired.

Katharine Rigby
Starr-Washington Jr. H.S., Lancaster, Ohio

27

EASY MARZETTI

1   4-oz. package noodles
1 lb. ground beef
2 tbsp. shortening
1 lg. onion, chopped
1/2 green pepper, chopped
1   8-oz. can mushrooms
1/4 tsp. oregano
1 can tomato soup
1   6-oz. can tomato paste
1/2 c. water
1 tbsp. Worcestershire sauce
1/2 lb. sharp cheese, grated

Cook noodles according to package directions; drain. Cook ground beef in shortening until brown. Add onion, green pepper, mushrooms, oregano, soup, tomato paste, water, Worcestershire sauce and cheese. Add noodles; toss until well mixed. Place in 3-quart casserole. Bake in preheated 375-degree oven for 45 minutes. Yield: 8 servings.

Mrs. Ann Hohman
Juniata Valley H.S., Alexandria, Pennsylvania

JOHNNY MARZETTI

2 lb. ground beef
2 c. chopped green pepper
1 c. chopped celery
2 c. chopped onions
2 tsp. salt
1   8-oz. can tomato sauce
1   8-oz. can tomato sauce
    with mushrooms
1 can tomato soup
1   4-oz. can sliced mushrooms
    and liquid
1/3 c. chopped stuffed olives
1   1-lb. package broad noodles
2 c. grated American cheese

Saute ground beef in a large skillet. Add green pepper, celery, onions and salt; cook for 5 minutes. Add sauces, soup, mushrooms and olives; cook for 10 minutes. Cook noodles according to package directions; place in large roasting pan. Add sauce; stir gently until mixed. Sprinkle cheese on top. Bake in preheated 350-degree oven for 35 to 45 minutes. Yield: 12 generous servings.

Janelle Lehman
Hulbert H.S., Hulbert, Oklahoma

MOCK RAVIOLI

1/2 c. oil
2 lg. onions, chopped
1 1/2 lb. ground beef
2 cloves of garlic
1 c. tomato paste
2 c. water
1 tbsp. Italian seasoning
1 lb. bowknot pasta
1   10-oz. package frozen spinach, thawed
4 eggs, beaten
1 c. grated Italian cheese
1/4 c. parsley

Heat oil in skillet; add onions. Cook until brown. Add ground beef and cook until slightly browned. Add garlic, tomato paste, water and seasoning. Simmer for 30 minutes. Cook pasta according to package directions; drain. Combine spinach, eggs, cheese and parsley. Alternate layers of pasta, ground beef mixture and spinach mixture in a buttered casserole. Sprinkle additional grated cheese on top of casserole. Bake in preheated 325-degree oven for 40 minutes. Yield: 8 servings.

Mrs. Margaret Morgan
Austin H.S., Austin, Minnesota

OLD ENGLISH CASSEROLE

1 .8-oz. package noodles
1 1/2 lb. ground beef
1 lg. onion, chopped
1 tbsp. flour
1/2 tsp. salt
1/4 tsp. lemon pepper
1 can sliced mushrooms
1 can green beans, drained
1   15-oz. can tomato sauce
1 c. grated Cheddar cheese

Cook noodles according to package directions. Place noodles in a lightly greased 2-quart baking dish. Brown ground beef in large skillet. Remove beef to bowl; drain all but 1 tablespoon fat from skillet. Saute onion in fat until tender; add beef. Blend in flour, salt and lemon pepper. Stir in mushrooms and liquid, green beans and tomato sauce. Spoon mixture over noodles, spreading evenly; sprinkle with cheese. Bake in preheated 350-degree oven for 30 minutes.

Mrs. Mildred Blackwell
Lakeview H.S., Winter Garden, Florida

SICILIAN SUPPER

1 lb. ground beef
1/2 c. chopped onion
1   6-oz. can tomato paste
3/4 c. water
1/2 tsp. salt
1/4 tsp. pepper
3/4 c. milk
1   8-oz. package cream cheese,
    cubed
1/2 c. grated Parmesan cheese
1/2 c. chopped green pepper
1/2 tsp. garlic salt
2 c. noodles, cooked and drained

Cook ground beef in skillet until brown; drain. Add onion; cook until tender. Add tomato paste, water and seasonings; simmer for 5 minutes. Combine milk and cream cheese in saucepan over low heat; stir until smooth. Stir in 1/4 cup Parmesan cheese, green pepper, garlic salt and noodles. Place half the noodle mixture in 1 1/2-quart casserole. Cover with half the ground beef mixture. Repeat layers. Bake in preheated 350-degree oven for 20 minutes. Sprinkle with remaining Parmesan cheese. Yield: 6 servings.

Oleta Hayden
Milford H.S., Milford, Texas

SPANISH NOODLES

1 lb. ground beef
1 1/2 tsp. salt
1/8 tsp. pepper
2 tbsp. oil
1/4 c. chopped green pepper
1/4 c. chopped onion
3 c. tomatoes
1 1/2 tsp. sugar
2 c. noodles

Combine ground beef, salt and pepper; mix well. Heat oil in frying pan. Add beef, stirring to separate, and cook until brown. Add green pepper and onion; saute until limp. Place tomatoes, sugar and noodles in a saucepan; cook for about 5 minutes. Combine ground beef mixture and tomato mixture; mix well. Turn into greased casserole; cover. Bake in preheated 350-degree oven for about 40 minutes or until done. Add liquid, if needed.

Mable P. Nichols
Marjorie Stansfield Sch., Haledon, New Jersey

SPICY BEEF CASSEROLE

1 lb. ground beef
3/4 c. chopped onions
1 tsp. salt
1/2 tsp. seasoned salt
1/4 tsp. oregano
2 c. tomatoes
1/4 tsp. soda
1   8-oz. package noodles
1/2 lb. Cheddar cheese, cubed
1 can French-fried onions

Saute beef and onions in skillet for about 15 minutes. Add seasonings, tomatoes and soda. Cook noodles according to package directions; drain. Place 1/3 of the cooked noodles in a casserole. Cover with 1/2 of the beef mixture. Add 1/3 of the cheese. Add half the remaining noodles and the remaining beef mixture. Spread on remaining noodles and top with remaining cheese. Bake in a preheated 350-degree oven for 20 minutes. Place onions on top and bake for 10 minutes longer.

Sue Volkmer
Hemingford H.S., Hemingford, Nebraska

UNUSUAL BEEF CASSEROLE

4 c. medium noodles
1 tbsp. salad oil
1 c. chopped onion
1 lb. ground beef
1 tsp. salt
1/2 tsp. thyme
1/4 tsp. pepper
1 can cream of celery soup
1/2 c. milk
1 c. grated sharp cheese
2 eggs, beaten

Prepare noodles according to package directions. Place oil, onion, beef, salt, thyme and pepper in skillet; cook until beef loses red color. Do not brown. Combine soup and milk in bowl; stir until blended. Place 1/3 of the noodles in 1 1/2-quart casserole. Spread 1/2 of the meat mixture over noodles; top with half the soup mixture. Repeat layers, ending with noodles on top. Sprinkle with cheese. Pour eggs over top. Bake in preheated 350-degree oven until top is crisp.

Clara May Charlesworth
Northeast H.S., Pasadena, Maryland

VARIETY CASSEROLE

1   8-oz. package noodles
1 lb. lean ground beef
1 lg. onion, minced
2 tbsp. butter or margarine
1 can chicken broth
1 can corn
1 c. pitted ripe olives

Cook noodles according to package directions. Place noodles in baking dish. Saute beef and onion in butter. Add chicken broth, corn and olives. Stir into noodles. Bake, covered, in preheated 350-degree oven for 20 minutes. Remove cover; bake for 10 minutes longer or until brown. Yield: 8 servings.

Helen L. Giles
Susan Blach English Sch., Seldovia, Alaska

BEEF-EGGPLANT CASSEROLE

1 med. eggplant
1/4 c. margarine
1 lb. lean ground beef
1/3 c. chopped bell pepper
1/3 c. chopped onion
1/3 c. chopped celery leaves
1 c. packaged precooked rice
1 egg, slightly beaten
1 tsp. salt
1/4 tsp. pepper
2 c. well-buttered bread crumbs

Pare and slice eggplant, then cook in boiling salted water until tender. Drain and mash, then set aside. Melt margarine in skillet, then saute the ground beef, bell pepper, onion and celery leaves until beef is cooked but not browned and vegetables are tender. Combine beef mixture, eggplant, rice, egg, salt and pepper; mix well. Turn into buttered casserole. Top with bread crumbs. Bake in preheated 350-degree oven for 45 minutes or until browned.

Kathryn Frazior
Nederland H.S., Nederland, Texas

CANTONESE CASSEROLE

1   12-oz. package frozen rice
    pilaf in plastic bag
1 lb. ground beef
1/2 c. diced onion
1 c. diced celery

1 can cream of mushroom soup
1 can chicken with rice soup
1   2 1/2-oz. jar sliced mushrooms,
    drained
1/4 c. soy sauce
Chow mein noodles

Cook rice according to package directions only until thawed. Cook ground beef, onion and celery in large skillet until brown; drain off fat. Combine all ingredients except chow mein noodles; spoon into 2 1/2-quart casserole. Bake in preheated 350-degree oven for 35 to 40 minutes. Serve with chow mein noodles. Yield: 6 servings.

Mrs. Carole Phillips
Sierra Joint Union, Tollhouse, California

CHEROKEE CASSEROLE

1 lb. ground beef
1 tbsp. olive oil
1/2 c. chopped onion
1 c. packaged precooked rice
1/2 tsp. salt
1 can mushroom soup
4 slices cheese
6 olives, sliced

Cook ground beef in hot olive oil in iron skillet until brown. Add onion to ground beef; cook on medium heat for 5 minutes. Add rice, salt and mushroom soup to ground beef mixture; simmer for 5 minutes. Pour into casserole; top with cheese and olives. Bake in preheated 400-degree oven for 3 to 5 minutes or until cheese is melted.

Mrs. Janet Scott
Meade Co. H.S., Brandenburg, Kentucky

CHINESE HAMBURGER

1 lb. ground beef
1 c. chopped celery
2 med. onions, chopped
1 can cream of mushroom soup
1 can cream of chicken soup
1 1/2 soup cans water
1 1/2 tsp. soy sauce
1 c. instant rice
1 can chow mein noodles

Cook ground beef, celery and onions in skillet until beef is brown. Add the mushroom soup, chicken soup, water and soy sauce; simmer for 15 minutes. Stir in the rice. Spoon into a shallow baking dish. Sprinkle noodles over top. Bake in preheated 350-degree oven for about 20 minutes or until bubbly.

Mrs. Joanne Litz
Tulare Western H.S., Tulare, California

HAMBURGER-ZUCCHINI CASSEROLE

6 tomatoes, peeled and sliced
4 c. sliced zucchini
Salt
1 1/2 lb. ground beef
2/3 c. rice
1/4 c. chopped onion
1/4 c. chopped green pepper
1 c. tomato juice
Pepper to taste
2 tbsp. chopped parsley
1 c. shredded Cheddar cheese

Arrange half the tomatoes in a greased 9 x 13-inch baking dish. Arrange half the zucchini over tomatoes; sprinkle with 1/2 teaspoon salt. Combine ground beef, rice, onion, green pepper and tomato juice in bowl; mix well. Add 1 teaspoon salt, pepper and parsley. Spoon ground beef mixture evenly over zucchini. Cover with remaining zucchini; add remaining tomatoes. Sprinkle with 1/2 teaspoon salt. Cover with foil. Bake in preheated 375-degree oven for 1 hour and 30 minutes or

until rice is done and vegetables are tender. Remove cover; sprinkle with cheese. Bake for 15 minutes longer.

Mrs. Jo Anne Ward
Hobson H.S., Hobson, Montana

MEXIBEEF

1/4 c. butter
1 c. chopped onion
1 lb. ground beef
1 tbsp. flour
1 1/2 tsp. chili powder
1 tsp. salt
1/8 tsp. pepper
1 c. milk
1/2 c. sliced pitted ripe olives
1 c. shredded Cheddar cheese
3 c. hot cooked rice
Green pepper rings (opt.)

Melt butter in frypan. Add onion and beef; cook, stirring and crumbling beef, until onion is transparent. Blend in flour, chili powder, salt and pepper. Add milk; cook, stirring, until sauce is thickened. Add olives. Fold 1/2 of the cheese into rice; spoon rice mixture over bottom and into a border around sides of shallow 1 1/2-quart casserole. Fill center of casserole with beef mixture; sprinkle with remaining cheese. Bake in preheated 350-degree oven for 20 to 25 minutes or until hot. Garnish with green pepper rings. Yield: 6 servings.

Mexibeef

RED-WHITE AND BLUE TART

3 c. sifted all-purpose flour
3/4 c. sugar
1 c. butter
2 eggs, separated
1 env. unflavored gelatin
1/8 tsp. salt
1/3 c. evaporated milk
1/4 c. sherry
1 No. 2 can cherry pie filling
1 No. 2 can blueberry pie filling

Sift flour and 1/2 cup sugar together into bowl; cut in butter until mixture is crumbly. Stir in egg yolks until pastry holds together; knead on floured surface until smooth. Press 3/4 of the pastry into bottom and 1 1/2 inches up side of two 9-inch removable-rim cake pans or springform pans. Cut four 7 3/4 x 1 1/2-inch cardboard strips and cover with foil. Press 2 strips into each pan gently to divide pan into thirds. Divide remaining pastry into fourths; press on one side of each divider. Bake at 375 degrees for 25 minutes or until lightly browned. Remove strips carefully and cool crusts thoroughly. Soften 1 envelope gelatin in 1/3 cup cold water in top of double boiler; stir over boiling water until dissolved. Stir in remaining sugar and salt. Combine evaporated milk and sherry; stir in gelatin mixture. Chill until slightly thicker than consistency of unbeaten egg white. Add egg whites and beat for about 8 minutes or until mixture begins to hold shape. Divide and turn into center sections of tart shells. Chill. Sprinkle remaining gelatin over 1/2 cup cold water in saucepan; stir over low heat until dissolved. Mix half the gelatin with cherry pie filling; mix remaining gelatin with blueberry pie filling. Divide fillings and spoon into remaining sections of tart shells to create red, white and blue stripe in each. Chill until firm.

PINEAPPLE-LOBSTER APPETIZERS

1 fresh pineapple
3 green peppers, seeded
12 2-oz. South African rock
*   lobster-tails*

Remove rind and crown of pineapple and cut pineapple into 36 bite-sized pieces. Cut green peppers into 72 pieces. Refrigerate until chilled. Drop lobster-tails into boiling, salted water. Bring to a boil again and cook for 2 minutes. Drain immediately and dip in cold water. Cut away underside membrane and remove lobster meat in 1 piece. Cut each piece into 3 crosswise slices. Refrigerate until chilled. String 1 slice lobster, 2 pieces of green pepper and 1 piece of pineapple alternately on each of 36 small skewers. Arrange on platter and chill until serving time. Serve with desired dips. Yield: 36 appetizers.

SHRIMP PETITES

1/2 lb. cooked shrimp
1 9 1/4-oz. package pie crust mix
4 slices crisp-cooked bacon, crumbled
2 slices Swiss cheese, finely
*   chopped*
2 eggs, slightly beaten
2/3 c. evaporated milk
2 tbsp. flour
1/4 tsp. Tabasco sauce
1/4 tsp. salt
Dash of pepper

Shell and devein shrimp, then chop. Small shrimp may be left whole. Prepare pie crust mix according to package directions. Roll out thin on a lightly floured surface; cut with a 2 3/4-inch round cutter. Press pastry into 24 1 3/4 x 1-inch muffin pans. Place shrimp in pastry cups; sprinkle with bacon and cheese. Combine remaining ingredients and pour over shrimp mixture carefully. Bake at 425 degrees for 25 minutes or until set and pie crust is done. Yield: 24 petites.

HOSTESS PATE

1 3 or 4-oz. can chopped mushrooms
1 env. unflavored gelatin
1 10 1/2-oz. can beef bouillon
2 tbsp. brandy
1 tsp. Worcestershire sauce
2 5-oz. cans liver spread
1/2 c. pitted ripe olives
1/4 c. parsley leaves

Drain liquid from mushrooms; place in blender container. Sprinkle gelatin over liquid. Heat 1/2 cup bouillon to boiling point; add to liquid. Cover and process at low speed until gelatin dissolves. Add remaining bouillon and remaining ingredients; cover. Process at high speed until smooth. Pour into 4-cup mold. Chill for about 4 hours or until firm. May be chilled overnight. Unmold and serve with crisp crackers. Yield: 3 1/3 cups.

Photograph for these recipes on page 33.

FIESTA DAY SHRIMP POT

1 1/2 lb. fresh or frozen shrimp
1/2 c. olive or salad oil
3 tbsp. chopped onion
1/4 c. chopped green pepper
1 clove of garlic, minced
1 1/2 c. converted rice
2 1/2 c. water
1 1/2 tsp. salt
1/2 tsp. oregano
1/4 tsp. pepper
1/4 c. lemon juice
3/4 c. tomato sauce
1 10-oz. package frozen succotash,
  partially thawed
1 10-oz. package frozen baby okra,
  partially thawed
3/4 c. frozen green beans, partially
  thawed

Thaw shrimp; clean and set aside. Heat olive oil in a large, deep heatproof casserole. Add onion, green pepper, garlic and rice; cook, stirring constantly, until rice is lightly browned. Add water, seasonings, lemon juice, tomato sauce and vegetables; blend gently. Cover. Cook over low heat for 15 minutes. Uncover; arrange shrimp on surface. Cover; cook for 10 minutes longer or until rice is tender and shrimp are pink. Serve from casserole. May be prepared in skillet, if desired. Yield: 8-10 servings.

Photograph for this recipe on page 34.

COWBELLE CASSEROLE

2 c. sliced potatoes
1 tbsp. sugar
1 tbsp. salt
1/2 tsp. pepper
1/2 c. rice
1 1/2 lb. hamburger
1 lg. onion, sliced or chopped
1 c. sliced carrots
4 c. tomatoes, coarsely chopped

Arrange half the potatoes in a greased baking dish. Combine the sugar, salt and pepper; sprinkle over potatoes lightly. Add layers of half the rice, hamburger, onion slices, carrots and tomatoes, sprinkling each layer with sugar mixture. Repeat layers using remaining ingredients. Bake in a preheated 350-degree oven for 2 hours.

Marie L. Mohr
Wayne-Carroll H.S., Wayne, Nebraska

JAMBALAYA DIRTY RICE AND BEEF

3 tbsp. cooking oil or butter
1 c. long grain rice
3/4 c. chopped onions
1/2 c. chopped celery
1/2 sm. garlic pod, minced
1/4 tsp. red pepper
1/8 tsp. pepper
1 1/4 tsp. salt
1 tbsp. Worcestershire sauce
3 c. beef stock or broth
1 lb. ground beef

Heat cooking oil in 2-quart saucepan. Add rice; fry over medium heat until golden brown. Add onions, celery and garlic; saute until wilted, but not brown. Add seasonings, beef stock and ground beef; bring to a boil. Pour into casserole, then cover. Bake in preheated 400-degree oven for 30 minutes without removing cover.

Mrs. Ann Davis
Gentry H.S., Gentry, Arkansas

NORTH DAKOTA FLUFF

1 lg. onion, chopped
1/2 bell pepper, chopped
Butter
1 1/2 lb. ground round
Salt and pepper to taste
1 can whole kernel corn, drained
1 can tomato soup
1 can mushroom soup
1/4 c. rice

Saute onion and pepper in butter in skillet until tender; remove from skillet. Cook ground round in skillet, stirring, until brown. Season with salt and pepper. Stir in corn, soups, onion mixture and rice. Turn into casserole; cover. Bake in preheated 350-degree oven for 45 minutes. Uncover; bake for about 45 minutes longer or until brown.

Mrs. Joan Ericksen
Capitol View Jr. H.S., St. Paul, Minnesota

FOUR-IN-ONE-DISH

1 c. diced potatoes
1/2 c. cooked rice
1 lb. hamburger
1/3 c. diced onions
Salt and pepper to taste
2 c. tomato pieces

Place potatoes, rice, hamburger and onions in casserole. Season with salt and pepper. Pour tomato pieces over the hamburger mixture. Bake in preheated 350-degree oven for 40 to 45 minutes.

Sharon Ambler
Homer Dist. Sch. No. 208, Homer, Illinois

QUICK BEEF AND RICE CASSEROLE

1 c. rice
1 lb. ground beef
1 8-oz. can tomato sauce
2 c. tomato juice
2 c. boiling water
1 sm. bottle stuffed olives
1 tsp. salt
1/8 tsp. garlic salt
1/8 tsp. paprika
1/8 tsp. pepper

Combine all ingredients; mix well. Place in a greased 3-quart casserole. Bake in preheated 350-degree oven for 1 hour. Reduce oven temperature to 250 degrees and bake for 1 hour longer. Grated cheese may be sprinkled over top of beef mixture during the last 30 minutes of baking, if desired.

Mrs. Barbara S. Peterson
Lancaster H.S., Lancaster, Minnesota

RICE CASSEROLE ITALIANO

4 c. sliced zucchini
1 lb. lean ground beef
1 c. chopped onions
1 clove of garlic, crushed
1 tsp. salt
1 tsp. basil
1/2 tsp. oregano
1/4 tsp. pepper
2 c. cooked rice
1   8-oz. can tomato sauce
1 c. cottage cheese
1 egg, beaten
1 c. grated Cheddar cheese

Cook zucchini in boiling salted water for about 2 to 3 minutes; drain well. Saute ground beef, onions, garlic and seasonings until onions are tender. Stir in rice and tomato sauce. Blend cottage cheese and egg. Arrange half the zucchini slices in a buttered shallow 2-quart casserole; spoon on ground beef mixture. Spread cottage cheese over beef mixture. Top with remaining zucchini and sprinkle with Cheddar cheese. Bake in preheated 350-degree oven for 20 to 25 minutes or until bubbly. Yield: 6 servings.

Carolyn S. Heimbuch
Howard D. Crull Intermediate Sch.
Port Huron, Michigan

SPANISH BEEF-RICE

1 lb. ground beef
1 med. onion, chopped
1 c. chopped green pepper
2 c. canned tomatoes or tomato
   juice
1 c. rice
1 tsp. chili powder
1 tsp. salt
1/4 tsp. pepper

Cook ground beef in skillet, stirring, until brown. Add onion and green pepper; cook until tender. Drain off fat. Add tomatoes, rice, chili powder, salt and pepper; mix well. Turn into a casserole; cover. Bake in preheated 375-degree oven for 45 minutes or until rice is done.

Lynda Lillian Henderson
Washington Jr. H.S., Ogden, Utah

SIX-LAYER CASSEROLE

10 potatoes, sliced
Salt and pepper to taste
2 onions, sliced
1 green pepper, sliced
1 c. rice
2 lb. ground beef
1 No. 2 1/2 can tomatoes
1/2 c. water
1 tbsp. sugar
Butter

Cover the bottom of a buttered deep baking dish or casserole with a layer of potatoes. Season with salt and pepper. Top potatoes with a layer of onions, then a layer of green pepper. Spread rice over green pepper. Spread ground beef over rice, then season again. Pour tomatoes and water over top. Sprinkle sugar on top and dot with butter. Bake, covered, in preheated 325-degree oven for 3 hours. Yield: 6 servings.

Mrs. Ann J. Hilliard
Plant City Sr. H.S., Plant City, Florida

WESTERN MEAL-IN-ONE

1 lb. ground beef
1 tbsp. salad oil or bacon
   drippings
1 clove of garlic, minced or
   mashed
1 tsp. salt
1 lg. onion, finely chopped
1 green pepper, seeded and
   chopped
1 tsp. chili powder
1   1-lb. can tomatoes
1   1-lb. can kidney beans
3/4 c. rice
1/4 c. chopped ripe olives
3/4 c. shredded Cheddar cheese

Cook the ground beef in oil in skillet until brown, stirring to separate thoroughly. Add garlic, salt, onion, green pepper and chili powder; saute for 5 minutes or until vegetables are limp. Stir in tomatoes, kidney beans and rice; turn into a greased 2-quart casserole. Bake, uncovered, in a preheated 350-degree oven for 45 minutes. Sprinkle with olives and cheese; bake for 15 minutes longer or until cheese is melted. Yield: 8 servings.

Mrs. Eileen B. Yeakley
Martinsville Jr. H.S., Martinsville, Indiana

WINNEBAGO RICE

1 1/2 lb. ground beef
1 15-oz. can Libby's Spanish rice
1 pkg. green onion chip dip mix
Sharp cheese strips

Cook ground beef in skillet until browned; drain off fat. Stir in rice and onion dip mix, then place in oblong casserole. Arrange cheese strips close together in attractive design on beef mixture. Bake in a preheated 325 to 350-degree oven for 20 minutes.

Mrs. Marilyn Strack
Sanborn Comm. Sch., Sanborn, Iowa

STUFFED PEPPERS AND RICE

1 lb. ground beef
1 tsp. salt
1/2 tsp. pepper
2 lg. green peppers
1/2 c. rice
2 potatoes
1 can tomatoes
1/4 c. butter

Combine ground beef, salt and pepper; mix well. Cut each green pepper into 4 rings. Mix rice with seasoned ground beef; stuff into pepper rings. Lift with wide spatula; place in baking dish. Peel potatoes; cut into cubes. Place around pepper rings. Pour tomatoes over top; dot with butter. Cover. Bake in a preheated 400-degree oven for 1 hour. Yield: 4 servings.

Mrs. Caroline Bode
Robert E. Lee H.S., San Antonio, Texas

TEXAS HASH

1 lb. ground beef
3 lg. onions, sliced
1 lg. green pepper, chopped
1 1-lb. can tomatoes
1/2 c. rice
1 to 2 tsp. chili powder
2 tsp. salt
1/8 tsp. pepper

Place ground beef in a large skillet; cook and stir until light brown. Drain off fat. Add onions and green pepper; cook and stir until onions are tender. Stir in tomatoes, rice, chili powder, salt and pepper; heat through. Pour into ungreased 2-quart casserole; cover. Bake in preheated 350-degree oven for 1 hour. Yield: 4-6 servings.

Sister M. Josepha Book
Forest Park H.S., Ferdinand, Indiana

CHEESY SPAGHETTI BAKE

1/2 lb. ground beef
1/4 c. chopped onion
1 15-oz. can spaghetti sauce
  with mushrooms
1 6-oz. package spaghetti
2 tbsp. butter
4 tbsp. flour
1/4 tsp. salt
3/4 c. evaporated milk
1/3 c. water
1 c. shredded American cheese
2 tbsp. grated Parmesan cheese

Saute ground beef and onion in frying pan until brown; drain off fat. Add spaghetti sauce; simmer for 10 minutes. Break spaghetti into thirds. Cook according to package directions, then drain. Mix spaghetti into sauce. Melt butter in saucepan; stir in flour and salt to make a smooth paste. Add milk and water slowly, stirring constantly; cook over medium heat until thickened. Add 1/2 cup American cheese and the Parmesan cheese; stir until melted. Spread half the spaghetti mixture in 10 x 6 x 2-inch baking dish. Spoon all of the cheese sauce over the spaghetti; top with remaining spaghetti mixture and remaining 1/2 cup American cheese. Bake in preheated 350-degree oven for 15 to 20 minutes.

Mrs. Margery Creek
Francis Scott Key Jr. H.S.
Silver Spring, Maryland

EASY STEAKED SPAGHETTI

1/2 lb. ground beef
1 can cream of tomato soup
1 sm. chopped onion
1/2 green pepper, chopped
1/2 c. grated cheese
2 c. cooked spaghetti
Salt and pepper to taste

Mix all ingredients together and pour into a greased casserole. Bake in a preheated 375-degree oven for 40 minutes.

Ruth Allard
Lyndon Institute, Lyndon Center, Vermont

Stuffed Peppers Trinidad

STUFFED PEPPERS TRINIDAD

4 green peppers
2 tbsp. butter or margarine
3 tbsp. minced onion
1/2 lb. ground beef
1 c. cooked rice
1/2 tsp. salt
1/8 tsp. paprika
1 tsp. Angostura aromatic bitters
1 No. 303 can tomatoes

Cook green peppers in boiling water until just tender; drain. Melt butter in saucepan. Add onion; saute until tender, stirring frequently. Add ground beef; saute until well browned, stirring occasionally. Add rice, salt, paprika and bitters. Cut tops off of green peppers; remove seeds. Fill green pepper cases with beef mixture. Place green peppers in casserole; pour tomatoes around green peppers. Bake in preheated 350-degree oven for 15 to 25 minutes. Yield: 4 servings.

CHUCK CASSEROLE

1 lb. ground beef
3 tbsp. chopped onion
1/2 tsp. salt
1/4 tsp. pepper
1 can golden mushroom soup
1 pkg. Tater Tots

Spread ground beef in casserole. Sprinkle onion, salt and pepper over beef. Spoon soup over top. Push Tater Tots down into beef.

Cover casserole. Bake in preheated 350-degree oven for 1 hour.

Marjane Telck
Rock Springs Jr. H.S., Rock Springs, Wyoming

BEEF-POTATO BAKE

1 lb. ground beef
1/2 c. diagonally sliced celery
1/2 c. chopped onion
1   8 1/2-oz. can cut green beans,
    drained
1 can cream of celery soup
1/3 c. milk
1/2 tsp. salt
Dash of pepper
1   1-lb. package frozen potato
    rounds

Cook ground beef, celery and onion in skillet until brown; drain off fat. Turn into 1 1/2-quart casserole. Top with green beans. Combine soup, milk, salt and pepper; pour over green beans. Stand frozen potato rounds upright around the edge of the casserole. Bake in preheated 350-degree oven for 40 to 45 minutes. Yield: 4-6 servings.

Mrs. Ray R. Robertson
Maaison Schools, Madison, Nebraska

TATER TOT CASSEROLE

1 lb. ground beef
1 sm. onion, chopped
Salt and pepper to taste
1   10-oz. package Tater Tots
1 No. 300 can green beans,
    drained
1 can cream of celery soup
1 soup can milk

Fry ground beef and onion in skillet, stirring constantly until slightly browned. Season with salt and pepper. Place beef mixture in greased casserole; add Tater Tots and green beans. Combine soup and milk; stir until well mixed. Pour over top. Bake in a preheated 350-degree oven for 40 to 50 minutes. One 10-ounce package green beans, prepared according to package directions, may be used instead of canned beans. Yield: 6 servings.

Mrs. Gloria Smith
Valders H.S., Valders, Wisconsin

MEAL-IN-SIXTY-MINUTES CASSEROLE

1 1/2 lb. ground round
1 tsp. salt
1/4 tsp. pepper
1/4 c. chopped onion
1 No. 303 can French-style
    green beans, drained
1 can Cheddar cheese soup
1 1-lb. package Tater Tots

Season beef with salt and pepper. Add onion; mix well. Spread into 8 x 12-inch casserole. Arrange beans evenly over beef mixture. Spread Cheddar cheese soup over beans. Top with Tater Tots. Bake in preheated 350-degree oven for 1 hour. Yield: 6 servings.

Mrs. Paula Calhoun
Fisher H.S., Fisher, Illinois

TAGLIARINI

2 lb. hamburger
1/2 c. chopped green pepper
1 med. onion, chopped
2 tbsp. chili powder
1 tsp. salt
2 tbsp. (firmly packed) brown
    sugar
1 tsp. Worcestershire sauce
1 tsp. vinegar
1/2 tsp. mustard
1 sm. can tomato sauce
1 sm. can tomato paste
1 can whole kernel corn
1 sm. jar stuffed olives
Grated cheese

Cook the hamburger, green pepper and onion in a skillet until brown. Combine the chili powder, salt, brown sugar, Worcestershire sauce, vinegar, mustard, tomato sauce and tomato paste in a small bowl. Rinse the tomato paste can with 1 can water and add the water to the paste mixture. Add the liquid mixture, corn and olives to the hamburger mixture. Place in a baking dish. Bake in preheated 350-degree oven for 45 minutes. Remove from oven; top with grated cheese. Bake for about 10 minutes longer or until cheese melts.

Jeanette Hornbacher
Kennedy Pub. Sch., Kennedy, Minnesota

TASTY TAMALE PIE

2 lb. ground beef
2 lg. onions, chopped
2 c. milk
1 c. yellow cornmeal
1 No. 2 1/2 can tomatoes
1 No. 2 can whole kernel corn
1 No. 2 can olives, drained
2 tbsp. chili powder
2 tsp. salt
Pepper to taste
Butter

Fry ground beef and onions in a large oven-proof skillet until beef is done. Add milk and cornmeal; bring to a boil, stirring. Add tomatoes, corn, olives, chili powder, salt and pepper; mix well. Dot with butter. Bake in a preheated 325-degree oven, stirring occasionally. Add 1/2 to 1 cup tomato juice if more moist pie is desired.

Marguerite S. Darnall
Corona Sr. H.S., Corona, California

BEEFY-CHEESY BISCUIT CASSEROLE

1 1/4 lb. ground beef
1/2 c. chopped onion
1/4 c. diced green pepper
1 8-oz. can tomato sauce
1 1/2 to 2 tbsp. chili powder
3/4 tsp. garlic salt
1 8-oz. can refrigerated buttermilk
    or country-style biscuits
1 1/2 c. shredded Monterey Jack
    or sharp Cheddar cheese
1/2 c. sour cream
1 egg, slightly beaten

Brown beef in skillet, then drain off fat. Add onion, green pepper, sauce, chili powder and garlic salt; simmer for 10 minutes. Separate the 10 biscuits into halves. Place 10 halves in 9 x 9-inch pan. Combine 1/2 cup cheese, sour cream and egg; mix well. Remove beef mixture from heat; stir in sour cream mixture. Spoon over biscuits. Place remaining biscuit halves on top; sprinkle with remaining cheese. Bake in preheated 375-degree oven for 25 to 30 minutes or until biscuits are browned.

Connie Schlimgen
Edison Jr. H.S., Sioux Falls, South Dakota

STAR-STUDDED CASSEROLE

1 lb. ground beef
1 1-lb. can sliced carrots
1 3/4-oz. envelope French's brown
  gravy mix
1/4 c. catsup
1 tbsp. brown sugar
1 tbsp. French's prepared yellow
  mustard
2 or 3 slices bread, lightly buttered

Place ground beef in large skillet; cook until brown, stirring to crumble beef. Drain off excess fat. Pour liquid from carrots into measuring cup; add enough water to make 1 cup liquid. Stir gravy mix, carrots, carrot liquid, catsup, brown sugar and mustard into beef; bring to a boil over medium heat, stirring occasionally. Spoon into 1 1/2-quart shallow casserole. Trim crusts from bread. Cut stars from bread, using a small star-shaped cookie cutter; arrange over casserole. Bake in preheated 400-degree oven for 15 to 20 minutes. Yield: 4-6 servings.

CHEESEBURGER CASSEROLE

1 lb. ground beef
1/4 c. chopped onion
1 8-oz. can tomato sauce
1/4 c. catsup
1/2 tsp. salt
Dash of pepper
1 8-oz. package American cheese slices
1 8-oz. can refrigerated snowflake
  dinner rolls
1 tsp. sesame seeds

Brown ground beef and onion lightly in a skillet. Stir in tomato sauce, catsup and seasonings. Arrange alternate layers of the beef mixture and cheese slices in a 2-quart casserole. Place rolls around edge of casserole, then sprinkle with sesame seeds. Bake in preheated 400-degree oven for 20 to 25 minutes or until rolls are golden brown. Serve hot. Yield: 6 servings.

Mrs. John L. Puffenbarger
Buckhannon-Upshur H.S.
Buckhannon, West Virginia

Star-Studded Casserole

CREAMY GROUND BEEF CASSEROLE

1 1/2 lb. ground beef
1/4 c. chopped onions
1/4 c. milk
1 10 1/2-oz. can cream of
    mushroom soup
1/2 8-oz. package cream cheese,
    softened
1 1/2 tsp. salt
1/4 c. catsup
1 can refrigerator biscuits

Brown the ground beef and onions in skillet; drain. Combine milk, soup and cream cheese until blended; stir in salt, catsup and beef. Pour into 2-quart casserole. Bake, uncovered, in preheated 375-degree oven for 10 minutes. Place biscuits over top and bake for about 15 minutes longer or until biscuits are golden brown. Yield: 5-6 servings.

Jean Searcy
Silver Lake H.S., Silver Lake, Kansas

GROUND BEEF AND VEGETABLE CASSEROLE

1 1/2 lb. ground beef
1 sm. onion, chopped
2 tbsp. flour
1 can tomato soup
1 can cream of mushroom soup
1 3-oz. can sliced mushrooms
1/4 tsp. thyme
1 tsp. salt
1/4 tsp. pepper
3 diced potatoes
3 diced carrots
1 1/4 c. milk
1 1/2 c. biscuit mix
1 c. instant mashed potato flakes

Brown ground beef and onion in large skillet; stir in flour. Simmer, stirring frequently, for 15 minutes. Add soups, mushrooms, seasonings, diced potatoes and carrots. Pour into 9 x 13-inch casserole. Combine 1/2 cup milk and biscuit mix; stir in potato flakes and remaining milk. Spoon over top. Bake in preheated 350-degree oven for about 45 minutes or until vegetables are tender. Yield: 6-8 servings.

Allieta Nelson
Harrison H.S., Colorado Springs, Colorado

HAMBURGER CORN PONE PIE

1 lb. ground beef
1/3 c. chopped onion
1 tbsp. shortening
2 tsp. chili powder
3/4 tsp. salt
1 tsp. Worcestershire sauce
1 c. canned tomatoes
1 c. drained kidney beans
1 c. corn bread batter

Cook beef and onion in melted shortening until brown. Add seasonings and tomatoes. Cover; let simmer for 10 minutes. Add kidney beans; pour mixture into greased casserole. Top with corn bread batter, spreading carefully with wet knife. Bake in preheated 400-degree oven for 20 minutes.

Mrs. Clara Levins
Eastern Jr. H.S., Lynn, Massachusetts

TAMALE PIE

1 lb. ground beef
1/2 c. chopped onion
1 No. 303 can chili beans
1 No. 2 can tomatoes
1 1/2 tsp. chili powder
Salt to taste
1 tsp. oregano
2 tbsp. flour
2 tbsp. water

Cook beef and onion in frying pan until brown. Add beans, tomatoes, chili powder, salt and oregano; cook until heated through and flavors blended. Stir flour in water to make a smooth paste. Add to beef mixture; cook until slightly thickened. Pour into a greased 2-quart casserole.

Topping

1/2 c. flour
2 tsp. sugar
2 tsp. baking powder
1/4 tsp. salt
1/2 c. cornmeal
1 egg
1/3 c. milk
2 tsp. soft shortening

Sift flour, sugar, baking powder, salt and cornmeal together in a mixing bowl. Beat in egg, milk and shortening until just combined. Drop by spoonfuls onto ground beef mixture, then spread to cover top. Bake in preheated 400-degree oven for 20 minutes.

Louise Teague
Iola Jr. H.S., Iola, Kansas

MEAT LOAF CASSEROLE SUPREME

2 lb. ground beef
1/2 c. catsup
1 1/2 tsp. salt
2 onions, chopped
1 egg, beaten
3/4 tsp. pepper
3 c. bread cubes
1 c. string beans, drained
3 lg. stalks celery, chopped
1/2 tsp. poultry seasoning
1/2 c. water
2 tbsp. melted butter
3 c. mashed potatoes

Combine beef, catsup, 1 teaspoon salt, 1 chopped onion, egg and 1/2 teaspoon pepper; mix well. Pat out 1/2 to 3/4 inch thick on waxed paper. Combine bread cubes, beans, celery, poultry seasoning, water and the remaining onion, salt and pepper. Spoon onto beef mixture, then roll up as for jelly roll. Place in baking dish. Bake in a preheated 350-degree oven for 50 minutes. Remove from oven and pour off excess fat. Combine butter and potatoes; spread over top and sides of roll. Return to oven and bake for about 10 minutes longer or until potatoes are browned.

Jerrie Evans
Ontario H.S., Ontario, Oregon

86
GROUND BEEF TOPPED WITH MASHED POTATOES

1 lb. ground beef
1/4 c. chopped onion
1 10-oz. package frozen peas, thawed
1 2-oz. can mushroom pieces, drained
1 can celery soup
1 tsp. salt

Dash of basil
2 tsp. mustard
2 c. mashed potatoes

Cook beef and onion in skillet until brown; pour off excess drippings. Combine peas, mushroom pieces, soup, salt, basil, and mustard; stir into beef mixture. Place in 2-quart casserole; arrange mashed potatoes around top. Bake in a preheated 350-degree oven for 25 to 30 minutes.

Mary A. Vanloh
Chicago Christian H.S., Palos Heights, Illinois

QUICK SHEPHERD'S PIE

1/3 c. chopped onion
1 clove of garlic, crushed
1 to 2 tbsp. salad oil
1 1/2 lb. ground beef
1 10 1/2-oz. can cream of mushroom soup
1 8 1/4-oz. can sliced carrots, drained
1/2 c. chopped dill pickles
1/4 tsp. salt
1/8 tsp. pepper
1 6 to 7-serving env. instant mashed potatoes
2 tbsp. grated Parmesan cheese
2 tbsp. heavy cream
1 tbsp. chopped parsley

Saute onion and garlic in hot oil in large skillet until onion is tender, stirring frequently. Add ground beef; cook, stirring, until brown. Stir in undiluted soup, carrots, dill pickles, salt and pepper; simmer for 15 to 20 minutes, stirring occasionally. Prepare mashed potatoes according to package directions while beef mixture is simmering. Add cheese, cream and parsley to whipped potatoes and mix well. Place beef mixture in 1-quart ovenproof deep dish or casserole; spoon or pipe potato mixture over beef mixture around edge of dish. Brown under broiler; serve at once. Garnish with additional pickle slices. One 10-ounce package frozen carrots, cooked and drained, may be substituted for canned carrots. Dill salad cubes may be used instead of chopped pickles. Yield: 4-6 servings.

Photograph for this recipe on page 16.

Potato-Crowned Casserole

POTATO-CROWNED CASSEROLE

1 lb. ground beef
1 8-oz. can tomato sauce
1 tbsp. French's instant minced
  onion
1 tbsp. vinegar
1 tsp. French's barbecue seasoning
  or chili powder
1/2 tsp. salt
1 5-serving env. French's instant
  mashed potato granules
3 eggs, separated

Cook ground beef in casserole until brown, stirring to crumble beef; drain off excess fat. Stir tomato sauce, onion, vinegar, 1/2 teaspoon barbecue seasoning and salt into beef; bring to a boil, stirring occasionally. Spoon into 2-quart casserole. Prepare mashed potato granules according to package directions. Beat egg whites until stiff peaks form; beat egg yolks just until well blended. Stir egg yolks into potatoes, then fold in egg whites. Spread potato mixture over beef mixture; sprinkle with remaining barbecue seasoning. Bake in preheated 350-degree oven for 40 to 50 minutes or until deep golden brown and puffed.

SNOW-CAPPED HAMBURGER CASSEROLE

1 lb. hamburger
1 can tomato soup
1 can green beans, drained
Mashed potatoes

Brown hamburger in a skillet. Add soup; mix well. Pat into a casserole; cover with green beans. Dot the top with mashed potatoes. Bake in preheated 350-degree oven until potatoes are lightly browned.

Barbara Deane
Glenwood Springs H.S.
Glenwood Springs, Colorado

ENCHILADA CASSEROLE

2 lb. ground beef
1 can mushroom soup
1 can cream of chicken soup
1 can green chilies
1 can taco sauce
1 can evaporated milk
2 doz. tortillas
1 lb. grated cheese

Brown beef; drain off grease. Combine soups, green chilies, taco sauce and milk in saucepan; heat through. Stir in beef. Arrange layers of tortillas, beef mixture and cheese in casserole. Bake in preheated 350-degree oven for 30 minutes. Yield: 12 servings.

Mrs. Becky Lewis
Olney H.S., Olney, Texas

MEXICAN CASSEROLE

1   15-count pkg. tortillas
1   lb. ground beef
1   can Ro-Tel tomatoes
Chopped onions to taste
Salt and pepper to taste
1   can cream of mushroom soup
2   cans cream of chicken soup
1   lb. Cheddar cheese, shredded

Tear tortillas into pieces. Brown beef in a large frypan; add tomatoes, onions, salt and pepper. Mix beef mixture, soups and cheese together; add tortillas. Mix thoroughly. Place in casserole. Bake in preheated 350-degree oven for about 1 hour. Yield: 6-8 servings.

Lynda Herrin
Austwell-Tivoli H.S., Tivoli, Texas

TORTILLA-BEEF-CHEESE BAKE

1   1-lb. can refried beans
1/2 tsp. ground cumin
1/4 tsp. garlic salt
1   c. grated Monterey Jack cheese
3/4 lb. Italian sausage
1 1/2 lb. ground beef
3   cans green chile salsa
6   flour tortillas
3/4 lb. Colby longhorn cheese,
     grated
2   lg. fresh tomatoes, peeled
     and chopped
Sliced green onion tops
Shredded lettuce

Combine beans, cumin, garlic salt and Monterey Jack cheese in top of double boiler. Cook over hot water, stirring frequently, until cheese is melted. Keep mixture hot. Remove casing from sausage. Crumble sausage and beef into hot skillet; cook over medium heat until brown. Drain off grease, then add 2 cans chile salsa. Bring to a boil; reduce heat to moderate and cook, uncovered, until most of liquid evaporates. Spread tortillas with hot bean mixture; spread beef mixture over beans. Roll tortillas lightly; place, seam side down, in single layer in well-greased 9 x 12-inch baking dish. Pour remaining can of chile salsa over top and around sides of tortillas; sprinkle with longhorn cheese. Top with tomatoes and onion tops. Bake, uncovered, in preheated

350-degree oven for 30 minutes. Serve on shredded lettuce. Yield: 6 servings.

Mrs. P. Langston
Alamosa H.S., Alamosa, Colorado

GREEN CHILI PIE

1   lb. ground beef
2   cans cream of chicken soup
1   sm. can green chili peppers,
     drained and chopped
1   pkg. tortillas
1   c. chopped green onion tops
2   c. grated Cheddar cheese

Saute beef in large frypan until beef loses red color. Stir in soup and green chili peppers; set aside. Tear tortillas into small pieces. Line baking dish with a layer of tortillas; add a layer of beef. Sprinkle with part of the onion tops and grated cheese. Repeat layers, ending with cheese. Bake in preheated 350-degree oven for 30 minutes. Yield: 4 servings.

Mrs. Oleta M. Smith
O'Donnell H.S., O'Donnell, Texas

MORE

1/2 lb. pork sausage
1 1/2 lb. ground beef chuck
1   med. onion, chopped
1   lg. can tomatoes
1   sm. package egg noodles,
     cooked
Salt and pepper to taste
1   clove of garlic, minced or
     garlic powder to taste
1   pkg. frozen peas, cooked
1   sm. can pimento strips, drained
1   sm. can pitted ripe olives, drained
1   can button mushrooms

Brown sausage in large frying pan. Add beef and onion; cook until brown. Add tomatoes, noodles, salt, pepper and garlic; simmer for about 20 minutes. Place a layer of the beef mixture, then a layer of peas, pimento, olives and mushrooms in a 9 1/2 x 13 1/2-inch baking pan. Repeat, ending with a layer of beef mixture. Bake for 1 hour in a preheated 350-degree oven. This can be frozen no longer than 3 months.

Mrs. Evelyn Grabowski
Plant City Sr. H.S., Plant City, Florida

Italian-Style Veal Chops

Masterful Meat Casseroles

The heartiest casseroles — the ones you can always depend on to satisfy the biggest appetites in your family — begin with meat. In the following pages, you'll find a wealth of casserole recipes for veal, corned beef, luncheon meats, frankfurters, liver and many more.

For an outstanding veal casserole, try Veal Baked in Sour Cream made with boneless veal, chopped onions, sliced mushrooms and sour cream. Satisfy a man-sized appetite with Man-Style Meat and Potato Casserole. Or try the hearty Southern-style beef dish, Southern Meat Casserole made with stew meat, shredded cabbage and biscuits.

Also included are delicious, filling casseroles made with economical variety meats, such as Salami Casserole, Corned Beef Vegetable Casserole, Scalloped Potatoes with Spam, Tamale Casserole with Ripe Olives, and the best of old favorites, Beans and Franks.

In the recipes which follow, you'll find casseroles to please everyone in your family, and all make taste-tempting one-dish meals.

BATTER-UP BEEF CASSEROLE

1/4 c. butter or margarine
1 1/2 c. self-rising flour
1 1/2 c. milk
1 c. grated Cheddar cheese
2 tbsp. finely chopped onion
1 tbsp. sugar
2 1/2 c. beef stew

Melt butter in 8-inch square baking pan. Combine all ingredients except stew in a mixing bowl. Stir until blended. Pour batter over butter in pan; pour beef stew over batter. Do not stir. Bake in preheated 350-degree oven for about 1 hour or until golden brown. Yield: 6 servings.

Mrs. Miriam Toth
Castro Valley H.S., Castro Valley, California

SWISS STEAK WITH OLIVE-TOMATO SAUCE

1 2-lb. round steak, 1 in. thick
2 med. onions
1/2 c. flour

1 1/2 tsp. salt
1/2 tsp. pepper
3 tbsp. vegetable shortening
1/2 c. sliced pimento-stuffed
   olives
2 16-oz. cans tomatoes
1 tbsp. bottled thick meat sauce
1 bay leaf
1 tsp. light brown sugar
1/8 tsp. thyme leaves

Cut steak into serving pieces. Slice onions; separate into rings. Combine flour, salt and pepper; pound into steak with a tenderizing mallet or edge of a saucer. Heat shortening in large skillet. Add steak; cook until well browned on both sides. Arrange in large, shallow baking dish; place onion rings and olives over steak. Place tomatoes, meat sauce, bay leaf, brown sugar and thyme leaves in saucepan; mix well. Bring to a boil, breaking up tomatoes with back of a spoon. Pour over steak; cover. Bake in preheated 350-degree oven for 1 hour and 30 minutes to 2 hours or until steak is fork tender. Skim off any excess fat before serving. Yield: 6 servings.

Swiss Steak With Olive-Tomato Sauce

BEEF AND DUMPLING BAKE

2 lb. round steak, cut into cubes
1/3 c. flour
2 med. onions, sliced
2 bay leaves
1 4-oz. can sliced mushrooms
1 10 1/2-oz. can cream of chicken
  soup
1 10 1/2-oz. can onion soup
1 can water
1 tbsp. Worcestershire sauce
1 10-oz. package frozen peas or
  green beans
4 green pepper rings
1/2 c. chopped ripe olives
Parsley Dumplings

Dredge steak with flour; cook in small amount of fat in skillet until brown. Add onions, bay leaves, mushrooms, soup, water and Worcestershire sauce; cover. Bake in preheated 400-degree oven for 1 hour and 30 minutes. Remove bay leaves, then add peas, green pepper and olives. Drop dumplings by rounded teaspoonfuls over steak mixture; cover. Bake for 25 minutes longer.

Parsley Dumplings

1 egg
1/3 c. milk
2 tbsp. parsley flakes
2 tbsp. cooking oil
1/4 tsp. sage
1 c. flour
1 1/2 tsp. baking powder
1/2 tsp. salt

Combine the egg, milk, parsley flakes, cooking oil and sage in a medium-sized bowl; mix well. Combine flour, baking powder and salt; add to egg mixture. Stir only until lightly mixed.

Mrs. Beverly Carrington
Larkin H.S., Elgin, Illinois

BEEF AND NOODLE CASSEROLE

1 lb. round steak
2 c. noodles
1 pkg. dry onion soup mix
1 c. sour cream

Broil round steak until brown on both sides. Cook noodles according to package directions.

Trim fat from steak, then cut into 1-inch squares. Combine steak, noodles, soup mix and sour cream; toss until well mixed. Place in oiled baking dish. Bake in preheated 350-degree oven for 15 minutes.

Linda Ryan
Golden Plains H.S., Rexford, Kansas

MAN-STYLE MEAT AND POTATO CASSEROLE

1 1/2 c. beef, cut into strips
1/2 c. thinly sliced onion
2 tbsp. butter
1 c. cream of celery soup
1/3 c. milk
1 c. shredded cheese
Dash of pepper
3 c. cooked sliced potatoes
Paprika

Brown beef; cook onion in butter in a saucepan until tender. Blend soup, milk, 3/4 cup shredded cheese and pepper. Arrange alternate layers of potatoes, beef, onion and sauce in a 1 1/2-quart casserole. Sprinkle top with remaining cheese and paprika. Bake, uncovered, in a preheated 375-degree oven for about 30 minutes.

Mrs. Pat Willoughby
Hamlin H.S., Hamlin, Texas

CHINESE BEEF

1 lb. cubed round steak
1 c. finely chopped celery
2 sm. onions, finely chopped
1 can chicken-noodle soup
1 can cream of mushroom soup
2 soup cans hot water
1/2 c. rice
4 tsp. soya sauce

Trim fat from steak. Cook steak in small amount of fat in large frypan until brown. Remove and place in large casserole or roasting pan. Cook the celery and onions in the frypan until crisp-tender. Add soups, water, rice and soya sauce to the frypan and heat through. Pour into casserole and mix well. Bake in preheated 325-degree oven for 2 hours.

Rosalie Wentzell
Stettler Jr. H.S., Stettler, Alberta, Canada

CHOPPED BEEF AND YORKSHIRE PUDDING

1 c. flour
Salt to taste
1 c. milk
2 eggs
Freshly grated nutmeg
Dash of cayenne pepper
Dash of mace
1 1/2 lb. finely chopped beef
1 1/2 tbsp. grated onion
1 tsp. finely chopped parsley
1 tsp. chives
1/2 clove of garlic, finely chopped
Pepper to taste
Pinch of cloves

Sift flour and salt together; add milk gradually, stirring constantly, until smooth. Add eggs, one at a time, beating well after each addition. Season with nutmeg, cayenne pepper and mace; beat thoroughly. Combine beef, onion, parsley, chives and garlic; season with salt, pepper and cloves. Heat a well-greased large shallow baking pan in a preheated 450-degree oven until sizzling; pour in 1/2 of the batter. Spread on beef mixture quickly, using a wet spatula; pour remaining batter over the beef. Bake until the pudding rises and begins to brown. Reduce the oven temperature to 350 degrees; bake for 20 minutes longer or until pudding leaves the side of the pan. May be served with rich tomato sauce, brown sauce or mushroom sauce.

Shirley Belyea
Irvine Sch., Irvine, Alberta, Canada

ROUND STEAK IN CASSEROLE

1 1/2 lb. round steak
Flour
Salt and pepper to taste
1 can English peas
1 lb. fresh mushrooms
1 sm. onion, chopped
1 c. tomato juice

Cut steak into serving pieces; sprinkle with flour, salt and pepper. Pound flour mixture into steak. Sear in hot shortening in a skillet. Place in baking dish; add peas, mushrooms, onion and tomato juice, then cover. Bake in a preheated 300-degree oven for 2 hours.

Virginia S. McEwen
Coosa Co. H.S., Rockford, Alabama

HERITAGE BEEF-RICE CASSEROLE

1 1/2 lb. beef steak, cut in cubes
3 tbsp. cooking oil
1/2 c. chopped onion
3 c. cooked rice
1/2 c. sour cream
1 tsp. salt
1/2 c. catsup
1 c. cottage cheese
1/2 c. chopped sweet pickle
1/4 tsp. pepper
1 c. grated Cheddar cheese

Cook beef in hot oil in skillet until lightly browned on all sides; add onion. Simmer, covered, for about 20 minutes. Drain off grease. Add remaining ingredients except cheese, blending thoroughly. Turn into buttered 2-quart casserole. Sprinkle with cheese. Bake in preheated 350-degree oven for about 25 minutes. Yield: 8 servings.

Mrs. Patricia Langston
Alamosa H.S., Alamosa, Colorado

JIFFY STEAK CASSEROLE

1 lb. cube steak
Flour
Salt and pepper to taste
2 tbsp. fat
1 pkg. dry onion soup mix
1/2 c. rice

Dredge steak in flour; sprinkle with salt and pepper. Place in fat in casserole. Bake in preheated 400-degree oven until brown. Reduce heat to 350 degrees. Sprinkle soup mix over meat. Add 1 1/4 cups water. Add rice; cover. Bake for about 1 hour or until meat is tender and rice is done. Add water as needed. Yield: 4 servings.

Judith I. Jones
Richlands H.S., Richlands, North Carolina

STEAK AND RICE ORIENTAL

1 1/2 lb. round steak, cut in cubes
1 c. rice
1 can cream of mushroom soup
1 can cream of chicken soup
2 c. cold water
1 c. finely chopped celery
1/4 c. minced onion

1 tsp. salt
2 tbsp. soy sauce

Brown steak in skillet rubbed with shortening. Combine remaining ingredients; mix well. Add browned meat to rice mixture. Pour into greased casserole. Bake in a preheated 350-degree oven for 1 hour and 15 minutes. Yield: 5 servings.

Marjorie Harris
Greeley H.S., Greeley, Nebraska

SOUTHERN MEAT CASSEROLE PIE

1 lb. stew meat
Flour
Salt and pepper to taste
Garlic salt to taste
Oregano to taste
2 med. potatoes
1 can whole tomatoes
1 can peas and carrots
1 onion, chopped
1/4 head cabbage, shredded
8 drop biscuits

Dredge the stew meat in flour and seasonings. Brown in a small amount of fat in a Dutch oven. Cut potatoes in large chunks and add to meat. Add tomatoes, peas and carrots including liquid, onion and cabbage; add enough water to cover. Lower heat; cover. Cook until the potatoes are tender. Remove lid. Drop biscuits on top of stew. Bake in preheated 400-degree oven for 10 to 12 minutes or until biscuits are done. Canned biscuits may be used, if desired.

Sue Slusser
Agra H.S., Agra, Oklahoma

SWISS STEAK CASSEROLE

4 cubed steaks
Salt and pepper to taste
1/2 c. flour
2 tbsp. oil
1   10-oz. box frozen mixed
*   vegetables, thawed*
1/2 c. chopped onions
1/2 c. chopped green peppers
1/4 c. steak sauce
1 No. 300 can tomato sauce

Season steaks with salt and pepper; dredge lightly with flour. Heat oil in a large skillet; brown steaks in oil. Place steaks in a shallow baking pan; arrange vegetables around and on top of the steaks. Combine steak sauce and tomato sauce; pour over vegetables. Cover baking pan. Bake in a preheated 300-degree oven for 1 hour or until vegetables and steaks are tender. Serve with mounds of fluffy mashed potatoes. Yield: 4 servings.

Mrs. Maxine Thompson
Washington H.S., East Chicago, Indiana

VEGETABLE-BEEF CASSEROLE

2 lb. beef, cut in 1-in. cubes
1/3 c. flour
1 tbsp. salt
1/2 c. chopped onion
1/3 c. shortening
2 c. hot water
1 tbsp. Worcestershire sauce
4 c. diced vegetables
1 recipe pastry for 1-crust pie

Dip beef cubes in flour seasoned with salt; brown beef and onion in shortening in skillet. Add water; cook over low heat for about 30 minutes. Add Worcestershire sauce and vegetables; cook for about 20 minutes or until vegetables are almost tender. Place in casserole. Roll pastry 1/8 inch thick. Cut in strips; weave across beef filling. Trim strips even with edge of casserole. Place 3/4-inch strip of pastry around edge of casserole, covering ends of latticed pastry strips. Flute with fingers or a fork. Bake in preheated 425-degree oven for 20 to 25 minutes. Yield: 6 servings.

Sister Mary Rosario, SC
Archbishop Alter H.S., Kettering, Ohio

SHOPPER'S CASSEROLE

1 1/2 lb. lean stew meat
1 can onion soup
1 can cream of mushroom soup

Cut the stew meat in 1-inch cubes. Combine stew meat and soups in casserole. Bake in preheated 300-degree oven for 3 hours and 30 minutes. Yield: 6 servings.

Phyllis Fry
Orrville H.S., Orrville, Ohio

51

EASY BAKED STEW

1 1/2 lb. lean beef
2 tsp. salt
1/4 tsp. basil leaves
1/4 tsp. pepper
2 stalks celery
4 carrots
2 onions
1 can tomato soup
1/2 soup can water
3 potatoes

Cut the beef in 1 1/2-inch cubes; place in a 3-quart casserole. Sprinkle with salt, basil and pepper. Cut the celery in diagonal slices. Cut the carrots in half lengthwise, then cut in half crosswise. Cut onions in 1/2-inch slices, then add celery, carrots and onions to casserole. Combine soup and water; stir until well blended. Pour soup mixture over beef and vegetables, tossing to coat all ingredients. Cover tightly. Bake in preheated 300-degree oven for 3 hours. Peel and cube the potatoes, then add to casserole. Bake for 45 minutes longer. Yield: 5-7 servings.

Mrs. Gloria Smith
Valders H.S., Valders, Wisconsin

EASY OVEN STEW

1 lb. stew meat
1/2 c. red wine
1   10 1/2-oz. can consomme
3/4 tsp. salt
1/8 tsp. pepper
1 med. onion, peeled and sliced
1/4 c. fine dry bread crumbs
1/4 c. flour

Combine meat, wine, consomme, salt, pepper and onion in casserole. Combine the bread crumbs and flour; pour over top of meat mixture, then cover. Bake in preheated 300-degree oven for 3 hours.

Mrs. Joanne Litz
Tulare Western H.S., Tulare, California

FIVE-HOUR STEW

1 to 1 1/2 lb. beef cubes
1 can whole potatoes
1 can whole onions
1 c. sliced carrots
1 can tomato soup

1/2 soup can water
Salt and pepper to taste

Combine beef cubes, potatoes, onions and carrots in a large bowl. Combine the soup and water in a small bowl; stir until blended. Add the soup mixture to the beef mixture and season. Place in a casserole; cover. Bake in a preheated 250-degree oven for 5 hours. Other vegetables may be added, if desired.

Barbara J. Ebner
Middletown Area H.S., Middletown, Pennsylvania

FAVORITE BEEF STEW

1 to 2 lb. stew meat
2 beef bouillon cubes
2 c. hot water
2 tbsp. tapioca
2 med. onions, sliced
2 tbsp. bread crumbs
1 sm. can mushrooms

Cook stew meat in a frypan, turning until all sides are brown; place in a casserole. Dissolve the bouillon cubes in hot water, then add bouillon, tapioca, onions, bread crumbs and mushrooms to steak. Bake, covered, in preheated 350-degree oven for 4 hours. Serve with mashed potatoes, rice or noodles.

Connie Ramlow
Zanesville H.S., Zanesville, Ohio

SPICY OVEN BEEF STEW

2 lb. stew meat
1 lg. can tomatoes
8 carrots, cut in lg. chunks
1 c. celery chunks
1/2 pkg. onion soup mix
1 tbsp. sugar
1 tbsp. salt
1/2 c. cooking sherry
3 tbsp. tapioca
2 slices bread, cubed
Dash of marjoram
Dash of rosemary
Dash of thyme
1 pkg. frozen peas, cooked

Combine all ingredients except the peas in a baking dish; cover. Bake in a preheated 225 to 250-degree oven for 5 hours and 40 minutes. Remove from oven; stir in peas. Return to oven and bake for 20 minutes longer. Yield: 6-8 servings.

Mary Cay Ross
Mahtomedi Middle Sch., Mahtomedi, Minnesota

CORNED BEEF-VEGETABLE CASSEROLE

    5 to 6 med. potatoes, cooked and
        sliced
    1 can corned beef, broken up
    1 med. onion, chopped
    1 can green beans or peas, drained
    1 can cream of celery or
        mushroom soup
    2 tbsp. milk

Place a layer of potatoes in a greased casserole. Combine the corned beef, onion and green beans in a bowl; toss to mix well. Cover the potato layer with a layer of half the corned beef mixture. Place remaining potatoes in a layer over the corned beef mixture, then add the remaining corned beef mixture. Combine the soup and milk; mix thoroughly.

Spread soup mixture over top. Bake in preheated 350-degree oven for 20 to 30 minutes.

Anne M. Thurbide
Villa Madonna Sch.
Bras d'or, Nova Scotia, Canada

YANKEE CABBAGE ROLLS

    4 lg. cabbage leaves
    1   15 1/2-oz. can corned beef
        hash
    1   10 1/2-oz. can Franco-American
        chicken gravy
    1/2 c. sliced cooked carrots
    1/2 tsp. caraway seed

Cook cabbage in boiling, salted water for several minutes to soften; drain. Divide hash among cabbage leaves. Fold in sides of leaves; roll up, securing with toothpicks, if necessary. Place, seam side down, in shallow 10 x 6 x 2-inch baking dish. Pour gravy over cabbage rolls; stir carrots and caraway seed into gravy. Bake in preheated 350-degree oven for 30 minutes or until hot. Yield: 4 servings.

Yankee Cabbage Rolls

HIBERNIAN HODGEPODGE

1   3/4-oz. envelope French's brown
gravy mix
1 c. water
1   10-oz. package frozen peas and
carrots
1   10-oz. package frozen lima beans
1   12-oz. can corned beef, cut in
chunks
1/4 c. Widmer's Burgundy or
claret (opt.)
1   5-serving env. French's instant
mashed potato granules
1 tbsp. French's instant minced
onion
1 tsp. French's parsley flakes
1 hard-cooked egg, sliced (opt.)

Combine gravy mix, water, peas and carrots
and lima beans in large saucepan. Heat to boiling point; simmer for 5 to 10 minutes or until
lima beans are tender. Stir in corned beef and
Burgundy; spoon into 2-quart casserole. Prepare mashed potatoes according to package
directions; stir in onion and parsley flakes.
Spoon around edge of casserole. Bake in preheated 400-degree oven for 20 to 25 minutes;
garnish with sliced egg to form shamrock
shape. Yield: 6 servings.

REUBEN CASSEROLE

1   12-oz. can corned beef
1/4 c. Thousand Island dressing
1   1-lb. can sauerkraut
1/2 lb. Swiss cheese, grated
1/4 c. margarine
6 slices rye bread

Crumble corned beef into well-greased 12 x
8-inch baking dish. Dot with Thousand Island
dressing. Drain sauerkraut well and spread
over the top. Cover with cheese. Melt margarine. Tear rye bread into crumbs. Toss with
margarine and sprinkle over surface of casserole. Bake in preheated 350-degree oven for
30 minutes or until hot and bubbly.

Mrs. Carolyn K. Simpson
Burbank Sr. H.S., Burbank, California

Hibernian Hodgepodge

CRUSTY CORNED BEEF CASSEROLE

1   12-oz. can corned beef
1   16-oz. can green beans,
    drained
1/2 c. chili sauce
1 tbsp. prepared mustard
1 pkg. corn bread mix
1/2 c. pitted chopped ripe olives

Preheat oven to 400 degrees. Break up corned beef into baking dish. Add beans, chili sauce and mustard; stir well. Prepare corn bread mix according to package directions; add olives. Spoon batter over corned beef mixture. Bake for 40 minutes.

Helen Giles
Susan Bloch English Sch., Seldovia, Alaska

MOUSSAKA

1 c. finely chopped onion
1 1/2 lb. ground lamb or chuck
1 clove of garlic, crushed
Butter
1/2 tsp. dried oregano leaves
1 tsp. dried basil leaves
1/2 tsp. cinnamon
Salt
Pepper
2   8-oz. cans tomato sauce
2 eggplant
2 tbsp. flour
2 c. milk
2 eggs
1/2 c. grated Parmesan cheese
1/2 c. grated Cheddar cheese
2 tbsp. dry bread crumbs

Saute the onion, lamb and garlic in 2 tablespoons butter in Dutch oven, stirring, for about 10 minutes or until brown. Add oregano, basil, cinnamon, 1 teaspoon salt, a dash of pepper and tomato sauce; bring to a boil, stirring constantly. Reduce heat; simmer, uncovered, for 30 minutes. Cut the unpared eggplant in half lengthwise, then cut crosswise in 1/2-inch thick slices. Place in broiler pan; sprinkle lightly with salt. Brush with 1/2 cup melted butter. Broil 4 inches from source of heat for 4 minutes on each side or until golden. Melt 2 tablespoons butter in medium saucepan; remove from heat. Stir in the flour, 1/2 teaspoon salt and dash of pepper. Add milk gradually. Bring to a boil, stirring constantly. Cook and stir until thickened; remove from heat. Place the eggs in a small bowl; beat with a wire whisk. Add a small amount of the hot white sauce, beating with the whisk. Return the egg mixture to the saucepan; stir until well mixed. Set aside. Place a layer of overlapping eggplant slices in a shallow 2-quart baking dish; sprinkle with 2 tablespoons each of the Parmesan and Cheddar cheeses. Stir the bread crumbs into the lamb mixture, then spoon over the eggplant in casserole. Sprinkle with 2 tablespoons each of the cheeses. Add the remaining eggplant, overlapping the slices and cover with the reserved sauce. Sprinkle the remaining cheeses on top. Bake in a preheated 350-degree oven for 35 to 40 minutes or until golden brown. Cool slightly before serving. Cut in squares.

Elizabeth Ann Seefeldt
Dakota Comm. Unit H.S., Dakota, Illinois

ARMENIAN-STYLE LAMB

6 carrots, peeled
8 med. potatoes, peeled and halved
1 eggplant, cut in chunks
2 onions, peeled and sliced
1 lb. squash, cut in 1/2-in. slices
4 fresh tomatoes, halved or
    1   28-oz. can tomatoes
Several sprigs of parsley, chopped
1 bay leaf
1 clove of garlic, minced
2 tsp. salt
1/2 tsp. pepper
6 lamb chops
1/4 c. all-purpose flour

Arrange carrots, potatoes, eggplant, onions and squash in deep baking dish or Dutch oven. Top with tomatoes. Combine parsley, bay leaf, half of garlic, 1 1/2 teaspoons salt and 1/4 teaspoon pepper; sprinkle over vegetables. Rub lamb chops with remaining garlic, salt and pepper. Arrange over vegetables. Bake, covered, in preheated 375-degree oven for 1 hour. Remove from oven. Mix flour with 1/2 cup water until smooth. Lift chops in several places and stir flour mixture into pan juices. Bake, uncovered, for 20 minutes longer, or until gravy is thickened. If using canned tomatoes, drain and reserve 1/2 cup to use with flour. Yield: 6 servings.

Mrs. Marie Heltzel
Union Co. H.S., Lake Butler, Florida

Lamb Manicotti Delight

LAMB MANICOTTI DELIGHT

    1 lb. ground lamb
    1 10-oz. package frozen spinach
    1 12-oz. carton cream-style
       cottage cheese
    1 egg, slightly beaten
    1 tsp. oregano
    1/4 tsp. pepper
    1/4 tsp. instant minced garlic
    2 tsp. salt
    1 8-oz. package manicotti
    1/3 c. chopped onion
    1/4 c. cooking oil
    1/4 c. flour
    1 3/4 c. milk
    1/2 c. water
    1/2 c. grated Parmesan cheese

Cook lamb in large skillet until brown; drain. Cook spinach according to package directions while lamb is cooking; drain. Add to lamb. Add cottage cheese, egg, oregano, pepper, garlic and 1 teaspoon salt; mix well. Chill. Cook manicotti according to package directions until just tender. Saute onion in cooking oil until tender while manicotti is cooking. Add flour and remaining salt to onion; stir until mixed. Add milk and water gradually, stirring constantly; cook, stirring, until thick and bubbly. Add Parmesan cheese; stir until combined. Reserve 1/2 cup sauce; pour remaining sauce into large, shallow baking dish, spreading evenly. Stuff manicotti with lamb mixture; place manicotti side by side in single layer over sauce. Pour reserved sauce over manicotti; sprinkle with additional Parmesan

cheese, if desired. Cover. Bake in preheated 350-degree oven for about 20 minutes. Uncover baking dish; bake for 10 minutes longer. Yield: 6 servings.

LAMB AND VEGETABLE BAKE

    1 lg. onion, sliced
    1 lg. tomato, sliced
    1/2 c. chopped celery
    4 lamb neck slices, about
       1 in. thick
    1 tsp. salt
    1/4 tsp. pepper
    1/2 c. stock or bouillon

Arrange onion, tomato and celery in shallow baking dish. Top with lamb. Sprinkle with salt and pepper. Pour stock over lamb and vegetables. Bake in preheated 350-degree oven for 30 to 45 minutes or until lamb is tender.

Sister Carmela Belzile, scim
V.B.D.H.S., Van Buren, Maine

CREAMY LIVER CASSEROLE

    1 sm. onion, sliced
    2 tbsp. fat
    1 lb. liver, cut in sm. pieces
    4 tbsp. flour
    1 c. milk or water
    Salt and pepper to taste
    1 can peas
    1 c. cooked rice or bread crumbs

Saute onion slices in fat in frypan until brown. Remove onion, then add the liver and saute until brown. Remove liver. Stir flour into the pan juices to make a smooth paste. Add the milk, stirring constantly; cook until smooth and thick. Stir in seasonings. Place peas in casserole; add liver, rice and gravy. Arrange onion slices over top. Bake in preheated 350-degree oven for 20 to 30 minutes.

Mrs. Jeannette Hargroves
Abingdon H.S., Abingdon, Virginia

CHOPPED LIVER IN CASSEROLE

    1 1/2 qt. boiling water
    2 tsp. salt
    3/4 c. rice
    2 slices bacon, diced
    1/3 c. sliced onion

1 tbsp. chopped green pepper
1 c. tomato juice
1/2 lb. parboiled liver, chopped
1/8 tsp. pepper
1 tbsp. butter or margarine

Combine boiling water and 1 1/4 teaspoons salt in saucepan. Add rice; cook until tender. Fry bacon in large frying pan until golden brown; remove from pan. Cook onion and green pepper in bacon drippings until tender; stir in tomato juice, rice, liver, bacon, remaining salt and pepper. Pour into well-greased 1 1/2-quart casserole; dot with butter. Cover casserole. Bake at 350 degrees for 1 hour.

Mrs. Marion Price Elkin
East Duplin H.S., Beulaville, North Carolina

BEANS AND FRANKS

9 frankfurters
9 slices American cheese
1/3 c. molasses
1/2 c. chopped onion
1 family-size can pea beans
Catsup

Cut a lengthwise slash in frankfurters halfway through. Place 1/2 slice of cheese in each frankfurter. Combine molasses, onion and pea beans; mix well. Spoon bean mixture in a greased casserole. Place remaining cheese over top of bean mixture. Arrange frankfurters over cheese; cover frankfurters with catsup. Bake in preheated 350-degree oven for 45 minutes.

Mrs. Dorothy J. Hemenway, Home Ec. Dept. Head
W. Boylston Jr.-Sr. H.S.
W. Boylston, Massachusetts

WIENER QUICKIE

3 med. tomatoes
Flour
6 wieners
1 med. green pepper, sliced
1 can whole kernel corn
1 lg. onion, thinly sliced
1/2 tsp. salt
1/4 tsp. pepper
1 clove of garlic, minced

Cut the tomatoes in 1-inch thick slices; dredge slices in flour. Cut the wieners in 1/2-inch pieces. Arrange tomato slices, wieners, green pepper slices, corn and onion slices in alternate layers in a greased 1 1/2-quart casserole. Sprinkle each layer with salt, pepper and garlic. Bake, covered, in a preheated 350-degree oven for 30 minutes. Yield: 4-6 servings.

Lynnell Holland
Chiloquin H.S., Chiloquin, Oregon

WIENERS ITALIAN

4 or 5 manicotti
4 or 5 frankfurters or meat loaf
  mixture
3 c. Ragu spaghetti sauce
  with mushrooms
1/2 c. grated Cheddar cheese

Cook manicotti in boiling, salted water until almost tender; drain well. Slip 1 frankfurter into each manicotti. Spread 1/2 cup spaghetti sauce in shallow oblong baking dish; place stuffed manicotti on top of the sauce. Pour remaining sauce over manicotti; sprinkle with cheese. Bake in preheated 350-degree oven for 30 minutes. Yield: 4-5 servings.

Erma Ehrler Goehring
Harbor Creek H.S., Harbor Creek, Pennsylvania

SCALLOPED POTATOES WITH SPAM

6 med. potatoes
3 tbsp. margarine
2 tbsp. flour
3 c. milk
1 tsp. salt
1/4 tsp. pepper
2 tbsp. chopped onion
1/2 to 1 c. cubed Spam

Peel the potatoes and slice thin. Cook in a small amount of boiling salted water for about 15 minutes or until just tender. Melt margarine in a saucepan, then blend in flour. Stir in the milk gradually. Add salt and pepper; cook and stir until thickened. Place half the potatoes in a greased 2-quart casserole; cover with half the onion. Spoon half the white sauce over onion, then add the Spam in an even layer. Repeat layers of potatoes, onion and white sauce; cover. Bake in a preheated 350-degree oven for about 1 hour. Uncover; bake for about 15 minutes longer or until top is browned. Yield: 4-6 servings.

Mrs. Hilda J. Finch
Fort Edward H.S., Fort Edward, New York

SPAM AND VEG-ALL CASSEROLE

1 can Spam
2 c. wide egg noodles
1   16-oz. can Veg-All
1 can cream of mushroom soup
1/2 c. milk
1 tsp. minced onion (opt.)

Cut Spam into 9 or 10 slices; cut each slice in a triangle. Place in 1 1/2-quart casserole. Place in 425-degree oven while preparing noodles. Cook noodles in boiling water for 5 minutes and drain. Combine noodles, vegetables with liquid, soup, milk and onion. Reduce oven temperature to 350 degrees. Remove 6 or 7 slices of Spam from casserole. Pour noodle mixture over remaining Spam. Arrange reserved slices on top. Bake for 30 minutes.

Mrs. Kristen Roudybush
Grand Valley Comm. Sch., Kellerton, Iowa

KRAUT HEIDELBERG

1 can luncheon meat
1/4 c. margarine
1 lg. onion, chopped
2 cloves of garlic, minced
2 tbsp. flour
2 tsp. sugar
1 can beef broth
1 c. canned tomato juice
1 c. tomato paste
1 can sauerkraut, drained
1 c. sour cream

Cut luncheon meat into 1/4-inch slices and then into strips. Cook in margarine in skillet until browned. Add onion and garlic; cook until tender. Stir in flour and sugar. Add beef broth, tomato juice and paste. Cook, stirring constantly, until thickened. Spread sauerkraut into baking dish. Pour meat sauce over top. Bake in a preheated 350-degree oven for 40 minutes. Pour sour cream over top, swirling lightly with a fork. Bake for 5 minutes longer.

Dorotha Hurst
Baytown Jr. Sch., Baytown, Texas

SALAMI CASSEROLE

6 tbsp. butter
1/2 c. flour
1 tsp. salt
Dash of pepper
4 c. milk

4 c. grated sharp Cheddar cheese
10 med.-sized cooked potatoes
8 hard-cooked eggs, sliced
1 lb. salami, cut in strips

Melt butter in saucepan. Blend in flour, salt and pepper. Add milk slowly. Cook and stir until thickened. Stir in cheese. Slice potatoes 1/2 inch thick. Place 1/2 of the potatoes in casserole. Add a layer of eggs and a layer of salami. Cover with half the cheese sauce. Repeat layers ending with cheese sauce. Bake in preheated 350-degree oven for about 20 minutes or until brown and bubbly.

Leah K. Massey
Smithville Middle Sch., Smithville, Indiana

FAVORITE CASSEROLE

1 can cream of mushroom soup
1 can hominy, drained and rinsed
1 can tamales in tomato sauce
2 cans Vienna sausages
Cheese wedges (opt.)

Mix mushroom soup and hominy together. Place tamales in baking dish; pour soup mixture over tamales. Arrange Vienna sausages and cheese wedges on top. Bake, covered, in a preheated 350-degree oven for 1 hour.

Mrs. Marie Freeman
Doyle H.S., Knoxville, Tennessee

TAMALE CASSEROLE WITH RIPE OLIVES

1 can tamales
1 No. 303 can creamed corn
1 No. 303 can ripe pitted olives
1 No. 303 can whole kernel corn, drained
Salt and pepper
1 pkg. Doritos or corn chips
Milk (opt.)

Remove wrapping from tamales and cut into pieces, if desired. Arrange half the creamed corn, ripe olives and whole kernel corn in layers in a 2-quart casserole. Add seasonings to taste, then add the tamales. Sprinkle with half the Doritos. Repeat the layers and top with remaining Doritos. Pour in milk if a moist casserole is desired. Bake in a preheated 375-degree oven for 40 to 45 minutes. Serve hot.

Cynthia Atkins
Altoona-Midway Jr.-Sr. H.S., Buffalo, Kansas

CHOP SUEY CASSEROLE

1 1/2 lb. veal and pork, cubed
1 med. onion, diced
1 c. diced celery
2 tbsp. green pepper
2 tbsp. pimento
1/2 c. uncooked rice
1 can cream of mushroom soup
1 can cream of chicken soup
1 soup can water
1 can mixed chow mein vegetables
1 can bean sprouts
1 sm. can water chestnuts, sliced
1 can mushrooms
3 to 4 tbsp. soy sauce
Salt and pepper to taste
Chow mein noodles

Cook veal, pork and onion in skillet until brown. Add remaining ingredients except noodles; mix well. Turn into casserole; cover. Bake in preheated 350-degree oven for 1 hour and 30 minutes. Uncover and sprinkle with chow mein noodles. Bake for 30 minutes longer.

Mrs. Karin Bargar
Pattengill Jr. H.S., Lansing, Michigan

ITALIAN-STYLE VEAL CHOPS

3 tbsp. olive oil
3 tbsp. butter
8 veal chops, 3/4 in. thick
1 1/2 c. thinly sliced fresh carrots
1 c. finely chopped fresh celery
1 c. chopped fresh tomatoes
1/2 c. finely chopped fresh onion
1 1/2 tsp. salt
1/4 tsp. ground pepper
1/3 c. chopped fresh parsley
2 med. fresh tomatoes
1/2 tsp. basil leaves

Heat oil and butter in large skillet. Add veal chops; cook over moderate heat until brown on both sides. Remove from skillet. Add carrots, celery, chopped tomatoes and onion to skillet; sprinkle with salt and pepper. Cook over low heat, stirring to blend in brown particles from bottom of skillet, until vegetables are glazed. Arrange vegetable mixture in bottom of large, shallow casserole; top with single layer of veal chops. Sprinkle with parsley. Cut each tomato into 4 slices; place 1 slice on each chop. Sprinkle with basil; cover. Bake in pre-

heated 350-degree oven for 30 minutes. Remove cover; bake for 15 minutes longer or until veal is tender. Yield: 8 servings.

Photograph for this recipe on page 46.

VEAL BAKED IN SOUR CREAM

1 1/2 lb. boneless veal,
cut in cubes
1 1/2 tbsp. butter
1 tbsp. chopped onion
1/2 lb. sliced mushrooms
1 tbsp. flour
3 tbsp. water or stock
3/4 c. sour cream
1/2 tsp. salt
1/8 tsp. pepper

Brown veal in butter in skillet; transfer to an ovenproof baking dish. Saute the onion and mushrooms in skillet; stir in flour, water, sour cream, salt and pepper. Pour mushroom sauce over veal; cover. Bake in preheated 250-degree oven for 1 hour. Yield: 4 servings.

Sister Mary Benedict
Mt. St. Benedict Sch., Crookston, Minnesota

VEAL HOT DISH

1 lb. veal steak, cubed
3 tbsp. butter
3 med. onions, sliced
1 1/2 c. diced celery
1/2 c. rice
1 sm. can mushrooms
1/4 green pepper, diced
3 tbsp. soy sauce
1 can mushroom soup
1 can chicken-rice soup
2 soup cans water
1/2 tsp. salt
Pepper to taste
1/2 c. salted chopped almonds

Cook veal in butter in skillet until brown. Remove to casserole. Cook onions in same skillet until tender. Combine veal, onions, celery, rice, mushrooms, green pepper, soy sauce, soups, water, salt and pepper in skillet; mix well. Spoon into baking dish. Bake in preheated 350-degree oven for 1 hour. Sprinkle almonds on top; bake for 30 minutes longer.

Mrs. Joan Ericksen
Capitol View Jr. H.S., St. Paul, Minnesota

High Hat Chicken Supper

Perky Poultry Casseroles

Poultry casseroles are an economical and delicious way to please family and guests at mealtime. Chicken and turkey have outstanding flavor appeal when combined with other foods and seasonings in taste-tempting casseroles. In the following pages, you'll find mouth-watering poultry casseroles for all occasions.

Company dinners are perfect occasions for serving such poultry delights as Chicken and Dressing Company Casserole made with chicken, minced onion, celery, bread crumbs and cream of chicken soup, or Delicious Chicken and Asparagus Casserole made with chicken breasts, asparagus, cream of chicken soup, lemon juice and Cheddar cheese. Add Italian flair to supper parties with Chicken Tetrazzini, a delicious combination of chicken, bacon, green pepper and macaroni.

Try any or all of the following casseroles, confident that all are trusted by innovative home economics teachers.

AMISH TURKEY CASSEROLE

1 med. onion, finely chopped
2   1-lb. loaves bread, cubed
1 c. butter, melted
4 eggs, well beaten
1 1/2 qt. milk
1 tbsp. salt
1 tbsp. celery salt
2 tbsp. flaked parsley
2 1/2 lb. cooked turkey, finely cut

Saute onion and bread cubes in melted butter. Combine eggs, milk, salt, celery salt and parsley; blend well. Add to bread mixture. Fold in turkey. Place in greased casserole. Bake in preheated 350-degree oven for 1 hour.

Mrs. Lucy B. Bickel
Eastern Lebanon Co. H.S.
Myerstown, Pennsylvania

DAISY'S TURKEY DIVAN

1/4 c. butter
1/4 c. flour
1 1/2 c. turkey broth
1/8 tsp. nutmeg
1/2 c. sour cream
1/2 c. Parmesan cheese
2 pkg. frozen broccoli spears
1 lb. cooked turkey or chicken

Melt butter in a saucepan; stir in flour until smooth. Add broth; cook, stirring constantly, until thickened. Stir in nutmeg, sour cream and cheese. Cook broccoli according to package directions. Arrange broccoli in baking dish; cover with turkey. Pour sauce over turkey. Bake in preheated 375-degree oven for 30 minutes. Yield: 4-5 servings.

Mrs. Hazel R. Johnson
Central Jr. H.S., Sheridan, Wyoming

COMPANY TURKEY PIE

1/2 c. chopped onion
2 tbsp. butter
1 c. sliced mushrooms (opt.)
1/8 tsp. thyme
1/8 tsp. curry powder
Salt to taste
Pepper to taste (opt.)
1 can cream of mushroom soup
Turkey gravy or milk
1 can whole kernel corn
2 c. chopped cooked turkey

Turkey stuffing
1 thick crust puff or short pastry

Cook onion gently in butter until clear and soft; add mushrooms, thyme, curry powder, salt and pepper. Dilute soup to consistency of thick cream with gravy, then stir into onion mixture. Add corn, turkey and desired amount of stuffing. Pour into casserole; top with pastry crust. Slash small vents in pastry for steam to escape. Bake in preheated 425-degree oven until browned.

Mrs. Norma McCullough, Home Mgt. Consultant
Dept. of Ed., Govt. of the Northwest Territories
Fort Smith, Northwest Territory, Canada

SCALLOPED TURKEY

3 tbsp. butter or poultry fat
2 tbsp. chopped onion
3 tbsp. flour
1 c. chicken broth
1/2 tsp. salt
1/8 tsp. pepper
2 c. cooked cut-up turkey or
    chicken
1/2 to 1 c. cooked vegetables
Potato chips

Melt butter in skillet; add onion and saute until soft. Add flour; blend well. Add broth gradually and cook for 5 minutes, stirring constantly. Season with salt and pepper. Mix turkey and vegetables in a baking dish; pour sauce over top and mix well. Cover with crushed potato chips. Bake in preheated 350-degree oven for 25 to 30 minutes. Yield: 4 servings.

Sister Tabitha Kaup
Ryan H.S. Inc., Omaha, Nebraska

MAKE-AHEAD TURKEY CASSEROLE

6 slices bread
2 c. diced cooked turkey
1/2 c. chopped onion
1/2 c. chopped celery
1/4 c. chopped green pepper
1/2 c. mayonnaise
3/4 tsp. salt
Dash of pepper
2 eggs, beaten
1 1/2 c. milk
1 can cream of mushroom soup
1/2 c. shredded Cheddar cheese

Trim the crusts from 4 slices of bread. Set bread aside and cube the crusts. Cube the remaining 2 slices bread and combine with crust cubes. Place in 8-inch square baking dish. Combine turkey, onion, celery, green pepper, mayonnaise, salt and pepper. Spoon over bread cubes. Arrange the 4 trimmed slices of bread over turkey mixture. Combine the eggs and milk; pour over all. Cover and chill for 1 hour or overnight. Stir the mushroom soup until smooth, then spread over all. Bake in preheated 350-degree oven for 55 minutes. Sprinkle cheese on top; bake for 5 minutes longer.

Mrs. Deborah Wheeler
Cabot H.S., Cabot, Vermont

EASY TURKEY CASSEROLE

3 to 4 c. diced cooked turkey
1/4 c. diced onions
1 1/2 to 2 c. poultry dressing or
    cracker crumbs
1 can cream of celery soup
Salt and pepper to taste

Place turkey, onions and dressing in buttered casserole. Add the soup; season with salt and pepper. Bake in preheated 350-degree oven for 30 to 35 minutes.

Sharon Ambler
Homer Sch., Homer, Illinois

TURKEY TETRAZZINI

8 oz. spaghetti
1/4 c. butter or margarine
1/2 c. flour
2 1/2 c. chicken broth
1 c. light cream
1 1/4 tsp. salt
Dash of pepper
1/2 tsp. meat tenderizer
1 6-oz. can mushrooms, drained
1/4 c. chopped green pepper
2 c. diced cooked turkey or
    chicken
1/2 c. shredded Parmesan cheese

Cook spaghetti in boiling salted water until just tender; drain. Melt butter; blend in flour to make a smooth paste. Stir broth into flour mixture gradually; add cream. Cook and stir until thickened and smooth. Add seasonings; mix well. Add spaghetti, mushrooms, green pepper and turkey; place in 11 1/2 x 7 1/2 x 1 1/2-inch baking dish. Sprinkle with Parmesan cheese. Bake in preheated 350-degree oven for about 25 minutes or until hot. Yield: 6 servings.

Mrs. Marie Heltzel
Union Co. H.S., Lake Butler, Florida

TEXAS RANCH CASSEROLE

1 can cream of chicken soup
1 can cream of mushroom soup
1/2 can Ro-Tel tomatoes
    with green chilies
1/2 can chicken broth
1 doz. tortillas, torn in sm. pieces
2 c. cooked chopped turkey or
    chicken
1 onion, chopped
2 c. grated cheese

Combine chicken and mushroom soups; add tomatoes and chicken broth. Arrange alternate layers of tortillas, turkey, onion, sauce and cheese in baking dish. Bake in preheated 350-degree oven for 45 minutes to 1 hour.

Mrs. L. A. Boyd
Vernon H.S., Vernon, Texas

TURKEY-CRANBERRY CASSEROLE

2 tbsp. butter
1/2 c. sugar
1 tsp. lemon juice
2 c. cranberries
4 to 5 c. cubed cooked turkey
2 c. bread crumbs
2 tbsp. finely chopped onion
Salt and pepper to taste
2 c. milk
2 eggs, slightly beaten
Summer savory or poultry seasoning

Melt butter in casserole; blend in sugar and lemon juice, then add cranberries. Place turkey over the cranberry mixture. Combine bread crumbs, onion, seasonings, milk, eggs and summer savory in mixing bowl; mix well. Spread over turkey. Bake in a preheated 400-degree oven for about 45 minutes. Yield: 4-6 servings.

Rosalie Wentzell
Stettler Jr. H.S., Stettler, Alberta, Canada

TURKEY MORNAY

6 slices toasted bread
6 slices turkey
1 can asparagus spears, drained
1 c. medium white sauce
1 c. grated Cheddar cheese

Place toast in 9 x 15-inch baking dish. Arrange slices of turkey on toast. Place the asparagus spears over turkey. Combine sauce and cheese; heat until cheese is melted. Pour over asparagus. Bake in preheated 325-degree oven until heated through. Yield: 6 servings.

Pauline K. Brown
Lone Wolf H.S., Lone Wolf, Oklahoma

HIGH HAT CHICKEN SUPPER

1/3 c. butter
Flour
1 1/4 tsp. salt
Dash of pepper
1 tsp. instant minced onion
1/2 tsp. basil
1 2/3 c. evaporated milk
1 c. chicken broth
1 tbsp. lemon juice
2 c. diced cooked chicken
2 tbsp. chopped pimento
1 tsp. baking powder
2 eggs, separated
2 tbsp. melted butter

Melt butter in medium saucepan over low heat. Blend in 1/2 cup flour, 1 teaspoon salt, pepper, onion and basil; stir in 1 cup evaporated milk and chicken broth gradually, keeping mixture smooth. Cook over medium heat, stirring, until thickened. Stir in lemon juice, chicken and pimento; turn into buttered 1 1/2-quart baking dish. Set aside. Combine 2/3 cup flour with remaining salt and baking powder in bowl. Beat egg yolks slightly, then beat in remaining evaporated milk and melted butter. Add to flour mixture, mixing lightly. Beat egg whites until stiff, but not dry; fold into flour mixture. Pour over chicken mixture. Bake in preheated 425-degree oven for 15 minutes or until golden brown. Yield: 6 servings.

Photograph for this recipe on page 60.

CHICKEN AND MUSHROOM BAKE

1 3-lb. chicken
Seasoned flour
1/4 c. butter
3/4 c. cooked fresh mushrooms
1 10 1/2-oz. can mushroom or
   chicken soup
1 c. sour cream

Cut chicken into serving pieces; dredge with seasoned flour. Melt butter in shallow baking pan; arrange chicken in pan in single layer,

Chicken And Mushroom Bake

skin side down. Bake in preheated 350-degree oven for 30 minutes. Remove from oven; turn chicken skin side up. Combine mushrooms, soup and sour cream; pour over chicken. Return to oven; bake for 40 to 45 minutes longer or until chicken is tender. Three 1-pound chicken breasts, halved, may be used instead of cut up chicken. Canned mushrooms may be substituted for fresh. Yield: 6 servings.

Photograph for this recipe on page 64.

DELICIOUS CHICKEN AND ASPARAGUS CASSEROLE

2 chicken breasts, skinned and
    boned
1/4 tsp. pepper
1 1/2 tsp. monosodium glutamate
2 tbsp. corn oil
2 10-oz. packages frozen asparagus
1 10-oz. can cream of chicken soup
1/2 c. mayonnaise
1 tsp. lemon juice
1/2 tsp. curry powder
1 c. shredded sharp Cheddar cheese

Cut chicken breasts into bite-sized pieces; sprinkle with pepper and monosodium glutamate. Pour corn oil into 10-inch frypan; place over medium heat. Add chicken pieces; saute for about 6 minutes. Remove from pan; drain on paper toweling. Cook asparagus according to package directions for 4 to 5 minutes; drain. Line 9 x 9-inch baking dish with asparagus; place chicken over asparagus. Combine chicken soup, mayonnaise, lemon juice and curry powder; pour over chicken. Sprinkle cheese over top; cover with foil. Bake in preheated 375-degree oven for 30 to 35 minutes.

Patricia Austin
Allegheny-Clarion Valley H.S.
Foxburg, Pennsylvania

BAKED CHICKEN SOUFFLE

9 slices bread, crusts removed
4 c. diced cooked chicken or turkey
1/2 lb. fresh white mushrooms,
    sliced
1/4 c. butter
1 can water chestnuts, sliced
1/2 c. mayonnaise

9 slices process cheese
4 eggs, well beaten
2 c. milk
1 tsp. salt
1 can cream of mushroom soup
1 can cream of celery soup
1 jar pimento pieces
2 c. buttered coarse bread crumbs

Line a large flat baking pan with bread. Top with chicken. Saute mushrooms in butter for 5 minutes; spoon over chicken. Add chestnuts with liquid; dot with mayonnaise. Top with cheese. Combine eggs, milk and salt; pour over the cheese. Combine soups; add pimento, then spoon over top. Refrigerate overnight. Bake in preheated 350-degree oven for 1 hour and 30 minutes. Top with buttered crumbs; bake for 15 minutes longer or until crumbs are browned. Yield: 9-10 servings.

Barbara Gaylor, Supervisor
Home Economics Special Projects
Work Study and Co-op Unit
Michigan Department of Education
Lansing, Michigan

CHICKEN-RICE GOODNESS

2 10-oz. packages frozen broccoli
    spears
1/2 c. shredded American cheese
6 lg. slices or 2 c. cubed
    cooked chicken
Salt and pepper to taste
1 c. cooked rice
2 tbsp. butter
2 tbsp. flour
1 c. milk
1 tbsp. lemon juice
1 c. sour cream

Cook broccoli according to package directions; drain well. Arrange in 11 x 7 x 1 1/2-inch baking dish. Sprinkle with 1/2 of the cheese; top with chicken. Season with salt and pepper, then spoon on rice. Melt butter in a saucepan; stir in flour to make a smooth paste. Stir in milk; cook until smooth and thick. Add lemon juice and sour cream; mix well. Pour over rice; top with remaining cheese. Bake in a preheated 400-degree oven for 15 to 20 minutes. Yield: 6 servings.

Marilyn Counce
Bartlett H.S., Bartlett, Tennessee

WINE-MARINATED BUTTERFLIED LEG OF LAMB

    1   7 to 8-lb. leg of lamb
    1 1/2 c. dry red wine
    1/2 c. orange juice
    1/2 c. chili sauce
    1/4 c. salad oil
    2 cloves of garlic, crushed
    1 bay leaf, crumbled
    1 tsp. salt
    1 tsp. basil
    1/4 tsp. pepper
    1 lg. onion, sliced
    1/2 c. orange marmalade
    2 tbsp. cornstarch

Have lamb boned and butterflied at market. Place lamb in large, shallow baking dish. Combine wine, 1/2 cup water, orange juice, chili sauce, oil, garlic, bay leaf, salt, basil, pepper and onion; pour over lamb. Cover. Chill, turning occasionally, for 12 hours or overnight. Remove lamb from marinade; reserve marinade. Grill lamb over coals, about 6 inches from source of heat, for 25 to 30 minutes on each side or until meat thermometer registers 160 to 170 degrees when inserted in thickest part. Strain reserved marinade into saucepan; blend in marmalade. Combine cornstarch with 3/4 cup water; add to marinade mixture, blending well. Cook, stirring constantly, until sauce is thickened and clear. Add more wine if sauce is too thick. Carve lamb; serve with sauce. Yield: 12 servings.

Photograph for this recipe on page 67.

HOLIDAY FRUIT BREAD

    1 pkg. date bread mix
    1 No. 2 can apple pie filling
    1 c. chopped pecans

    1/3 c. orange juice
    1 tbsp. brandy flavoring
    1/8 tsp. cinnamon

Prepare date bread mix according to package directions, reducing water to 2/3 cup and adding 1 cup apple pie filling and pecans with the dry mix. Turn into two 1-quart molds, greased and floured on bottom only. Bake at 350 degrees for 1 hour to 1 hour and 10 minutes. Cool for 10 minutes; remove from molds. Cool. Bread may be baked in 8 x 4-inch or 9 x 5-inch loaf pan, if desired. Combine remaining pie filling, orange juice, brandy flavoring and cinnamon in saucepan; cook over medium heat, stirring occasionally, until thoroughly heated. Serve with bread.

Photograph for this recipe on page 68.

PEACH AND PISTASCHIO PARFAITS

    1 pkg. vanilla frosting and
       filling mix
    3/4 tsp. almond flavoring
    8 drops of green food coloring
    1 No. 2 can peach pie filling
    1 tbsp. sherry flavoring
    1/2 c. chopped pistaschio nuts
    6 to 8 maraschino cherries, drained

Prepare frosting and filling mix according to package directions, adding almond flavoring and food coloring with the water. Reserve 1/2 cup frosting mixture. Mix pie filling with sherry flavoring. Layer pie filling mixture, remaining frosting mixture and pistaschio nuts alternately in parfait glasses; top each with reserved frosting mixture. Garnish with additional pistaschio nuts and a cherry. Refrigerate until serving time. Yield: 6-8 servings.

Photograph for this recipe on page 68.

FROSTY MINCE MOLD

1 pkg. yellow cake mix
1 No. 2 can mince pie filling
1 pkg. vanilla frosting and
    filling mix
1 egg white
2 tsp. brandy flavoring

Prepare cake mix according to package directions. Place in 2 greased and floured 9-inch round layer pans. Bake according to package directions; cool completely. Freeze one layer for use at another time. Reserve and refrigerate 2/3 cup pie filling. Prepare frosting and filling mix according to package directions; reserve and refrigerate 1 cup. Beat egg white until soft peaks form. Combine remaining pie filling and frosting with egg white and flavoring; pack into a 1-quart ring mold. Freeze for at least 4 hours or overnight. Unmold onto plate rinsed with cold water; slip onto cooled cake layer. Spread reserved frosting over side of cake layer and lower edge of frozen mixture. Freeze until 20 minutes before serving. Spoon reserved pie filling into center of ring mold; cut into wedges to serve. Yield: 6-8 servings.

Photograph for this recipe on page 68.

HOLIDAY TARTS

1 roll refrigerated sugar or lemon
    sparkle cookies

Slice cookie dough 1/8 inch thick. Place paper baking cups over back of muffin pans or custard cups. Arrange three cookies over each cup, edges overlapping and about 1/2 of the round extending below edge of cup bottom. Let stand at room temperature for 15 minutes; press to seal edges and mold slightly. Bake at 375 degrees for 10 to 12 minutes; cool. Remove paper liners. Fill shells with desired filling. Tarts may be prepared 2 hours before serving and stored in refrigerator. Yield: About 22 tart shells.

Peach Glace Tarts

2 tbsp. cornstarch
2 tbsp. red cinnamon candies
1 No. 2 can peach pie filling

Combine 1 cup water, cornstarch and candies in small saucepan; cook, stirring constantly, until thick and clear. Cool. Spoon pie filling into tart shells; spread cinnamon glace over filling. Garnish with sweetened whipped cream and red cinnamon candies.

Apple Tarts

Green colored sugar
2 3-oz. packages cream cheese
1 c. confectioners' sugar
1/2 c. heavy cream
1 tsp. grated orange rind
1 No. 2 can apple pie filling

Prepare 21 sugar cookie tarts. Cut stars, with cookie cutter, from remaining cookie slices; sprinkle with green colored sugar. Place on cookie sheet. Bake at 375 degrees for 5 to 7 minutes or until golden brown. Make small hole for candle in center of each while warm; cool for 2 minutes. Remove from cookie sheet. Soften cream cheese in bowl. Add confectioners' sugar; mix well. Beat heavy cream until thick; fold whipped cream and orange rind into cream cheese mixture. Spread 1 tablespoon over bottom and side of each tart shell; spoon pie filling into tarts. Top with star cookies; insert small candles in center.

Lemon-Sour Cream Tarts

1 No. 2 can lemon pie filling
1 c. sour cream
1/4 c. confectioners' sugar

Reserve 1/4 cup lemon pie filling; spoon remaining filling into tart shells. Combine sour cream, confectioners' sugar and reserved lemon filling; beat until smooth. Top lemon filling with dollop of sour cream mixture; garnish with red and green candied cherries.

Cherry-Almond Tarts

1 No. 2 can cherry pie filling
2 tsp. almond extract
Confectioners' sugar
1 3-oz. package cream cheese,
    softened

Combine pie filling and almond extract; spoon into tart shells. Dust a cookie sheet with confectioners' sugar. Spread cream cheese 1/4 inch thick on cookie sheet; chill. Cut stars from cream cheese with small cutter dipped in confectioners' sugar; place stars on filling in tart shells.

Photograph for this recipe on page 68.   **69**

EASY CHICKEN-BROCCOLI CASSEROLE

1   2 1/2 to 3-lb. chicken, disjointed
1 pkg. frozen broccoli, thawed
4 med. potatoes, quartered
1 can cream of mushroom soup
Salt and pepper to taste

Arrange chicken, broccoli and potatoes in large baking dish; cover with mushroom soup. Sprinkle with salt and pepper; cover baking dish with foil. Bake in preheated 350-degree oven for 1 hour or until chicken is done. Yield: 4 servings.

Candice Pickens
Kemp Jr.-Sr. H.S., Kemp, Texas

CRUSTY CHICKEN AND BROCCOLI CASSEROLE

2 10-oz. packages frozen broccoli
4 c. diced cooked chicken
2 10-oz. cans cream of chicken
*   soup*
1 c. mayonnaise
1 tsp. curry powder
2 tbsp. lemon juice
1 c. bread crumbs
1/2 c. melted butter

Cook broccoli according to package directions until partially tender; drain. Arrange in greased 11 x 7-inch pan. Arrange chicken on top of broccoli. Combine soup, mayonnaise, curry powder and lemon juice; spread over chicken. Combine crumbs and butter; sprinkle over soup mixture. Bake in a preheated 350-degree oven for 50 minutes.

Mrs. Marlys Folkers
Cedar Falls H.S., Cedar Falls, Iowa

CLASSIC CHICKEN DIVAN

2 10-oz. packages frozen chopped
*   broccoli*
3 chicken breasts, cooked and boned
1 c. mayonnaise
2 cans cream of mushroom soup
1 sm. jar sliced pimentos
1 tbsp. lemon juice
1/4 to 1/2 tsp. curry powder
1/2 c. grated mild Cheddar cheese

1/2 c. soft bread crumbs
1 tbsp. melted butter

Cook broccoli according to package directions; drain well. Arrange broccoli and chicken breasts in a casserole. Combine mayonnaise, soup, pimentos, lemon juice and curry powder; pour over the chicken. Sprinkle cheese over the soup mixture. Combine bread crumbs and butter; sprinkle over the cheese. Bake in preheated 350-degree oven until bubbly and the cheese is melted.

Mrs. Frances Clark
North Side H.S., Jackson, Tennessee

CHICKEN AND BEEF CASSEROLE

8 chicken breasts, boned
8 strips bacon
1 8-oz. package chipped beef
1 4-oz. can mushrooms
1 can cream of chicken soup or
*   1 c. sour cream*

Wrap each chicken breast with one slice of bacon. Line 9 x 13-inch baking dish with chipped beef. Place chicken on beef. Combine mushrooms and soup; pour over chicken. Bake, covered, in preheated 350-degree oven for 3 hours.

Emily Rickman
Home Economics Education Services
State Dept. of Education, Richmond, Virginia

CHICKEN AND BROCCOLI WITH SAUCE

2 pkg. frozen broccoli
1 to 3 carrots, sliced
Salt to taste
4 chicken breasts
2/3 c. mayonnaise
1/2 c. shredded Cheddar cheese
1 tsp. lemon juice
1/2 c. evaporated milk
1 can cream of chicken soup
Bread crumbs

Cook broccoli according to package directions until crisp-tender; drain well. Cook carrots in a small amount of boiling salted water until crisp-tender; drain well. Place broccoli and carrots in casserole. Arrange chicken breasts on top. Sprinkle with salt to taste. Combine mayonnaise, cheese, lemon juice, milk and soup; mix well. Pour over chicken; sprinkle with bread crumbs. Bake in a preheated 350-degree oven for 1 hour.

Susan N. Benjamin
Austin Area Sch., Austin, Pennsylvania

CHICKEN-ALMOND BAKE

1 c. cream of celery soup
1/4 c. milk
1 c. diced chicken
1/2 c. minced celery
1 sm. onion, minced
1/2 c. blanched almonds
1/4 tsp. Worcestershire sauce
1 c. Chinese noodles

Blend celery soup and milk together in a mixing bowl; add chicken, celery, onion, almonds and Worcestershire sauce. Arrange half the noodles in baking dish; pour chicken mixture over noodles. Top with remaining noodles. Bake in preheated 350-degree oven for 30 to 35 minutes or until heated through and bubbly.

Mrs. Jane H. Osborne
Goodlettsville H.S., Goodlettsville, Tennessee

Chicken Baked In Chivy Sour Cream

CHICKEN BAKED IN CHIVY SOUR CREAM

2 tbsp. white vinegar
2 tsp. sugar
1 1/2 c. Basic Sour Cream Sauce
2 tbsp. butter
4 chicken breasts, halved
2 chicken legs
2 chicken thighs
Flour
Paprika

Add vinegar and sugar to sour cream sauce; mix well. Melt butter in baking dish. Dredge chicken pieces with flour; dip into sour cream mixture, coating thoroughly. Place chicken in baking dish, skin side up; sprinkle with paprika. Bake in preheated 400-degree oven for 1 hour. Yield: 4 servings.

Basic Sour Cream Sauce

1 pt. sour cream
2 tbsp. chopped chives
1/2 tsp. tarragon leaves
1/2 tsp. salt

Blend sour cream with chives, tarragon leaves and salt. Yield: 2 cups.

CHICKEN-CHIP BAKE

2 c. cubed cooked chicken
2 c. sliced celery
3/4 c. mayonnaise or salad dressing
1/3 c. toasted slivered almonds
2 tsp. grated onion
2 tbsp. lemon juice
1/2 tsp. monosodium glutamate
1/2 tsp. salt
1/2 c. shredded American cheese
1 c. crushed potato chips

Combine all ingredients except cheese and potato chips in mixing bowl. Spoon lightly into 1 1/2-quart casserole. Sprinkle with cheese, then with potato chips. Bake in preheated 425-degree oven for 20 minutes or until heated through. Yield: 5-6 servings.

Kathleen Burchett
Home Economics Area Supervisor
Bristol, Virginia

CHICKEN CAN-CAN

1   4 to 5-lb. chicken, cooked
1 can cream of chicken soup
1 can cream of celery soup
1 can cream of mushroom soup
1   14 1/2-oz. can evaporated milk
1 lg. can chow mein noodles
1/3 c. butter
1/2 c. slivered almonds

Remove bones from chicken; cut chicken into small pieces. Combine soups and milk in a large bowl; mix until smooth. Add chicken and noodles; mix well. Turn into 9 x 13-inch baking dish. Melt butter in small frypan; add almonds and brown lightly. Spoon over top of casserole. Bake in preheated 350-degree oven for 1 hour.

Edna Doperalski
Wamego H.S., Wamego, Kansas

CHICKEN LIVERS WITH RICE

1/4 c. butter or margarine
3 tbsp. minced onion
1   5-oz. package precooked rice
1/2 lb. thawed frozen or fresh
   chicken livers
Seasoned flour
1 can cream of chicken soup
1/2 c. milk

1 tbsp. chopped parsley
Pinch of dried basil

Melt 1 tablespoon butter in saucepan; add onion. Cook until tender. Add to rice, then cook according to package directions. Cut livers into 1-inch pieces. Roll chicken livers lightly in flour. Saute in remaining butter in skillet until browned on each side. Combine livers, rice, soup and remaining ingredients in 1 1/2-quart casserole. Bake in preheated 375-degree oven for 30 minutes or until hot and bubbly. Yield: 5-6 servings.

Gertrude Chambers
Westmont Jr. H.S., Westmont, Illinois

CHICKEN AND CHEESE CASSEROLE

4 c. diced cooked chicken
4 c. chicken broth
1 1/2 c. diced celery
1 c. diced process cheese
1 lg. onion, diced
1 can cream of chicken soup
1 1/2 tsp. pepper
2 tsp. salt
4 c. Pepperidge Farm herb-seasoned
   stuffing mix

Combine all ingredients except 1 cup stuffing mix in a 3-quart baking dish. Sprinkle remaining stuffing mix over top. Bake, uncovered, in a preheated 350-degree oven for 45 minutes. Yield: 8-10 servings.

Mrs. Frances VanLandingham
Greene Central H.S., Snow Hill, North Carolina

DELUXE CHICKEN-ALMOND CASSEROLE

3 lb. chicken legs, thighs or breasts
Flour
1/4 c. oil
1/4 c. chopped onion
4 c. chicken stock or bouillon
1 lg. can tomatoes
1/2 c. slivered almonds
1   4-oz. can mushrooms
2 tbsp. parsley flakes
Cheese slices

Dredge chicken with flour, then brown in the oil in skillet. Remove chicken and place in casserole. Brown onion in skillet drippings; remove with slotted spoon and place over chicken. Add 1/2 cup flour to the skillet drippings and stir until well blended. Stir in the stock gradually. Add tomatoes; cook, stirring, until thickened. Add almonds, mushrooms and parsley; pour over chicken. Bake in preheated 350-degree oven for 1 hour. Cover with cheese slices and return to oven until cheese is melted. May serve with rice, if desired.

Katharine Rigby
Starr-Washington Jr. H.S., Lancaster, Ohio

CREAMED CHICKEN AND MUSHROOMS

1 c. diced cooked chicken
1 can cream of mushroom soup
1 can cream of chicken soup
1 can chow mein noodles
2 tbsp. chopped parsley

Combine chicken, soups, 2/3 can noodles and parsley. Pour into greased casserole. Sprinkle remaining noodles over top. Bake in preheated 350-degree oven for 35 minutes. Serve on toast. Yield: 5 servings.

Shirley Rose
New Germany Rural H.S.
New Germany, Nova Scotia, Canada

FAMILY CHICKEN AND DRESSING

1 c. chicken fat
1/4 c. flour
4 1/4 c. chicken broth
1 tsp. salt
1/4 tsp. pepper
1 1/2 qt. dried bread cubes
1 1/4 tsp. sage
2 tbsp. chopped onion
4 c. coarsely cubed chicken

Melt 1/4 cup chicken fat in a saucepan; stir in the flour until smooth. Add 4 cups broth gradually; cook, stirring constantly, until thickened. Season with 1/4 teaspoon salt and the pepper. Combine the bread cubes, remaining chicken fat, sage, remaining salt, remaining broth and onion in a large mixing bowl; mix lightly. Add the gravy and chicken and mix lightly. Turn into 9 x 13 x 2-inch baking pan. Bake in preheated 350-degree oven for 1 hour.

Barbara Hebeler
Haakon Independent Sch., Akron, Iowa

FIVE-CAN CASSEROLE

1 10 1/2-oz. jar boned chicken
1 can cream of mushroom soup
1 can chicken and rice soup
1 6-oz. can evaporated milk
1 med. can chow mein noodles
2 c. buttered bread crumbs

Combine all ingredients, except bread crumbs, in the order listed. Place in a 2-quart casserole; cover with buttered crumbs. Bake in preheated 350-degree oven for 45 minutes. Yield: 6 servings.

Mrs. Margaret McIntosh
Lostant H.S., Lostant, Illinois

CHICKEN AND DRESSING COMPANY CASSEROLE

3 sm. fryers or 1 stewing chicken
1 onion
1 carrot
2 tsp. salt
1/2 c. butter
1/2 c. minced onion
1 c. minced celery
1 1/2 loaves bread
2 tsp. poultry seasoning
6 tbsp. (about) broth
2 cans cream of chicken soup
1 14 1/2-oz. can evaporated milk
Bread crumbs

Place fryers, onion, carrot and salt in large kettle. Pour in 2 quarts water and cook until fryers are tender. Remove fryers from broth and let cool. Remove skin and bones; cut chicken into bite-sized pieces. Melt butter in frypan. Add minced onion and celery; saute until transparent. Break bread into small pieces; add sauteed vegetables and poultry seasoning. Add broth to moisten. Heat soup and milk together, stirring until smooth. Place the bread mixture in a greased casserole; pour in half the soup mixture. Arrange the chicken over the soup mixture, then top with remaining soup mixture. Sprinkle with bread crumbs. Bake in a preheated 375-degree oven for 30 minutes. Yield: 12-15 servings.

Bonnie Muirbrook
Roy H.S., Roy, Utah

73

WASTE NOT-WANT NOT SCALLOPED CHICKEN CASSEROLE

1   5-lb. hen with giblets
1 lg. carrot, chopped
1 med. onion, sliced
Salt
1/2 c. margarine
6 sprigs of parsley, chopped
6 scallions and tops or
    1 med. onion, chopped
2 lg. pieces celery and tops,
    chopped
1   1-lb. loaf dry bread, crumbled
1/4 tsp. pepper
1 tsp. poultry seasoning
1 c. milk
1 c. flour
4 eggs, beaten slightly
1 c. bread crumbs
4 tbsp. melted margarine

Place hen, carrot, onion and 2 teaspoons salt in a large kettle; add 2 quarts boiling water. Bring to a boil, then let simmer for about 2 hours or until hen is tender. Let hen cool, then remove from broth. Chill the broth so the chicken fat will harden. Remove and reserve the chicken skin, then remove all bones. Set the chicken aside. Cook giblets in boiling salted water until tender. Grind the reserved chicken skin through a meat grinder; set aside. Grind the giblets through the meat grinder; set aside. Melt margarine in a heavy skillet. Add parsley, scallions and celery; saute for 5 minutes. Place bread pieces in a large bowl. Add sauteed vegetables; toss lightly. Add ground giblets, 1 teaspoon salt, pepper and poultry seasoning; mix well. Remove hardened fat from the chicken broth and set aside. Add 6 tablespoons chicken broth to the dressing mixture; toss lightly. Heat 4 cups chicken broth and milk together. Melt 1 cup reserved chicken fat in a large heavy saucepan. Margarine may be added to the fat to measure 1 cup, if needed. Stir in flour to make a smooth paste. Add broth mixture slowly, stirring constantly. Add 2 teaspoons salt; cook, stirring constantly, until thick. Stir part of the hot sauce into the eggs, then stir the eggs into the hot sauce. Cook, stirring constantly, for 3 or 4 minutes or until well blended and bubbly. Remove from heat; stir in reserved chicken skin. Place bread stuffing in greased large casserole; pour half the sauce over the stuffing. Top with chicken pieces; pour on remaining sauce.

Combine bread crumbs and melted margarine; sprinkle over sauce. Bake in a preheated 375-degree oven for 20 minutes or until heated through and crumbs are golden. Garnish with parsley and tomatoes, if desired.

Mrs. Paula Scutt
Kelowna Secondary Sch.
Kelowna, British Columbia, Canada

EASY DINNER CASSEROLE

2 med. potatoes
2 med. carrots
1 tsp. salt
1/2 tsp. pepper
Butter
2 chicken breasts
1 tsp. dried onion flakes
1 can mushroom soup

Slice potatoes; place in casserole. Slice carrots; place over potatoes. Season with salt and pepper. Dot with butter. Arrange chicken on top. Sprinkle with onion. Mix soup until smooth; pour over chicken. Cover. Bake in preheated 325-degree oven for 1 hour or until chicken is tender.

Mrs. Cheryl McClure
Fayette-Ware South Sch., Somerville, Tennessee

HOT BAKED CHICKEN SALAD CASSEROLE

2 c. chopped cooked chicken
2 c. chopped celery
1/2 c. chopped pecans or almonds
1/2 tsp. salt
2 tsp. onion, minced
1 tbsp. wine vinegar
1/2 c. grated cheese
1/4 c. French dressing
1/2 c. mayonnaise
1/3 c. sour cream
1/3 c. corn flake crumbs

Combine chicken, celery, pecans, salt, onion, vinegar and cheese is mixing bowl. Combine French dressing, mayonnaise and sour cream; pour over chicken mixture. Toss lightly. Pour into a greased casserole. Sprinkle crumbs over top. Bake in preheated 450-degree oven for 10 minutes. Yield: 6 servings.

Mrs. Barbara MacDougall
Dr. E. P. Scarlett Sr. H.S.
Calgary, Alberta, Canada

CHEESY CHICKEN CASSEROLE

1 1-lb. package elbow macaroni
1 cooked chicken, boned and cut up
1 onion, diced
2 cans mushroom soup
2 c. milk
1 c. diced Velveeta cheese
Bread crumbs or cracker crumbs

Cook macaroni according to package directions until just tender. Combine macaroni, chicken, onion, soup, milk and cheese; mix well. Place in greased casserole; refrigerate overnight. Bake in preheated 325-degree oven for 1 hour and 30 minutes. Sprinkle bread crumbs over top. Bake for 10 minutes longer or until brown.

Mrs. William Boggs
Orrville Sr. H.S., Orrville, Ohio

CHICKEN TETRAZZINI

2 slices bacon
1/2 c. minced onion
1/2 c. minced green pepper
2 c. grated American cheese
1/4 c. cut-up pimento
1/4 c. toasted sliced almonds
1 No. 2 can green peas
2 c. cut-up cooked chicken
1 8-oz. package macaroni

Cook bacon until brown and crisp. Remove from frypan; drain and crumble. Add onion and green pepper to bacon drippings. Cook until lightly browned. Add bacon, cheese, pimento, almonds, green peas and chicken. Cook macaroni according to package directions; add to chicken mixture. Toss until lightly mixed. Add chicken broth, if mixture seems dry. Bake in preheated 350-degree oven for 20 to 25 minutes. Yield: 8 servings.

Mrs. A. S. Rinehardt
Trinity Sr. H.S., Trinity, North Carolina

EASY CHICKEN CASSEROLE

1 env. Swiss recipe chicken noodle
   soup mix
2 c. cubed cooked chicken
1 c. cooked elbow macaroni
1 c. diced cooked carrots
2/3 c. diced green pepper
1 tbsp. grated onion
2 eggs, beaten
1 1/2 c. milk

Combine soup mix, chicken, macaroni, carrots, green pepper and onion in 1 1/2-quart casserole. Blend eggs and milk; pour over vegetable mixture. Place casserole in pan of hot water. Bake in preheated 350-degree oven for about 1 hour or until knife inserted in center comes out clean. Yield: 4-6 servings.

Easy Chicken Casserole

CHICKEN-MUSHROOM CASSEROLE

1 c. sliced mushrooms
2 tbsp. butter
1 lg. onion, chopped
1 clove of garlic, minced
1/2 green pepper, chopped
2 c. diced cooked chicken
1 6-oz. package wide noodles,
  cooked
1 c. chopped walnuts
1 c. chopped ripe olives
2 cans mushroom soup
1 1/2 c. water
Salt and pepper to taste
Garlic salt to taste
1/2 c. grated Parmesan cheese

Saute mushrooms for 3 minutes in butter; remove from skillet. Add onion, garlic and green pepper; cook until tender. Place mushrooms, onion mixture, chicken, noodles, walnuts and olives in casserole. Combine soup and water in bowl; mix well. Pour over chicken mixture. Season with salt, pepper and garlic salt. Bake in preheated 350-degree oven for 45 minutes to 1 hour. Sprinkle with grated Parmesan cheese.

Mrs. Sylvia Ebersold
Alma Area Schools, Alma, Wisconsin

COMPANY CHICKEN

3 c. cubed cooked chicken
1 c. minced celery
1/4 c. minced onion
1 c. cracker crumbs
2 to 3 tbsp. lemon juice
3/4 tsp. salt
1/2 tsp. pepper
1 c. chicken broth
1 1/2 c. fine noodles, cooked
1 c. slivered almonds

Mix the chicken, celery, onion, cracker crumbs, lemon juice and seasonings together lightly; turn into lightly greased casserole. Pour broth over top. Bake in preheated 350-degree oven for 30 minutes. Combine noodles and almonds; sprinkle over top of casserole. Bake for 10 minutes longer or until golden brown. Yield: 4 servings.

Mrs. Ethel M. Poley
Narrowsburg Central Rural Sch.
Narrowsburg, New York

CHICKEN PAPRIKASH

1 3 1/2-lb. frying chicken
1/4 c. butter
1/2 c. chopped onion
1/4 c. flour
2 tbsp. paprika
2 tsp. salt
1/4 tsp. pepper
1 13 3/4-oz. can chicken broth
2 c. sour cream
1 tbsp. Worcestershire sauce
1 8-oz. package medium noodles

Cut chicken into serving pieces. Melt butter in large frypan; saute chicken in butter until lightly browned. Remove chicken from frypan. Add onion to pan drippings; blend in flour, paprika, salt and pepper. Add chicken broth; cook, stirring constantly, until thick and smooth. Remove from heat; stir in sour cream and Worcestershire sauce. Cook noodles according to package directions while preparing chicken and sauce. Mix 1/2 of the sauce with noodles; pour into shallow 3-quart casserole. Arrange chicken on noodles; spoon remaining onion sauce over chicken. Bake in preheated 325-degree oven for about 1 hour or until chicken is tender and noodles hot and bubbly. Yield: 6 servings.

CHICKEN PUFF

1 1/2 c. flour
2 tsp. baking powder
1/2 tsp. salt
2 eggs, separated
1 c. milk
1 to 2 c. diced cooked chicken
2 tsp. scraped onion
1/4 c. grated carrot
2 tbsp. melted butter or chicken fat

Sift flour, baking powder and salt together. Add egg yolks to milk; beat. Add to flour mixture; mix until smooth. Add chicken, onion, carrot and butter. Beat egg whites until stiff; fold into chicken mixture. Turn into greased pan. Bake in preheated 425-degree oven for 25 minutes. Serve hot with gravy. Yield: 6 servings.

Mrs. John D. Hughes
Southern Columbia Area Schools
Catawissa, Pennsylvania

Chicken Paprikash

QUICK CHICKEN CASSEROLE

2 c. diced cooked chicken
2 c. diced celery
2 tbsp. grated onion
1/2 tsp. salt
1/2 c. sliced almonds
2/3 c. mayonnaise
1 c. potato chips
1/2 c. grated sharp Cheddar cheese

Combine chicken, celery, onion, salt, almonds and mayonnaise; mix well. Crush potato chips into baking dish. Pour chicken mixture over chips. Top with grated cheese. Bake in preheated 450-degree oven for 10 minutes or until heated through.

Helen L. Giles
Susan Bloch English Sch., Seldovia, Alaska

CHICKEN FINALE

2 c. noodles
1/4 c. chopped green peppers
1/4 c. minced onion
2 tbsp. butter
1 can cream of chicken soup
1 c. sour cream
1/4 c. milk
1/4 c. sliced ripe olives
1/2 tsp. salt
1/4 tsp. pepper
1 1/2 c. diced cooked chicken
1/4 c. blanched slivered almonds
1 tbsp. minced parsley

Cook noodles according to package directions. Saute green peppers and onion in butter until tender. Add soup, sour cream, milk, olives, salt, pepper and chicken. Stir in noodles. Turn into greased 1 1/2-quart casserole; sprinkle with almonds and parsley. Bake in preheated 350-degree oven for 35 to 40 minutes. Yield: 6 servings.

Mrs. Ann Hohman
Iuniata Valley H.S., Alexandria, Pennsylvania

HUNTINGTON CHICKEN

1 cooked chicken
1 lb. cheese, diced
2 8-oz. boxes noodles
1 c. cream
1 sm. jar pimento strips
4 c. chicken broth
Salt and pepper to taste
1 can mushrooms (opt.)

Remove bones from chicken; cut chicken in large pieces. Combine chicken, cheese, noodles, cream, pimento, chicken broth, seasonings and mushrooms; mix well. Place in greased deep casserole; cover. Bake in 375-degree oven for 1 hour.

Maurine R. Marble
St. Clair H.S., St. Clair, Minnesota

77

CHICKEN-SPAGHETTI CASSEROLE

1 sm. onion, diced
3 chicken legs
1/2 c. diced celery
1   12-oz. package spaghetti,
*   cooked*
1   1-lb. can peas
1   1-lb. can sliced carrots
1 can cream of mushroom soup
1 c. milk
1 c. bread crumbs
1 c. grated cheese

Cook onion in small amount of fat until brown. Cook chicken and celery in boiling water for about 20 minutes; drain. Strain broth; reserve celery. Remove chicken from bones. Place spaghetti, chicken, onion, celery, peas and carrots in 2-quart casserole; mix. Add undiluted soup and milk; stir well. Bake in preheated 400-degree oven for 30 minutes. Sprinkle bread crumbs and grated cheese over casserole. Reduce oven temperature to 350 degrees; bake for 15 minutes longer.

Constance Henry
Milton H.S., Milton, Vermont

MARY'S QUICK CHICKEN TETRAZZINI

1   10 3/4-oz. can cream of
*   mushroom soup*
1   10 3/4-oz. can Cheddar cheese
*   soup*
1/2 sm. onion, grated
1 1/2 to 2 c. cooked diced chicken
1   8-oz. package spaghetti, cooked
1/2 c. Parmesan cheese
Paprika

Combine soups, onion and chicken in a large bowl, then stir in spaghetti. Turn into a casserole; sprinkle with Parmesan cheese and paprika. Bake in preheated 400-degree oven for 20 minutes. Yield: 4-6 servings.

Mary Woodruff
Hotchkiss H.S., Hotchkiss, Colorado

CREAMY CHICKEN-NOODLE CASSEROLE

2 c. diced cooked chicken
2 c. noodles, cooked
1 can cream of chicken soup
1/3 c. sour cream
1/3 c. water

2 tbsp. chopped pimento
2 tbsp. chopped parsley

Combine chicken, noodles, soup, sour cream, water, pimento and parsley; toss to mix well. Place in a greased 1 1/2-quart casserole. Bake in preheated 350-degree oven for 20 minutes.

Mrs. Nan Tate
Milton H.S., Alpharetta, Georgia

BETTY'S CHICKEN CASSEROLE

2 c. diced cooked chicken
1   5-oz. package egg noodles,
*   cooked*
1 can mushroom soup
1 c. milk
1 c. grated cheese

Combine chicken, noodles, soup, milk and cheese; mix well. Pour into buttered casserole. Bake in preheated 350-degree oven for 30 minutes.

Mrs. Betty Ambrose
Robert Lee H.S., Midland, Texas

MISSISSIPPI CHICKEN CASSEROLE

1   3 to 3 1/2-lb. fryer
1 sm. box crackers
1/2 c. margarine
1/2 pt. sour cream
1 can cream of mushroom soup
1/2 c. chicken broth
Paprika

Boil chicken in lightly salted water until tender. Remove from broth and debone; chop chicken into bite-sized pieces. Crush crackers; mix with melted margarine. Spread in 8-inch square baking dish. Combine sour cream, soup and broth; mix until smooth. Add chicken; mix well. Pour over cracker crumbs; sprinkle with paprika. Bake in preheated 350-degree oven for 25 to 30 minutes. Yield: 6-8 servings.

Mrs. Rachel E. Nicholson
Union H.S., Union, Mississippi

CHICKEN-CAULIFLOWER CASSEROLE

4 chicken breasts
1 head cauliflower, separated into flowerets

2 tbsp. butter
2 tbsp. flour
1 c. milk
1/4 tsp. salt
1/8 tsp. pepper
1/2 c. Ritz cracker crumbs
1/2 c. American cheese strips

Place chicken in large saucepan; cover with water. Bring to a boil; reduce heat and simmer until tender. Remove chicken from bones; cut into chunks. Cook cauliflower in small amount of water until tender; drain. Melt butter in a saucepan; stir in flour until smooth. Add milk gradually; cook, stirring constantly, until thickened. Season with salt and pepper. Sprinkle crumbs in a greased casserole. Place chicken and cauliflower in casserole; pour sauce over top. Cover with cheese strips. Bake in preheated 350-degree oven for 15 to 20 minutes or until heated through and bubbly.

Mrs. Carol Allen
Russell H.S., Russell, Kentucky

QUICK CHICKEN AND STUFFING SCALLOP

1 8-oz. package herb-seasoned
    stuffing mix
3 c. cubed cooked chicken
1/2 c. butter or margarine
1/2 c. flour
1/4 tsp. salt
Dash of pepper
4 c. chicken broth
6 eggs, slightly beaten
1 c. mushroom soup
1/4 c. milk
1 c. sour cream
1/4 c. chopped pimento

Prepare stuffing mix according to package directions for dry stuffing; spread in 13 x 9-inch baking dish. Top with chicken. Melt butter in a large saucepan; blend in flour and seasonings to make a smooth paste. Add broth, stirring constantly; cook until mixture thickens. Stir a small amount of the hot mixture into eggs; stir eggs into hot mixture. Pour over chicken. Bake in preheated 325-degree oven for 40 to 45 minutes or until a knife inserted in center comes out clean. Let stand for 5 minutes, then cut in squares. Combine mushroom soup, milk, sour cream and pimento in a saucepan; heat thoroughly, stirring

constantly. Serve with the chicken and stuffing squares.

Mrs. Linda Anderson
Somonauk H.S., Somonauk, Illinois

EASY CHICKEN DIVINE

2 10-oz. packages frozen asparagus or
    broccoli
2 c. sliced cooked chicken
2 cans cream of chicken soup
1 c. mayonnaise
1 tsp. lemon juice
1/2 tsp. curry powder
1/2 c. shredded sharp process cheese
Bread crumbs
Melted butter or margarine

Cook asparagus in boiling salted water until tender; drain. Arrange asparagus in greased 11 1/2 x 7 1/2 x 1 1/2-inch baking dish; place chicken on top. Combine soup, mayonnaise, lemon juice and curry powder; pour over chicken. Sprinkle with cheese. Combine bread crumbs and butter; sprinkle over soup mixture. Bake in a preheated 350-degree oven until heated through and bubbly.

Mrs. Miriam Toth
Castro Valley H.S., Castro Valley, California

CHICKEN COBBLER

2 c. diced chicken
1 c. cooked rice
2 c. chicken broth
1 tbsp. minced onion
1 tbsp. minced celery
1/4 c. margarine
1 c. flour
2 tsp. baking powder
1 tsp. salt
Pepper to taste
1 tbsp. sugar
1 c. milk
Paprika (opt.)

Mix chicken, rice, broth, onion and celery. Melt margarine in round baking dish in preheated 350-degree oven. Mix flour, baking powder, salt, pepper and sugar; stir in milk. Pour into baking dish. Place chicken mixture over flour mixture; sprinkle paprika over top. Bake for 50 minutes.

Florence T. Shaffer
Berwick Area Sr. H.S., Berwick, Pennsylvania

Louisiana Yam-Chicken Cherry Bake

LOUISIANA YAM-CHICKEN-CHERRY BAKE

> 1 3-lb. fryer
> Salt and pepper to taste
> Monosodium glutamate (opt.)
> Butter or margarine
> 1 c. chicken broth or bouillon
> 1/2 tsp. aromatic bitters
> 2 16-oz. cans Louisiana yams
> 1 tbsp. cornstarch
> 1/2 tsp. grated lemon peel
> 1/4 c. rose wine
> 1 16-oz. can pitted dark sweet
>   cherries, drained

Cut chicken into serving pieces; place in lightly buttered 3-quart baking dish. Sprinkle with salt, pepper and monosodium glutamate; dot each piece with about 1/4 teaspoon butter. Combine broth with 1/4 teaspoon bitters; pour over chicken. Bake in preheated 400-degree oven for 1 hour to 1 hour and 15 minutes or until chicken is fork tender. Remove baking dish from oven; drain all drippings into a cup measure. Skim off fat; there should be about 1/4 cup drippings left. Drain yams; reserve syrup. Combine drippings and 1 cup reserved yam syrup in saucepan; bring to a boil. Blend cornstarch with 1 tablespoon yam syrup; stir into boiling syrup mixture quickly. Boil for 30 seconds. Remove from heat; stir in lemon peel, wine and remaining bitters. Add yams and cherries to chicken; pour syrup mixture over all, covering each piece to glaze. Re-turn to oven; bake for 10 minutes longer. Yam syrup may be substituted for wine, if desired. Yield: 4 servings.

CHICKEN CASSEROLE WITH CHEESE PINWHEEL

> 1 c. long grain rice
> 1/2 c. chopped onion
> 1/4 c. butter or margarine,
>   melted
> 2 1/4 c. chicken broth
> 1/2 c. chopped green pepper
> 1/2 c. diced celery
> 1 1/2 c. cut-up chicken
> 1 3-oz. can sliced mushrooms,
>   drained
> 2 slices sharp American process
>   cheese, diagonally halved
> Sliced ripe olives

Saute rice and onion in butter in medium skillet, stirring occasionally. Add chicken broth; cover and cook for 10 minutes. Add green pepper and celery; cook, covered, for 10 to 15 minutes longer or until rice is tender, stirring occasionally. Add chicken and sliced mushrooms; mix well. Transfer to 1 1/2-quart casserole. Bake, covered, in preheated 350-degree oven for 15 to 20 minutes or until heated through. Remove casserole from oven; top with halved cheese slices forming a pinwheel design. Return to oven until cheese begins to melt. Garnish with sliced ripe olives. Yield: 5-6 servings.

Kathleen Burchett
Area Supervisor, Home Economics Ed.
Bristol, Virginia

CHICKEN CONTINENTAL

6 lb. chicken pieces
2/3 c. seasoned flour
1/2 c. margarine
2 cans cream of chicken soup
5 tbsp. grated onion
2 tsp. salt
Dash of pepper
2 tbsp. chopped parsley
1 tsp. celery flakes
2 2/3 c. water
2 2/3 c. Minute rice
1 tsp. paprika

Roll chicken in seasoned flour; saute in margarine in Dutch oven until browned. Remove chicken. Combine soup, onion and seasonings in Dutch oven, mixing well; blend in water. Bring to a boil over medium heat, stirring constantly. Place rice in casserole. Reserve 2/3 of the soup mixture; pour remaining soup over rice. Add chicken; pour reserved soup over chicken. Bake, covered, at 375 degrees for about 35 to 40 minutes or until chicken is tender. Yield: 8 servings.

Barbara J. Ebner
Middletown Area H.S., Middletown, Pennsylvania

CHICKEN LA CREALLO

2 lb. chicken pieces
1/4 c. oil
4 c. bouillon
2 c. rice
1 green pepper, chopped
1 tomato, chopped
1 tbsp. vinegar
1 tsp. paprika
1 tsp. seasoned salt
Salt and pepper to taste

Brown chicken pieces in hot oil; place in baking pan. Add bouillon and cover. Bake in preheated 350-degree oven until chicken is tender. Add rice and remaining ingredients; bake for 30 minutes longer. More bouillon may be added if rice becomes too dry.

Deloris Hutton
Howell H.S., Howell, Michigan

CHICKEN ON MUSHROOM RICE

1 can cream of mushroom soup
1 soup can milk
1 c. rice
1/2 env. dry onion soup mix
1 fryer, disjointed

Blend mushroom soup and milk; reserve 1/2 cup soup mixture. Combine remaining soup mixture, rice and soup mix in bowl; mix well. Pour into ungreased 2-quart baking dish. Arrange chicken on rice mixture. Pour reserved soup mixture over chicken; cover. Bake in preheated 350-degree oven for 1 hour. Uncover; bake for 15 minutes longer. Yield: 6 servings.

Mrs. Deborah Tunstall Tippett
Jordan Matthews H.S., Siler City, North Carolina

CHICKEN WITH WILD RICE

1 pkg. wild rice
2 chickens, cut up
2 pkg. onion soup mix
2 cans cream of mushroom soup
2 cans cream of chicken soup
2 soup cans water

Arrange rice in a layer in large casserole; place chicken on top. Combine soup mix, soups and water in a large bowl; stir until well blended. Pour over top of chicken; cover. Bake in preheated 350-degree oven for 2 hours and 30 minutes. Yield: 8-10 servings.

Mary Rogers
Benjamin Russell H.S., Alexander City, Alabama

EASY CHICKEN AND RICE

1/4 c. margarine
1 1/2 c. rice
1 chicken, disjointed
Salt to taste
1 can cream of chicken soup
1 can onion soup
1 soup can water

Melt margarine in baking dish. Spread rice evenly in dish. Place chicken on rice; season with salt. Spread soups over chicken. Pour water over all; cover. Bake in preheated 350-degree oven for 1 hour or until chicken is tender.

Mrs. Essie Milligan
Caney H.S., Caney, Oklahoma

CLUB CHICKEN CASSEROLE

1/4 c. butter or margarine
1/4 c. flour
1 c. chicken broth
1   14 1/2-oz. can evaporated milk
1/2 c. water
1 tbsp. salt
3 c. cooked rice
1 1/2 c. diced cooked chicken
1   3-oz. can sliced mushrooms
1/4 c. chopped pimento
1/3 c. chopped green pepper
1/2 c. blanched slivered almonds

Melt butter in heavy saucepan; stir in flour to make a smooth paste. Add broth, milk and water, stirring constantly; cook over low heat until thick. Add salt; mix well. Arrange half the rice, chicken, vegetables and sauce in greased baking dish. Repeat layers, then sprinkle with almonds. Bake in preheated 350-degree oven for 30 minutes. Yield: 8-10 servings.

Joyce Johnson
Manteca H.S., Manteca, California

CREOLE CASSEROLE

1/2 c. butter or cooking oil
1 fryer, disjointed
Salt
Pepper and red pepper to taste
Paprika
1/2 c. finely chopped onion
1 1/2 c. rice

Melt butter in roaster. Season chicken pieces with salt, pepper and red pepper; sprinkle with paprika. Place chicken in roaster; turn pieces in butter. Sprinkle chopped onion over chicken. Add rice, 3 cups water and 1 1/4 teaspoons salt; cover. Bake in preheated 325-degree oven for 1 hour and 30 minutes without stirring.

Sister Vivian Dekerlegand, M.S.C.
Opelousas Catholic H.S., Opelousas, Louisiana

COMPANY CHICKEN AND RICE

1 1/2 c. rice
1 can cream of chicken soup
1 can cream of mushroom soup

1 can cream of celery soup
2 tbsp. onion flakes
3/4 c. milk
Salt
Pepper to taste
8 serving pieces chicken
1/2 c. butter, melted

Combine rice, soups, onion flakes, milk, 1 teaspoon salt and pepper. Pour into a greased 9 x 13-inch baking dish. Sprinkle chicken pieces with salt; dip into melted butter. Arrange over rice mixture. Cover loosely with foil. Bake in preheated 300-degree oven for 2 hours. Uncover and bake for 30 minutes longer. Casserole may be prepared ahead and frozen. Allow 30 minutes longer baking time for frozen casserole.

Helen C. Hollinger
Celina Jr. H.S., Celina, Ohio

CRUNCHY CHICKEN CASSEROLE

1 cooked chicken, cubed
1 c. finely chopped celery
1/2 c. slivered almonds
1/4 tbsp. lemon juice
3 hard-boiled eggs, chopped
1 can cream of chicken soup
2 tsp. minced onion
1/2 tsp. salt
1/4 tsp. pepper
1/2 c. mayonnaise
3/4 c. cooked rice
2 c. crushed potato chips

Combine all ingredients except 1/2 cup potato chips. Place in casserole; top with remaining potato chips. Bake in a preheated 450-degree oven for 15 minutes. Yield: 6 servings.

Agnes D. Ingram
West Montgomery Sch.
Mount Gilead, North Carolina

FAMILY CHICKEN CASSEROLE

1 can cream of chicken soup
1 can cream of mushroom soup
1 can cream of celery soup
1/4 c. butter
1 c. rice
3 frying chickens, cut in serving
   pieces

Salt and pepper to taste
1 sm. can mushrooms (opt.)

Combine soups in a bowl; stir until well mixed. Melt butter in a casserole. Add rice and mix well. Add 1/3 of the soup mixture; blend well. Place chicken pieces on top; add salt, pepper and mushrooms. Pour remaining soup mixture over top. Cover. Bake in preheated 325-degree oven for 1 hour and 30 minutes. Yield: 10-12 servings.

Joan M. Hughes
Southern Columbia Area Schools
Catawissa, Pennsylvania

LUSCIOUS CHICKEN

1 can cream of chicken soup
1 can cream of celery soup
1 can cream of mushroom soup
1 c. white wine
1 sm. can mushroom caps
1 sm. jar chopped pimentos
1/2 green pepper, chopped
1/2 onion, chopped
1 can water chestnuts, sliced
1 c. Minute rice
8 to 12 chicken breast halves
Parmesan cheese

Combine soups, wine, mushrooms, pimentos, green pepper, onion and water chestnuts. Arrange rice in 9 x 13-inch baking dish. Cover with 1/3 of the soup mixture. Arrange chicken breasts on soup mixture; cover with remaining soup mixture. Sprinkle generously with Parmesan cheese, then cover. Bake in preheated 350-degree oven for at least 2 hours. This can be made ahead and kept in the refrigerator or frozen until ready to bake.

Mrs. Phyllis Larson
Glen Crest Jr. H.S., Glen Ellyn, Illinois

ONE OF THOSE DAYS CASSEROLE

1/2 c. rice
1 fryer chicken, disjointed
1 pkg. dry vegetable soup mix
1 can cream of chicken soup
1   14-oz. can of chicken broth

Sprinkle rice in large buttered casserole. Place chicken over rice; sprinkle soup mix over chicken. Spoon cream soup over top. Pour chicken broth over entire mixture; cover.

Bake in preheated 350-degree oven for 1 hour and 30 minutes to 2 hours.

Linda Zylstra
Willapa Valley H.S., Menlo, Washington

SAUCY CHICKEN AND RICE

1/4 c. chopped onion
1/4 c. flour
1 tsp. salt
1/8 tsp. pepper
8 pieces chicken
1/4 c. long grain rice
1 c. water
1 can cream of mushroom soup

Cook onion in 3 tablespoons fat for about 5 minutes or until golden but not brown. Remove from pan. Place flour, salt and pepper in paper bag; add chicken pieces and shake to coat. Saute chicken in fat, turning to brown evenly. Remove from pan; place in large casserole. Combine rice, water, mushroom soup and onion in bowl, mixing until smooth. Pour over chicken; cover. Bake in preheated 325 to 350-degree oven for 1 hour or until done. Yield: 6 servings.

Mrs. Nannie C. Edwards
Oxford Area H.S., Oxford, Pennsylvania

YELLOW RICE AND CHICKEN

1 fryer, disjointed
1 onion, chopped
2 cloves of garlic, minced
4 tbsp. olive oil
1/4 c. canned tomatoes
1 qt. water
1 bay leaf
2 tbsp. salt
1 1/4 c. rice
Pinch of saffron
2 green peppers, chopped
1 sm. can English peas

Saute chicken, onion and garlic in oil in a Dutch oven until lightly browned. Add tomatoes and water; bring to a boil. Boil for 5 minutes. Add bay leaf, salt, rice, saffron and green peppers; stir thoroughly. Bake, covered, in 350-degree oven for 30 minutes. Garnish with peas before serving.

Blanche Young
Northeast H.S., North Little Rock, Arkansas

SHERRIED CHICKEN AND RICE

1 c. rice
6 chicken breasts
1 can cream of mushroom soup
1/2 c. cooking sherry
1/2 c. water

Arrange rice evenly in casserole. Place chicken on top. Combine soup, sherry and water and pour over chicken. Bake, covered, in preheated 350-degree oven for 2 hours and 30 minutes.

Mrs. Clara Levins
Eastern Jr. H.S., Lynn, Massachusetts

SOUPY SOUTHERN CASSEROLE

1 chicken
1 env. dry onion soup mix
2 cans cream of mushroom soup
2 c. rice
Salt and pepper to taste

Cook the chicken and soup mix in boiling salted water until chicken is tender. Cool; remove chicken from bone. Combine chicken, chicken broth, mushroom soup, rice, salt and pepper in casserole; cover. Bake in preheated 325-degree oven for about 1 hour, stirring occasionally.

Jo Ann Been
Devine H.S., Devine, Texas

SISTER MARY'S CHICKEN CASSEROLE

1   4-lb. roasting chicken, disjointed
1/4 c. Seasoned Flour
Olive or salad oil
1 sm. onion, chopped
1 clove of garlic, sliced
3 or 4 stalks celery, chopped
1 med. carrot, diced
1 1/2 c. hot chicken stock
1 c. sliced mushrooms
12 stuffed olives, sliced

Place chicken in paper bag with Seasoned Flour. Close bag and shake vigorously. Brown chicken in 1/4 cup oil in skillet. Place in casserole. Add onion, garlic, celery and carrot to skillet; cook over low heat for 10 minutes. Place vegetables over the chicken; add stock. Cover. Bake in preheated 325-degree oven for

1 hour and 30 minutes or until chicken is tender. Saute mushrooms in 2 tablespoons oil for 5 minutes; add olives. Spoon over chicken and bake for 5 minutes longer.

Seasoned Flour

1 c. flour
1 tbsp. salt
1/8 tsp. pepper

Combine flour, salt and pepper. Place desired amount in paper bag; add food to be floured and shake.

Sister Mary Benedict
Mt. St. Benedict Sch., Crookston, Minnesota

MARY'S CHICKEN CASSEROLE OLE

4 lg. cooked chicken breasts, deboned
8 corn tortillas
1 can cream of chicken soup
1 can cream of mushroom soup
1 c. milk
1 onion, finely chopped
1   7-oz. can Ortega green chili
*   salsa*
1 lb. Cheddar cheese, grated

Cut chicken breasts into bite-sized pieces. Cut tortillas into 1-inch pieces. Combine all ingredients except cheese, then turn into a greased 9 x 13-inch baking dish. Top with cheese. Refrigerate for 24 hours. Bake, covered, in preheated 300-degree oven for 45 minutes. Uncover and bake for 45 minutes longer.

Bonnie Miller
Elk Creek H.S., Elk Creek, California

CHICKEN CHALATES

1/4 c. chopped green pepper
1 sm. onion, diced
1 clove of garlic, crushed
2 to 3 tbsp. butter
1 pt. sour cream
3 to 4 tbsp. chicken broth
2 c. cooked cubed chicken
2 or 3 Ortega green chili peppers,
*   diced*
8 to 10 corn tortillas, torn in
*   bite-sized pieces*
1/2 c. grated Cheddar cheese

Saute green pepper, onion and garlic in butter. Combine sour cream with chicken broth in mixing bowl; add all ingredients except tortillas and cheese. Arrange alternate layers of sauce mixture and tortillas in baking dish. Top with cheese. Bake in preheated 325-degree oven for 35 to 40 minutes. Yield: 4 servings.

Donna Samsel
Las Plumas H.S., Oroville, California

MEXICAN CHICKEN

1 cooked hen or fryer, boned
1 onion, chopped
1 tsp. garlic salt
1 tsp. chili powder
1 can Rotel tomatoes with green
* chilies*
1/2 lb. Cheddar cheese, grated
1 pkg. tortillas
Chicken broth
1 can cream of chicken soup
1 can cream of mushroom soup

Dice chicken into a mixing bowl; add onion, garlic salt, chili powder and tomatoes. Reserve 1 cup cheese for topping; add remaining cheese to chicken mixture. Soften tortillas in chicken broth; line large baking dish. Add chicken mixture and about 1/2 cup broth. Spread both cans of soup on top. Sprinkle reserved cheese on top. Bake in preheated 350-degree oven for 30 minutes. Yield: 6 servings.

Mrs. Juanita Pitts
Linden-Kildare H.S., Linden, Texas

VEGETABLE-CHICKEN CASSEROLE

Butter or margarine
1/3 c. all-purpose flour
1 1/2 c. milk
1 1/2 c. grated Cheddar cheese
1 1-lb. can peas, drained
1 c. sliced cooked carrots
1 12-oz. can whole kernel corn,
* drained*
1 c. diced cooked chicken
1 1/2 c. seasoned mashed potatoes

Melt 1/3 cup butter in saucepan; blend in flour. Add milk gradually; cook over low heat, stirring constantly, until thickened. Add

cheese; cook for 5 minutes, stirring constantly. Combine cheese mixture, peas, carrots, corn and chicken; mix well. Turn into greased 2-quart casserole. Top with potatoes. Dot with 2 tablespoons butter. Bake in preheated 350-degree oven for 25 to 30 minutes.

Kathleen Williams
North Lamar H.S., Powderly, Texas

OVEN CHICKEN SALADS

4 c. cubed cooked chicken
2 c. thinly sliced celery
2 c. toasted 1/2-in. bread cubes
1 c. mayonnaise or salad dressing
1/3 c. Pet evaporated milk
1/4 c. drained pickle relish
1 tbsp. instant minced onion
1 tbsp. lemon juice
1 tsp. salt
3 drops of Tabasco sauce
1 c. grated American process cheese
1/4 c. whole blanched almonds

Place chicken, celery, bread cubes, mayonnaise, milk, pickle relish, onion, lemon juice, salt and Tabasco sauce in 3-quart bowl; mix well. Place in 6 greased individual baking dishes or shells. Place on large cookie sheet; sprinkle cheese, then almonds over salads. Bake in preheated 450-degree oven on center shelf for 10 to 12 minutes or until cheese melts and almonds are toasted. Yield: 6 servings.

Oven Chicken Salads

Hot Crab-Avocado Casseroles

Sensational Casseroles From The Sea

Seafood is always a welcome addition to any menu, and when served in extravagant casseroles, it makes a delicious one-dish meal.

The following selection of seafood casseroles offers new and exciting ideas for preparing both simple and fancy seafood delights. Tuna has an irresistible flavor when served in a Tuna-Tomato Casserole made with macaroni, tomatoes, chopped onion and cream of chicken soup. For shrimp enthusiasts, serve Shrimp Thermador, a delicious combination of cooked shrimp, sliced mushrooms and rice. Combine two outstanding seafood flavors in Seafood Fancy made with crab meat, shrimp, celery and chopped onions. Dinner guests will applaud a Crab Meat Souffle made with chopped onions, egg whites, crab meat and tomato paste.

These are only a few of the delicious selections found in the following array of seafood casseroles, all generously submitted by creative home economics teachers.

COMPANY SEAFOOD CASSEROLE

2 cans cream of mushroom soup
2 cans minced clams, drained
1 sm. can mushrooms
2 tsp. curry powder
2 tsp. Worcestershire sauce
2 tbsp. minced onion
2 8-oz. packages spinach noodles,
   cooked and drained

Combine all ingredients; pour into a greased casserole. Bake in preheated 350-degree oven for 35 to 45 minutes.

Avis Burge
South Central H.S., Union Mills, Indiana

LUNCHEON CLAMBAKE

4 eggs
2 c. milk
2 1/2 c. soda cracker crumbs
1/3 c. melted butter
2 10 1/2-oz. cans minced clams
   with liquid
1/4 c. minced onion
2 tbsp. minced green pepper
1/2 tsp. salt
1/2 tsp. Worcestershire sauce

Beat eggs well in mixing bowl; add milk and cracker crumbs. Let stand for 20 minutes. Add butter and remaining ingredients; mix well. Pour into a 9 x 9 x 2-inch baking pan. Bake in preheated 350-degree oven for 1 hour. Yield: 8 servings.

Mrs. Carol Edwards
Blair H.S., Blair, Wisconsin

CRAB CREOLE CASSEROLE

4 tbsp. butter or margarine
1/2 c. finely chopped onion
2 tbsp. all-purpose flour
1 1-lb. can tomatoes
1/4 c. chopped green olives
Salt and pepper to taste
1/4 tsp. thyme
1 tbsp. Worcestershire sauce
2 c. crab meat
2 c. cooked rice
3/4 c. bread crumbs

Melt 2 tablespoons butter in medium-sized saucepan. Add onion; cook until tender. Stir in flour until smooth. Add tomatoes, olives, salt, pepper, thyme and Worcestershire sauce. Bring to a boil; reduce heat. Simmer for 10 minutes. Place half the crab meat in greased 1 1/2-quart casserole; add half the rice. Pour half the sauce over rice; repeat layers. Sprinkle bread crumbs over top; dot with remaining butter. Bake at 350 degrees for 30 minutes or until crumbs are golden brown. Yield: 6 servings.

Sylvia Marsh
John C. Fremont H.S., Colorado Springs, Colorado

HOT CRAB-AVOCADO CASSEROLES

2 California avocados
Lemon juice
2 7 1/2-oz. cans crab meat
1/4 c. butter or margarine
3 tbsp. flour
1 tsp. salt
1/4 tsp. crushed red pepper
1/4 tsp. crumbled thyme
2 c. milk
2 tbsp. white wine
1/2 c. grated Parmesan cheese

Cut avocados into halves lengthwise; remove seeds. Peel avocados. Cut 4 or 5 lengthwise slices for garnish; dice remaining avocados. Coat sliced and diced avocado with lemon juice. Drain and flake crab meat. Melt butter in saucepan; blend in flour, salt, pepper and thyme. Stir in milk; cook over low heat, stirring, until mixture comes to a boil and is thickened. Stir in crab meat and wine; heat through. Stir in diced avocado; turn into 4 or 5 individual casseroles. Sprinkle with cheese. Broil for 2 minutes or until golden brown. Garnish with sliced avocado; serve at once. Yield: 4-5 servings.

Photograph for this recipe on page 87.

DEVILED CRAB CASSEROLE

1/2 c. chopped onion
1/4 c. chopped green pepper
3 tbsp. butter or margarine
3 tbsp. flour
1 1/2 c. half and half
2 egg yolks, slightly beaten
Dash of cayenne pepper
1/2 tsp. salt
2 tsp. Worcestershire sauce
1 tbsp. prepared mustard
1 tbsp. finely chopped chives
2 7 3/4-oz. cans crab meat or tuna

1 c. soft bread crumbs
2 tbsp. melted butter

Saute onion and green pepper in the butter until tender in a saucepan. Add flour; mix until smooth. Stir in half and half gradually; cook over medium heat, stirring constantly. until sauce thickens. Stir a small amount of hot sauce into egg yolks; add to remaining sauce in pan. Cook, stirring constantly, for 2 minutes. Remove from heat; add cayenne pepper, salt, Worcestershire sauce, mustard and chives. Mix well. Stir in crab meat. Spoon into buttered 1-quart casserole. Combine bread crumbs and melted butter; sprinkle over crab mixture. Bake in a preheated 375-degree oven for 20 to 25 minutes.

Susan J. Thomas
Mascenic Regional Sch.
New Ipswich, New Hampshire

HOT CRAB DISH

2 c. shredded Velveeta cheese
3 c. medium white sauce
4 egg yolks, beaten
2 c. fresh or canned crab meat
1/4 c. melted butter
1/2 c. bread crumbs

Add cheese to white sauce; stir until melted. Add to egg yolks gradually; stir in crab meat. Place in greased casserole. Mix butter and bread crumbs; sprinkle over crab meat mixture. Bake at 350 degrees for 30 minutes. Remove from heat; let stand for about 10 minutes before serving.

Donna Rasmussen
Central Middle Sch., Montevideo, Minnesota

EASY CRAB MEAT SOUFFLE

1 c. chopped onions
2/3 c. butter
1/2 c. flour
2 tsp. salt
1 tsp. pepper
1 c. evaporated milk
1/2 c. tomato paste
8 eggs, separated
3/4 lb. crab meat

Saute onions in butter until soft. Add flour, salt and pepper; cook over low heat until smooth, stirring constantly. Stir in milk and tomato paste and cook until thickened, stir-

ring constantly. Stir small amount of sauce into beaten egg yolks; stir back into sauce. Remove from heat; add crab meat and mix well. Cool to room temperature. Beat egg whites until stiff. Fold crab meat mixture into egg whites gently. Place in 2 buttered 1 1/2-quart souffle dishes. Bake at 350 degrees for 30 to 35 minutes; serve immediately.

Helen Giles
Susan Bloch English Sch., Seldovia, Alaska

OVERNIGHT CRAB SOUFFLE

8 to 10 slices bread, crusts removed
1 c. crab
1/2 c. mayonnaise
1 sm. onion, chopped
1 c. chopped celery
4 eggs, beaten
2 1/2 c. milk
1 can cream of mushroom soup
1 c. grated cheese

Break up half the bread and place in buttered casserole. Combine crab, mayonnaise, onion and celery; place over bread. Break up remaining bread over crab mixture. Combine eggs and milk in a bowl; pour over bread. Cover; refrigerate overnight. Bake, uncovered, in preheated 325-degree oven for 1 hour. Stir soup to blend, then pour over casserole. Top with cheese. Bake for 15 minutes longer. Yield: 4 servings.

Marilyn Mills Anderson
North Central H.S., Spokane, Washington

PLAN-AHEAD CRAB MEAT CASSEROLE

1 lb. crab meat, drained
1 4-oz. package shredded Cheddar
   cheese
1 c. uncooked shell macaroni
1 hard-cooked egg, chopped
1 c. mushroom soup
1 c. milk
1 tbsp. chopped chives

Mix crab meat, cheese, macaroni and egg. Mix soup and milk; add to crab meat mixture. Add chives and mix well. Place in a greased casserole; cover. Refrigerate for at least 8 hours or overnight. Bake at 350 degrees for 1 hour. Yield: 6 servings.

Ruth M. Mounts
Rahway Jr. H.S., Rahway, New Jersey

FESTIVE CRAB MEAT CASSEROLE

1 2-oz. can pimentos
6 tbsp. butter
4 tbsp. flour
1/2 tsp. salt
2 c. milk
1 6 1/2-oz. can crab meat
1/4 c. minced green pepper
1 c. chopped celery
2 hard-cooked eggs, diced
1/2 c. diced cheese
1/4 tsp. paprika
1/3 c. bread crumbs

Drain and chop the pimentos. Melt 4 tablespoons butter. Add flour and salt; cook, stirring, until smooth. Add milk; cook, stirring, until thickened. Stir in the crab meat, green pepper, celery, pimentos and eggs; place in casserole. Sprinkle cheese on top. Melt remaining butter. Add paprika and bread crumbs; mix well. Sprinkle over cheese. Bake at 350 degrees for 20 minutes.

Borghild Strom
Pattengill Jr. H.S., Lansing, Michigan

PAULLINA CRAB CASSEROLE

3 cans crab meat
1/4 c. chopped mushrooms
1 green pepper, finely chopped
1 pimento, finely chopped
4 green onions, minced
2 tomatoes, peeled and chopped
2 tbsp. butter
1 c. cream
1 tbsp. chopped parsley
Salt and pepper to taste
Buttered crumbs

Pick over crab and remove any shell and cartilage. Combine with mushrooms, green pepper, pimento, onions and tomato. Saute in butter for 10 minutes. Add cream; cook over low heat for 5 minutes. Add parsley, salt and pepper. Place in shallow casserole or scallop shells. Cover with crumbs. Bake in preheated 350-degree oven for 30 to 45 minutes. Garnish with lemon. Yield: 6-8 servings.

Mrs. Elizabeth Peterson
Paullina Comm. Sch., Paullina, Iowa

BAKED SHRIMP AND CHEESE DELIGHT

1/4 lb. mushrooms
2 tbsp. butter or margarine

1 lb. fresh cooked shrimp or
   2 5 3/4-oz. cans shrimp, drained
1 1/2 c. cooked rice
1 1/2 c. shredded cheese
1/2 c. evaporated milk or cream
3 tbsp. catsup
1/2 tsp. Worcestershire sauce
Salt and pepper to taste

Slice mushrooms; saute in butter for 10 minutes. Mix lightly with shrimp, rice and cheese. Combine milk, catsup, Worcestershire sauce and seasonings. Add to shrimp mixture. Pour into casserole. Bake in preheated 350-degree oven for 25 minutes.

Mrs. Karl Moos
Marion Steele H.S., Amherst, Ohio

GOLDEN SHRIMP PUFF

10 slices bread
6 eggs
3 c. milk
2 tbsp. minced parsley
3/4 tsp. dry mustard
1/2 tsp. salt
2 c. shredded American cheese
2 c. cleaned cooked or canned shrimp

Remove crusts from bread; cut slices into cubes. Combine eggs, milk and seasonings in bowl; beat until well blended. Stir in bread cubes, cheese and shrimp. Pour into 11 x 7 x 1 1/2-inch baking dish. Bake, uncovered, in preheated 325-degree oven for 1 hour or until center is set. Serve immediately. Yield: 8 servings.

Beth Tveiten
Gonvick H.S., Gonvick, Minnesota

JIFFY SHRIMP MEAL

1 can shrimp soup
3/4 c. hot water
1/2 c. diced celery
1/2 c. diced green pepper
1 tsp. chopped parsley
2/3 c. instant rice
1 8-oz. package frozen cleaned
   shrimp, thawed
1/2 tsp. salt
Dash of pepper
1/2 c. sliced ripe olives
1/4 c. toasted slivered almonds
1 tsp. curry powder

Combine soup, water, celery and green pepper in a saucepan; cook over low heat for 10 minutes. Add the remaining ingredients and turn into a buttered 1 1/2-quart casserole. Cover. Bake in a preheated 350-degree oven for 25 minutes. Yield: 6 servings.

Mrs. Shirley Shepherd Allen
Redford H.S., Detroit, Michigan

MRS. DUHON'S SHRIMP CASSEROLE

1/2 c. butter or margarine
1/2 c. chopped bell pepper
1/2 c. chopped onion
1/2 c. sliced celery
1/2 clove of garlic, minced
2 c. fresh cleaned shrimp, chopped
2 tbsp. chopped green onion
2 tbsp. chopped parsley
1 tsp. salt
1/2 tsp. pepper
1/2 tsp. paprika
1 sm. jar pimentos, drained and
    chopped
1 can cream of mushroom soup
2 c. cooked rice
1/2 c. dry bread crumbs

Melt butter in skillet; add bell pepper, onion, celery and garlic and cook until tender. Add shrimp, green onion, parsley, salt, pepper and paprika; cook until shrimp turns pink. Stir in pimentos, soup and rice; pour into casserole. Top with crumbs and cover. Bake in a preheated 375-degree oven for 45 minutes. Yield: 6 servings.

Mrs. Ann McDonald
Jane Long Jr. H.S., Houston, Texas

SHRIMP-SPINACH AND EGG CASSEROLE

1/4 c. butter
1/4 c. flour
2 c. milk
1/2 tsp. Worcestershire sauce
1/2 tsp. salt
Pepper to taste
Dash of Tabasco sauce
1 c. grated American sharp cheese
2 boxes frozen chopped spinach
1 lb. cooked cleaned shrimp
6 deviled eggs

Melt butter in saucepan; stir in flour until smooth. Add milk gradually; cook, stirring constantly, until thick and smooth. Add Worcestershire sauce, salt, pepper, Tabasco sauce and

cheese; stir until cheese is melted. Cook spinach according to package directions until just tender; drain. Place spinach in 13 x 9-inch baking dish. Arrange shrimp over spinach, then eggs over shrimp. Pour sauce over all. Bake in preheated 450-degree oven for 15 minutes or until bubbly and lightly browned. Yield: 6 servings.

Marcia Codner
Mission Jr. H.S., Bellevue, Nebraska

CHARLESTON SHRIMP BAKE

1 1/2 lb. medium fresh shrimp
1/4 c. Blue Bonnet margarine
1/4 c. fine dry bread crumbs
1 1/2 c. chopped green pepper
1/4 c. chopped onion
4 c. stale bread cubes
1 1/2 tsp. salt
1/8 tsp. pepper
1 1-lb. can tomatoes

Shell and devein shrimp. Melt margarine in large skillet. Remove 1 tablespoon margarine; mix with bread crumbs thoroughly. Set aside. Add green pepper and onion to margarine remaining in skillet; cook over medium heat, stirring occasionally, for about 5 minutes or until tender. Stir in bread cubes, salt, pepper, undrained tomatoes and shrimp. Turn into oblong 2-quart baking dish; sprinkle with bread crumb mixture. Bake in preheated 350-degree oven for 25 to 30 minutes or until shrimp are done. Yield: 4-6 servings.

Charleston Shrimp Bake

MY FAVORITE SHRIMP CASSEROLE

8 hard-cooked eggs
1/2 tsp. prepared mustard
2 drops of Tabasco sauce
1/2 c. mayonnaise
1/4 tsp. sugar
Salt and pepper to taste
1/2 c. butter
1/2 c. flour
1 qt. milk
1 tbsp. dry mustard
1 tbsp. seasoned salt
1 tbsp. Worcestershire sauce
1/2 c. shredded sharp Cheddar cheese
1 tsp. garlic salt or 1 clove of garlic,
  pressed
1 tbsp. catsup
1/4 c. dry sherry or vermouth
2 tbsp. parsley flakes
2 lb. shrimp, cooked and cleaned
Buttered cracker crumbs

Cut eggs in half lengthwise; remove yolks. Mash yolks in a bowl; add prepared mustard, Tabasco sauce, mayonnaise, sugar, salt and pepper. Mix well. Fill egg whites with yolk mixture. Set aside. Melt butter in saucepan; stir in flour until smooth. Add milk gradually; cook, stirring constantly, until thickened. Add remaining ingredients except crumbs; mix. Place half the egg halves in baking dish. Cover with half the shrimp sauce. Repeat layers. Cover with buttered cracker crumbs. Bake in preheated 350-degree oven for 25 to 30 minutes or until bubbly and browned.

Mrs. Lois W. Gerald
Whiteville Sr. H.S., Whiteville, North Carolina

SHRIMP BOAT SPECIAL

2 15-oz. cans macaroni with cheese
  sauce
1 c. diced cooked shrimp
1 c. minced celery
1 tbsp. lemon juice
Dash of pepper
1/4 c. buttered bread crumbs

Combine all ingredients except crumbs in a 1 1/2-quart casserole. Sprinkle crumbs over top. Bake in preheated 400-degree oven for 20 minutes. Yield: 4 servings.

Mrs. Beverly A. Reed
Stamford Central Sch., Stamford, New York

WARM DAY CALIFORNIA CASSEROLE

3 12-oz. packages frozen shrimp,
  thawed
3 tbsp. butter or margarine
2 tsp. curry powder
1 c. chopped celery
1/2 c. chopped onion
1 8 3/4-oz. can crushed pineapple
2 c. water
1 1/2 tsp. salt
1 1/2 c. packaged precooked rice
2 California avocados

Peel and devein shrimp. Melt butter in large skillet. Add curry powder; cook until brown, stirring occasionally. Add celery and onion; cook until tender-crisp. Add shrimp to curry mixture; cook, covered, for 5 minutes. Add undrained pineapple and water; bring to a boil. Stir in salt and rice. Remove from heat. Cover; let stand for 10 minutes. Cut avocados lengthwise into halves; remove seeds and peel. Dice 1 avocado; stir into shrimp mixture. Turn into casserole. Cut remaining avocado crosswise into crescents; arrange on top of casserole. Serve at once. Yield: 6-8 servings.

SHRIMP-MUSHROOM CASSEROLE

1/2 lb. mushrooms, sliced
2 tbsp. butter
3 tbsp. chopped onion
1 lb. shrimp, cooked and cleaned
1 1/2 c. cooked rice
1 1/2 c. shredded Cheddar cheese
3 tbsp. catsup
1/2 tsp. Worcestershire sauce
1/2 c. heavy cream
Dash of Tabasco sauce
Salt and pepper to taste

Saute mushrooms in butter; add onion and cook until tender. Combine all ingredients; mix well. Turn into casserole. Bake in preheated 350-degree oven for 25 minutes. Yield: 4-5 servings.

Sister M. Magdalene
Our Lady of Mount Carmel Sch.
Wyandotte, Michigan

SHRIMP THERMIDOR

1/2 c. sliced canned mushrooms
1/2 stick margarine

Warm Day California Casserole

1/4 c. flour
1 tsp. salt
1/2 tsp. dry mustard
1/2 tsp. cayenne pepper
1 1/2 c. (about) milk
2 c. cooked shrimp
1 c. cooked rice
Parmesan cheese to taste
Paprika

Saute mushrooms in margarine for 5 minutes. Blend in flour, salt, mustard and cayenne pepper. Add milk slowly and cook, stirring constantly, until thick. Stir in shrimp. Arrange rice in a baking dish, then pour shrimp mixture over top. Sprinkle with cheese and paprika. Bake in a preheated 400-degree oven for 10 to 12 minutes. Serve immediately. Yield: 6 servings.

Mrs. Rachel E. Nicholson
Union H.S., Union, Mississippi

CRAB MEAT-SHRIMP CASSEROLE

3/4 c. finely chopped celery
3/4 c. finely chopped onions
3/4 c. finely chopped bell pepper
1/2 tsp. salt
1/8 tsp. freshly ground pepper
1 tsp. Worcestershire sauce
1 c. bread crumbs
1 c. mayonnaise
1   6 1/2-oz. can crab meat, drained
1   6 1/2-oz. can shrimp, drained
Progresso seasoned crumbs

Mix celery, onions, bell pepper, salt, ground pepper, Worcestershire sauce, bread crumbs and mayonnaise in a bowl. Add crab meat; mix well. Devein shrimp. Add to crab meat mixture and mix thoroughly. Place in a greased casserole. Sprinkle with Progresso seasoned crumbs. Bake at 350 degrees for 45 minutes. May be placed in 6 crab shells and baked for 30 minutes, if desired. Yield: 6 servings.

Mrs. L. Kervin Rush
State Sch. for Spastic Children
Alexandria, Louisiana

SHRIMP AND CRAB CASSEROLE

1 lb. cleaned shrimp
1 lb. crab meat
1 green pepper, diced
1 sm. onion, chopped
1 c. chopped celery
1 c. mayonnaise
1 tsp. Worcestershire sauce
1/2 tsp. salt
1/4 tsp. red pepper
1/2 c. bread crumbs
1 tbsp. margarine

Combine ingredients in order listed; mix well. Place in casserole; cover. Bake in preheated 350-degree oven for 40 minutes. Yield: 6 servings.

Mrs. David L. Beveridge
East Carteret H.S., Beaufort, North Carolina

SHRIMPLY SUPER

2 lb. shrimp
1 sm. can crab meat
1 1/2 c. tomato juice
1 can cream of celery soup
Dash of Tabasco sauce
2 tbsp. Worcestershire sauce
1 c. shell macaroni, cooked

Boil shrimp in seasoned boiling water for 12 to 15 minutes; peel and devein. Flake crab meat; mix with shrimp. Combine tomato juice, soup, Tabasco sauce and Worcestershire sauce; mix well. Mix with shrimp mixture and macaroni; place in 2-quart casserole. Bake in preheated 375-degree oven for 30 minutes. Yield: 6 servings.

Dorotha Hurst
Baytown Jr. H.S., Baytown, Texas

LOBSTER-CRAB MEAT AU GRATIN

2 or 3 boxes frozen lobster-tails
2 tbsp. butter
2 tbsp. flour
1/2 c. milk
1/2 c. cream
1 egg yolk, beaten
1/4 tsp. pepper
1 c. grated Parmesan cheese
1 sm. onion, chopped fine
1 7-oz. package frozen King crab,
    thawed
Bread crumbs
Paprika

Cook lobster-tails according to package directions; remove shells. Cut lobster into pieces. Melt butter in a heavy saucepan; stir in flour to make a smooth paste. Add milk and cream gradually, stirring constantly; cook until smooth and thick. Stir a small amount of hot sauce into egg yolk; stir egg yolk into hot sauce. Add pepper and cheese; cook until well combined. Saute onion in hot fat until clear. Stir lobster, crab meat and onion into cheese sauce; pour into casserole. Sprinkle with bread crumbs and paprika. Bake in preheated 400-degree oven until bubbly and the top is browned. Serve with rice.

Joan Joslin
Staley Jr. H.S., Rome, New York

SCALLOPED OYSTERS

1 1/2 pt. oysters
1/2 tsp. salt
1/3 tsp. pepper
1/3 c. butter or margarine,
    melted
3 c. soda cracker crumbs
3/4 c. milk

Drain oysters and reserve liquid. Sprinkle oysters with salt and pepper. Combine butter and crumbs. Arrange alternate layers of oysters and crumb mixture in greased baking dish. Combine milk and reserved oyster liquid. Pour over top. Bake in preheated 350-degree oven for 30 to 45 minutes.

Mrs. Karl Younginer
Fitzgerald Jr. H.S., Fitzgerald, Georgia

SEAFOOD AU GRATIN

1 sm. onion
1 clove of garlic
1 bay leaf
2 tbsp. salt
2 lb. shrimp
1/2 lemon, sliced
1 c. evaporated milk
4 tbsp. butter
4 tbsp. flour
1 tsp. Worcestershire sauce
Dash of cayenne pepper
1 can mushrooms
3/4 c. grated Cheddar or American
    cheese
2 med. lobster-tails, cooked
Buttered bread crumbs

Fill kettle 2/3 full with water. Add onion, garlic, bay leaf and salt; simmer for 30 minutes. Add shrimp and lemon slices; boil until shrimp is tender. Drain and let cool; shell and devein shrimp. Combine milk and 1 cup water in saucepan; heat thoroughly. Melt butter in top of double boiler; stir in flour to make a smooth paste. Stir in hot milk, seasonings, mushrooms and cheese; cook until thickened and cheese is melted. Remove lobster meat from shells; cut into pieces. Stir shrimp and lobster into cheese sauce; pour into baking dish. Sprinkle with buttered bread crumbs. Bake in preheated 350-degree oven for 30 minutes.

Marilyn Kanne
Brookside Jr. H.S., Albert Lea, Minnesota

SEAFOOD CASSEROLE DELUXE

4 c. cooked shrimp
1 7-oz. can lobster
1 6 1/2-oz. can crab meat
2 1/2 c. sliced celery
2/3 c. chopped onion
1 c. mayonnaise
2 tsp. Worcestershire sauce
1 tsp. salt
1/2 tsp. pepper
1 1/2 c. fine dry bread crumbs
1/3 c. melted margarine
2 slices lemon
Parsley

Cut shrimp in half lengthwise. Flake lobster and crab meat; add to shrimp. Mix in celery, onion, mayonnaise, Worcestershire sauce, salt and pepper. Spread seafood mixture in 1 1/2-quart casserole. Combine bread crumbs and margarine; sprinkle over casserole. Bake in preheated 350-degree oven for 30 to 35 minutes or until lightly browned. Garnish with lemon slices and parsley.

Linda Adams
Millersburg Area Schools
Millersburg, Pennsylvania

SEAFOOD CASSEROLE A LA GLATT

1 clove of garlic, minced
2 tbsp. peanut oil
1/2 green pepper, chopped
1 stalk green celery, chopped
12 sm. button mushrooms
1 1-lb. can stewed tomatoes
1 6-oz. package Spanish rice mix
1 13 1/2-oz. can chicken broth
1 10-oz. package frozen Italian-style
   vegetables
1/2 tsp. crumbled leaf savory
1 1-lb. package frozen fillet of
   sole, thawed
1 1-pt. can steamed clams in shells

Saute garlic in hot oil; add green pepper, celery and mushrooms. Add tomatoes, rice mix, broth, frozen vegetables and savory; bring to a boil, stirring frequently. Pour into 2-quart casserole. Cut sole into 1-inch cubes; add sole, clams and 1/2 cup clam liquid to casserole. Bake, covered, in preheated 400-degree oven for 20 minutes.

Saralee Glatt
Woodburn Jr. H.S., Woodburn, Oregon

SEAFOOD HEARTY

1 6-oz. package long grain and
   wild rice
4 tbsp. butter
2 tbsp. flour
1/2 tsp. salt
1/4 tsp. pepper
2 c. milk
Several drops of Tabasco sauce
1/4 c. pimento, cut in strips
1 4-oz. can sliced mushrooms,
   drained
1/2 c. thinly sliced green pepper
1/2 c. sliced thinly onion
1/2 lb. shrimp, cooked and cleaned
1/2 lb. crab meat, cut in chunks

Cook rice according to package directions. Melt 2 tablespoons butter in saucepan; blend in flour, salt and pepper. Add milk slowly, stirring constantly; cook until sauce is smooth and thickened. Add Tabasco sauce, pimento and mushrooms. Saute green pepper and onion in remaining butter until tender. Add to cream sauce; stir in shrimp and crab meat. Spoon rice into 2-quart casserole; pour cream sauce over all. Bake in preheated 350-degree oven for 40 minutes. Yield: 6 to 8 servings.

Jane S. Dakin
Memorial H.S., Millbury, Massachusetts

BAKED FLOUNDER FILLET SUPREME

2 lb. flounder fillets
Seasoned salt to taste
1 lg. tomato
6 slices Swiss cheese
1 4-oz. can mushrooms, drained
   and juice reserved
2 sm. onions, sliced
2 tbsp. butter
1 1/2 tbsp. flour
1/4 c. parsley flakes
Salt to taste
6 tbsp. sherry
1 c. light cream
2 c. rice, cooked

Sprinkle flounder fillets with seasoned salt; roll as for jelly roll. Cut tomato into 6 slices; cut cheese slices in half. Arrange half the flounder rolls in casserole; top with half the tomato slices. Place half the cheese slices over tomato slices; repeat layers. Saute mushrooms and onion slices in butter; stir in flour, parsley flakes and salt. Add enough reserved mushroom liquid to the sherry to measure 1/2 cup liquid. Add sherry mixture and cream to mushroom mixture; stir well. Bring to a boil; pour over cheese slices. Bake in preheated 400-degree oven for 20 minutes. Serve with rice. Yield: 6 servings.

Mrs. Bill Dobrinski
Duchesne H.S., St. Charles, Missouri

CUCUMBER FLOUNDER ROLLS

4 cucumbers
2 tbsp. wine vinegar
1 tsp. salt
1/8 tsp. sugar
2 tbsp. butter or margarine
3 tbsp. chopped fresh onion
1 1/2 c. soft bread crumbs
1/4 c. chopped fresh parsley
1 tsp. snipped fresh dill
1 tbsp. fresh lemon juice
6 lg. flounder fillets
Shrimp-Cucumber Sauce

Pare cucumbers; cut in half lengthwise. Scoop out seeds with spoon. Cut cucumber into cubes. Mix wine vinegar, salt and sugar in large bowl. Add cucumbers; mix well. Marinate at room temperature for 30 minutes. Drain; pat dry. Reserve 1 1/2 cups cucumbers for sauce. Melt butter in large skillet. Add onion; cook, stirring, until tender. Add bread crumbs, parsley, dill and lemon juice; simmer for 10 minutes, stirring frequently. Add remaining cucumbers to stuffing mixture; cook over low heat for 5 minutes. Place 1/4 cup stuffing on each flounder fillet; roll up, securing ends with food picks. Place in shallow 1 1/2-quart casserole; pour Shrimp-Cucumber Sauce over all. Bake in preheated 325-degree oven for 20 to 30 minutes. Yield: 6 servings.

Shrimp-Cucumber Sauce

3 tbsp. butter or margarine
2 tbsp. chopped fresh onion
1/4 c. flour
2 c. milk
3 tbsp. white wine
1/4 tsp. snipped fresh dill
1/4 tsp. salt
1/2 lb. cleaned fresh shrimp

Melt butter in large saucepan. Add onion; cook, stirring, until tender. Blend in flour. Stir in milk; cook, stirring constantly, until mixture comes to a boil and thickens. Stir in wine, reserved cucumber, dill, salt and shrimp; simmer for 5 minutes. Yield: 6 cups.

FISH IMPERIAL CASSEROLE

1/2 c. chopped green pepper
1 tbsp. butter
1/2 tsp. salt
1/4 tsp. pepper
1/4 tsp. dry mustard
1 tsp. Worcestershire sauce
1/4 c. mayonnaise
1 lb. baked red snapper or flounder,
    flaked
1/3 c. chopped pimento
1/2 tsp. paprika
2/3 c. soft bread crumbs
2 tbsp. melted butter

Saute green pepper in butter for 1 minute. Combine green pepper, salt, pepper, mustard,

Worcestershire sauce and mayonnaise; add red snapper. Turn into 1-quart casserole or 4 individual baking dishes. Combine pimento, paprika, bread crumbs and melted butter; sprinkle over top. Bake in preheated 350-degree oven for 30 minutes. Yield: 4 servings.

Mrs. Vernal Mobley Alexander
Gaffney Sr. H.S., Gaffney, South Carolina

SEAFOOD FANCY

1   6 1/2-oz. can crab meat
1   4 1/2-oz. can shrimp
1 c. chopped celery
1/2 c. chopped onion
1/2 c. chopped green pepper
1 c. mayonnaise
1 1/2 tsp. Worcestershire sauce
1/2 tsp. salt
Dash of pepper
1 c. soft bread crumbs
2 tbsp. melted butter

Combine all the ingredients except bread crumbs and butter. Turn into a 1-quart casserole. Combine crumbs and melted butter, then sprinkle over top of casserole. Bake in a preheated 350-degree oven for 45 to 50 minutes. Yield: 6 servings.

Karen Chamberlain
Varina H.S., Richmond, Virginia

FISH IN A DISH

1   3-oz. package long grain and
      wild rice mix
1 tbsp. butter
1/2 c. beer
1 egg, well beaten
2 lb. frozen flounder fillets,
      thawed
Salt to taste
Paprika
1   10-oz. package broccoli spears,
      partially cooked
1   1 1/4-oz. package hollandaise
      sauce mix, prepared

Preheat oven to 350 degrees. Cook rice with butter in beer until tender; let cool. Stir in egg. Season fillets with salt; sprinkle with pa-

prika. Place 1 or 2 broccoli spears on each fish fillet. Spoon part of the rice over the broccoli; roll as for jelly roll. Secure with toothpicks. Place rolls in baking dish. Bake, uncovered, for 25 to 30 minutes. Serve with hollandaise sauce. Fillets, broccoli and rice mixture may be placed in baking dish in layers and baked, if desired. Yield: 5-6 servings.

Mrs. Sandra Graman
Middletown H.S., Middletown, Ohio

HALIBUT CASSEROLE

1 lb. frozen halibut, thawed
2 bay leaves
1/4 c. butter
1/4 c. flour
2 c. milk
1/4 c. grated onion
1 c. grated cheese
1 can cream of celery soup
1 c. buttered bread crumbs

Place halibut in saucepan with bay leaves and a small amount of water; simmer until tender. Remove skin and bones and break into small pieces into a 2-quart casserole. Melt butter in saucepan; stir in flour until smooth. Blend in milk gradually. Cook, stirring constantly, until thick and smooth. Stir in onion. Pour over halibut. Cover with cheese. Spoon soup over top; sprinkle with bread crumbs. Bake in a preheated 300-degree oven for 1 hour.

Marilynn Manning
Mountain View Jr.-Sr. H.S.
Mountain View, Wyoming

QUICK TUNA-BROCCOLI BAKE

2 pkg. frozen broccoli
1 lg. can tuna, drained
1 can cream of mushroom soup
Potato chips

Cook broccoli according to package directions; drain. Place in baking dish or casserole. Add tuna to soup; toss lightly. Pour over broccoli. Top with crushed potato chips. Bake in a preheated 350-degree oven for 15 minutes.

Mrs. Donnabelle Pech
Lincoln Comm. H.S., Lincoln, Illinois

CAROLE'S PACIFIC CASSEROLE PIE

1 box frozen peas
2 7-oz. cans tuna, drained and
   flaked
1 can cream of chicken soup
3 med. tomatoes, sliced
1 pkg. potato chips, crushed
2 tbsp. grated sharp cheese

Cook peas according to package directions. Arrange half the tuna, soup, peas, tomatoes and chips in casserole, then repeat layers. Sprinkle with cheese. Bake in preheated 350-degree oven for 30 minutes. Serve with rice or creamed potatoes. Yield: 6 servings.

Mrs. Mary Ada Parks
Anna-Jonesboro Comm. H.S., Anna, Illinois

COMPANY TUNA BAKE

1/2 lb. macaroni
1 3-oz. package cream cheese
1 can cream of mushroom soup
1 sm. can tuna, drained and flaked
1 1/2 tbsp. chopped pimento
1 tbsp. chopped onion
1 tbsp. prepared mustard
1/3 c. milk
1/2 c. dry bread crumbs
2 tbsp. melted margarine

Cook macaroni according to package directions; drain. Soften cream cheese; blend in the soup with electric or rotary beater. Stir in tuna, pimento, onion, mustard, milk and macaroni; turn into a 1 1/2-quart casserole. Combine bread crumbs and margarine; sprinkle over top. Bake in preheated 375-degree oven for 20 to 25 minutes. Garnish with pimentos, flower petal fashion, around the center of casserole and with parsley. Yield: 4-5 servings.

Mrs. Loretta C. Bennett
Thomas Jefferson H.S., Alexandria, Virginia

SEASHELL CASSEROLE

1/2 c. chopped green pepper
1/2 c. chopped onion
2 tbsp. butter
2 cans Cheddar cheese soup
1/2 c. milk
1 c. chopped canned tomatoes

2 7-oz. cans tuna, drained
Dash of pepper
4 c. cooked sm. shell macaroni

Cook green pepper and onion in butter in a saucepan until tender. Stir in remaining ingredients. Pour into 1-quart casserole. Bake in preheated 350-degree oven for 30 minutes or until hot. Yield: 6 servings.

Esther Engelhardt
Mount Pleasant Comm. Sch.
Mount Pleasant, Iowa

TUNA-BROCCOLI-EGG CASSEROLE

1 pkg. frozen broccoli, cooked
1 7-oz. can tuna, drained and
   flaked
1 hard-cooked egg, sliced
1 can cream of mushroom soup
1/2 soup can milk
1 c. crushed potato chips

Place broccoli in a greased 1-quart casserole; top with tuna and sliced egg. Combine soup and milk; pour over tuna. Sprinkle potato chips on top. Bake in preheated 350-degree oven for 30 minutes. Yield: 4 servings.

Mrs. Mary Bray
Clinton Sr. H.S., Clinton, New York

TUNA DELIGHT

1/2 lb. seashell macaroni, cooked
1 can cream of mushroom soup
1/2 c. milk
1 1-lb. can whole tomatoes
1/4 c. tomato juice
1 9 1/4-oz. can tuna, drained
   and flaked
2 tsp. onion salt
1 4-oz. package shredded Cheddar
   cheese

Place cooked macaroni in 2-quart casserole. Combine soup, milk, tomatoes, tomato juice, tuna and onion salt together; mix thoroughly. Pour over the macaroni and mix well. Sprinkle cheese evenly over top. Bake, uncovered, in preheated 350-degree oven for 25 minutes. Yield: 4 servings.

Mrs. Lugenia Rozman
Warwick H.S., Lititz, Pennsylvania

KANSAS MACARONI-TUNA CASSEROLE

1 macaroni-cheese dinner mix
1 can tuna
1 can cream of mushroom soup
1 can peas or other vegetable
1/4 c. milk
2 tbsp. butter
Salt and pepper to taste

Cook macaroni dinner according to package directions. Combine tuna, soup, peas, milk, butter and seasonings in a 2-quart casserole. Add macaroni; mix well. Bake in preheated 350-degree oven for 30 to 35 minutes. Yield: 4 to 6 servings.

Cynthia Atkins
Altoona-Midway Jr.-Sr. H.S., Buffalo, Kansas

TUNA TREAT

1 lb. cooked elbow macaroni
2 cans tuna, drained and flaked
1 pkg. frozen peas and carrots,
    cooked and drained
2 cans cream of mushroom soup

Place macaroni in greased casserole. Combine tuna, vegetables and soup; mix well. Pour over macaroni; stir gently. Bake in preheated 375-degree oven for 20 minutes or until bubbly.

Eileen Kantor
MES Middle Sch., Yorktown, New York

NEW ENGLAND FISH CASSEROLE

1   6 1/2-oz. can tuna, drained and
    flaked
3 hard-cooked eggs, sliced
1 c. cooked frozen peas
2 tbsp. chopped onion
2 tbsp. chopped parsley
2 tbsp. butter
2 tbsp. flour
2 c. milk
1 tsp. salt
1/2 tsp. pepper
1 1/2 c. mashed potatoes
1/2 c. grated American or
    Cheddar cheese

Place tuna in a 2 1/2-quart buttered casserole. Arrange eggs, then peas over tuna. Cook onion and parsley in butter until soft and transpar-ent; blend in flour. Add milk gradually; cook over low heat, stirring constantly, until thick-ened. Add salt and pepper. Pour over peas. Arrange mashed potatoes around edge of cas-serole; sprinkle with cheese. Bake in preheated 350-degree oven for 25 to 30 minutes. Yield: 6 servings.

Susan Carothers
Franklin Reg. Sr. H.S., Murrysville, Pennsylvania

SHOPPER'S TUNA-NOODLE CASSEROLE

1   6-oz. package egg noodles
1 can cream of mushroom soup
1 c. milk
Salt and pepper to taste
1   7-oz. can tuna
1 tsp. cooking sherry (opt.)

Cook noodles in salted, boiling water until tender; drain. Place soup in saucepan; stir well. Add milk gradually, stirring constantly. Heat thoroughly. Season with salt and pepper. Add tuna and sherry; heat through. Add noo-dles; mix well. Place in greased 2-quart casse-role. Bake in preheated 350-degree oven for 20 minutes.

Kay Caskey
Manogue H.S., Reno, Nevada

TUNA AND NOODLES IN CASSEROLE

1 pkg. noodles
1 clove of garlic
1 c. medium white sauce
1 can tuna, flaked
1/2 tsp. salt
1 green pepper, finely cut
2 tbsp. melted butter
1 sm. can mushrooms, drained
1/8 tsp. pepper
2 tbsp. rum
3/4 c. grated cheese
1/4 c. crumbs

Cook the noodles and garlic in boiling salted water. Drain, rinse and drain again. Remove garlic. Combine noodles, sauce, tuna, salt, green pepper, butter, mushrooms, pepper, rum and 1/2 cup cheese; mix well. Turn into buttered casserole. Sprinkle with remaining cheese and crumbs. Bake in a preheated 350-degree oven for 45 minutes. Garnish with parsley and serve.

Lucille Huffman
New Castle H.S., New Castle, Virginia

SHANGHAI CASSEROLE

1 lb. lean ground beef
1 tsp. onion powder
1 tsp. garlic powder
1 c. sliced celery
1 c. cooked mixed vegetables
1   10 1/2-oz. can cream of mushroom
*   soup*
3 c. cooked rice
2 tbsp. soy sauce
1/4 tsp. pepper
1 c. Chinese noodles

Brown beef with onion and garlic powders in a lightly greased skillet. Add celery, mixed vegetables and soup; stir in rice, soy sauce and pepper. Turn into a greased 2-quart casserole; cover. Bake at 350 degrees for 25 minutes. Remove cover; top with noodles. Bake, uncovered, for 5 minutes longer. Yield: 6 servings.

Photograph for this recipe on page 101.

SHRIMP SALAD ACADIA

  1   *10-oz. package frozen broccoli*
     spears
Salad greens
3 c. cleaned cooked shrimp
1 1/2 c. diagonally sliced celery
1/2 med. red onion
Seven Seas Creole French dressing

Cook broccoli spears in boiling, salted water for 8 to 10 minutes or until tender but still firm; drain and chill. Remove stems; cut into thin strips. Separate buds to form bite-sized flowerets. Line 6 individual salad plates with greens; arrange flowerets, stems, shrimp and celery on greens. Slice onion and separate into rings. Top each salad with onion rings. Serve with French dressing. Yield: 6 servings.

CABBAGE-CARROT CARROUSEL

Carrot slices
3 c. shredded green cabbage
1/2 c. chopped green pepper
2/3 c. Seven Seas Creole French
    dressing
3 c. shredded red cabbage
Salad greens
Parsley sprigs

Notch carrot slices carefully with a knife in 4 or 5 places to form petals of a flower. Combine green cabbage, green pepper and 1/3 cup French dressing in large bowl; mix lightly. Toss red cabbage with remaining French dressing. Line a salad bowl with greens; pack red cabbage mixture around side and bottom of salad bowl. Pile green cabbage mixture in center; garnish with parsley sprigs. Insert a toothpick into center of each carrot slice; place on top of parsley. Remove toothpicks. Yield: 6-8 servings.

SHRIMP BUSH

3 c. cleaned cooked shrimp
4 hard-cooked eggs, chopped
1 1/2 c. finely chopped celery
1/2 c. Seven Seas Creole French
    dressing
Parsley sprigs
Pimento
Salad greens

Dice shrimp. Combine shrimp, eggs, celery, and French dressing in medium bowl; mix lightly. Press mixture firmly into small, deep bowl; chill for 2 to 3 hours. Unmold on cake stand or platter; garnish with parsley and pimento. Serve with salad greens. Yield: 6-8 servings.

SALADE JARDINIERE

  1   *1-lb. can whole baby carrots*
  1   *1-lb. can hearts of palm*
  1   *1-lb. can garbanzos or chick-peas*
1/2 c. thinly sliced scallions
3/4 c. Creole French dressing
Chicory or other curly greens

Drain carrots, hearts of palm and garbanzos. Slice carrots lengthwise; reserve half the carrots. Cut remaining carrots into 1-inch pieces. Cut hearts of palm into 1/4-inch slices; reserve half the slices. Combine remaining carrots and hearts of palm, garbanzos and scallions in large bowl. Add French dressing; mix lightly. Refrigerate for 2 to 3 hours or overnight. Line a salad platter with chicory; place salad on chicory. Decorate rim of salad platter with alternating slices of reserved hearts of palm and carrots; garnish with parsley sprigs. Two cups sliced, cooked carrots and 1 1/2 cups diagonally sliced celery may be substituted for canned carrots and hearts of palm. Yield: 6-8 servings.

Photograph for these recipes on page 102.

EFFIE'S TUNA CASSEROLE

1 c. noodles
1 tsp. salt
1 c. flaked tuna
1 can cream of mushroom soup
1 c. grated American cheese
2 tbsp. butter
Butter

Bring 1 quart water to a boil; add noodles and salt. Cook until tender; drain. Place 1/2 of the noodles in buttered baking dish. Place tuna on the noodles and spread half the soup over tuna. Add remaining noodles, then soup. Sprinkle cheese over top. Dot with butter and cover. Bake in a preheated 350-degree oven for 15 minutes. Remove cover; bake 15 minutes longer or until top is browned.

Effie Lois Greene
Potts Camp H.S., Potts Camp, Mississippi

SEAFOOD-NOODLE CASSEROLE

1 med. onion, minced
1 clove of garlic, minced
1/2 c. butter
1 tbsp. flour
2 4-oz. cans mushrooms with juice
1 tsp. Worcestershire sauce
1 can cream of chicken soup
1/4 c. sherry
2 7-oz. cans tuna, flaked
1 5-oz. can shrimp, drained
1 8-oz. package narrow noodles,
    cooked
1/2 c. Parmesan cheese

Saute onion and garlic in butter until tender. Stir in flour, then mushrooms, Worcestershire sauce, soup and sherry. Combine tuna, shrimp and noodles; add soup mixture and mix well. Turn into a buttered casserole; sprinkle with cheese. Bake in a preheated 350-degree oven until heated through and bubbly. Yield: 8 servings.

Mrs. Doris Burr
Sunset H.S., Hayward, California

TUNA SUPREME

1 8-oz. package med. noodles
1 6 3/4-oz. can tuna

1 can cream of chicken soup
3/4 c. milk or half and half
1 can sliced mushrooms
1 tbsp. chopped pimento
1 c. cooked peas
1 c. crushed potato chips

Cook noodles according to package directions; drain and set aside. Combine tuna, soup, milk, mushrooms, pimento and peas. Mix well. Stir in noodles. Pour into buttered casserole. Sprinkle potato chips over top. Bake in a preheated 350-degree oven for 30 minutes or until bubbly.

Wilma Sauer
John Page Jr. H.S., Madison Heights, Michigan

TUNA SURPRISE

3 tbsp. margarine
1 sm. onion, chopped
1 bell pepper, chopped
1/4 c. chopped celery
1 can Cheddar cheese soup
1 can cream of mushroom soup
2 6 1/2-oz. cans tuna
1 8-oz. package noodles, cooked

Melt margarine in a small frypan; add onion, bell pepper and celery. Saute until tender. Combine all ingredients in a casserole and mix well. Bake in a preheated 350-degree oven for 15 minutes or until bubbly. Yield: 6 servings.

Mrs. Kathleen Hudson
River Oaks Academy H.S., Belle Chasse, Louisiana

TUNA-TOMATO CASSEROLE

2 sm. onions, chopped
5 tbsp. chopped green pepper
1/4 c. butter
1 pkg. noodles
1 tsp. salt
1/2 tsp. pepper
1 1/2 cans cream of mushroom soup
1 can tomatoes
1 can tuna, drained
1 pkg. potato chips, crushed

Saute onions and green pepper in butter; cool. Cook noodles according to package directions;

drain. Add salt and pepper to soup. Arrange half the noodles, soup, onion mixture, tomatoes and tuna in casserole. Repeat layers. Top with potato chips. Bake in preheated 400-degree oven for 25 minutes.

Mrs. Jane H. Osborne
Goodlettsville H.S., Goodlettsville, Tennessee

SEAFOOD LASAGNA

1   1-lb. 2-oz. can tomatoes
1   8-oz. can tomato sauce
1   1 1/2-oz. package spaghetti
     sauce mix
1 tsp. oregano
1 tsp. sugar
1 clove of garlic, minced
1   9-oz. can tuna, drained
8 oz. lasagna
1 1/2 c. cottage cheese
2 c. mozzarella cheese
1/4 c. grated Parmesan cheese

Combine tomatoes, tomato sauce, spaghetti sauce mix, oregano, sugar and garlic in a 2-quart pan; simmer, uncovered, for 30 minutes, stirring occasionally. Stir in tuna. Cook lasagna according to package directions. Arrange half the lasagna in baking dish; cover with 1/3 of the tuna sauce. Add half the cottage cheese; cover with half the mozzarella. Repeat layers, ending with tuna sauce. Sprinkle Parmesan cheese over top. Bake in preheated 350-degree oven for 30 minutes. Remove from oven; let stand for 15 minutes. Cut into squares to serve. Yield: 8 servings.

Angela Johansen
Bd. of Ed., Sioux Falls, South Dakota

SPECIAL TUNA LASAGNA

1/2 lb. lasagna
1/2 c. chopped onion
1 clove of garlic, minced
2 tbsp. butter or margarine
2   6-oz. cans tuna, drained and
     flaked
1 can cream of celery soup
1/3 c. milk
1/2 tsp. crushed oregano
Dash of pepper
1 1/2 c. grated mozzarella cheese

2 c. grated Cheddar or American
     cheese
1/2 c. grated Parmesan cheese

Cook lasagna according to package directions; drain and cool slightly. Cook onion and garlic in butter in medium saucepan until tender. Add tuna, soup, milk, oregano and pepper; mix well and heat through. Arrange 1/3 of the lasagna in a 12 x 7-inch baking dish, then top with 1/2 of the tuna mixture, 1/2 of the mozzarella cheese and 1/2 of the Cheddar cheese. Repeat layers, then top with remaining lasagna. Sprinkle top with Parmesan cheese. Bake in preheated 350-degree oven for 30 to 35 minutes. Let stand for 10 to 15 minutes before cutting. Casserole may be frozen for later use, then bake frozen casserole at 400 degrees for 1 hour and 30 minutes. Yield: 6-8 servings.

Marilyn Staton
Roosevelt Jr. H.S., Coffeyville, Kansas

BLUE CHEESE AND TUNA CASSEROLE

3/4 c. rice
2 tbsp. butter or margarine
2 tbsp. all-purpose flour
1/4 tsp. salt
2 c. milk
1/3 c. crumbled blue cheese
2 lg. tomatoes, peeled and sliced
1   9 1/2-oz. can tuna, drained
     and flaked
Parsley

Preheat oven to 350 degrees. Cook rice according to package directions. Melt butter in 1 1/2-quart saucepan; blend in flour and salt. Cook over low heat until mixture is smooth, stirring constantly. Remove from heat; stir in milk. Heat to boiling point, stirring constantly. Add cheese; stir until melted. Place rice in casserole; pour 1 cup sauce over rice. Top with 6 slices of tomato and the tuna. Pour remaining sauce over tuna. Bake in preheated 350-degree oven for 20 minutes. Remove from oven; garnish with remaining tomato slices. Return to oven; bake for 10 to 15 minutes longer. Garnish with parsley. Yield: 6 servings.

Mrs. D. C. Livingston
Johnakin H.S., Marion, South Carolina

POTLUCK TUNA

3 tbsp. butter
1/4 c. chopped celery
2 tbsp. chopped onion
3 tbsp. all-purpose flour
1/2 tsp. salt
1/4 tsp. pepper
1 1/2 c. milk
1 1/2 c. shredded Cheddar cheese
1 7-oz. can tuna, drained and
   flaked
1 10-oz. package frozen peas and
   carrots, cooked and drained
1 8-oz. package refrigerator
   biscuits

Melt butter in a 2-quart saucepan; add celery and onion. Saute until tender. Stir in flour, salt and pepper. Remove from heat; stir in milk gradually. Cook over medium heat, stirring constantly, until thickened. Cook 2 minutes longer. Add cheese, tuna and vegetables; pour into casserole. Top with biscuits. Bake in preheated 350-degree oven for 20 to 25 minutes.

Violet Horne
Forest Hills H.S., Marshville, North Carolina

QUICK CRUNCHY TUNA CASSEROLE

1 can cream of mushroom soup
1/4 c. water
1 3-oz. can chow mein noodles
1 7-oz. can tuna, drained
1 c. chopped celery
1/2 c. cashews
1/4 c. chopped onions
Pepper to taste

Combine soup and water in mixing bowl; stir until smooth. Add 1 cup noodles, tuna, celery, cashews, onions and pepper; toss lightly. Pour in 10 x 6 x 1 1/2-inch baking pan. Sprinkle remaining noodles over top. Bake in preheated 375-degree oven for 15 minutes. Serve immediately. Yield: 4-6 servings.

Hazel Pielemeier
Loogootee H.S., Loogootee, Indiana

ORIENTAL TUNA CASSEROLE

1 10 1/2-oz. can cream of mushroom
   soup
1/4 c. water
2 c. chow mein noodles

1 7-oz. can tuna, drained
1 c. sliced celery
1/2 c. salted toasted cashews
1/4 c. sliced mushrooms
1/4 c. chopped onion
Dash of pepper

Combine cream of mushroom soup and water in a bowl; mix until smooth. Add 1 cup noodles, tuna, celery, cashews, mushrooms, onion and pepper; mix gently. Turn into a 10 x 6 x 1 1/2-inch baking dish. Sprinkle remaining noodles over top. Bake in preheated 375-degree oven for 30 minutes. Yield: 4 servings.

Robby Effron
Miller Jr. H.S., San Jose, California

SIX-CAN CASSEROLE

1 can tuna, drained
1 can asparagus with liquid
1 can chicken-noodle soup
1 can cream of chicken soup
1 can chow mein noodles
1 13-oz. can evaporated milk

Combine all ingredients; mix well. Pour into greased casserole. Bake, covered, in preheated 350-degree oven for 45 minutes. Uncover and bake for 15 minutes longer. Serve with warm buttered garlic toast.

Dean V. Twait
Brookside Jr. H.S., Albert Lea, Minnesota

EASY TUNA CASSEROLE

8 oz. spaghetti, cooked and drained
1 can cream of mushroom soup
1 sm. jar pimento, chopped
1 can tuna, drained
1 c. grated cheese
Salt and pepper to taste

Combine all ingredients in baking dish. Bake in preheated 350-degree oven for 30 minutes. Yield: 5 servings.

Candice Pickens
Kemp Jr.-Sr. H.S., Kemp, Texas

TUNA AND PEAS DELIGHT

3 c. medium white sauce
3/4 c. Cheddar cheese
1 16-oz. can peas, drained
1 6-oz. can tuna
1 7-oz. bag potato chips

Combine white sauce and cheese in saucepan; heat until cheese is melted. Add peas, tuna and about 3/4 of the potato chips; mix well. Place in casserole; crumble remaining potato chips over top. Bake in preheated 350-degree oven for 45 minutes.

Mrs. Mary Irish
Shawano H.S., Shawano, Wisconsin

TUNA TETRAZZINI

4 oz. spaghetti, broken
2 6 1/2-oz. cans tuna, drained
1 sm. jar pimento, chopped
1/4 c. chopped green pepper
1 sm. onion, chopped
1 can cream of mushroom soup
1/2 soup can water
1 3/4 c. grated sharp cheese

Cook spaghetti according to package directions. Combine all ingredients except 1/2 cup cheese; pour into casserole. Sprinkle remaining cheese over top. Bake in preheated 350-degree oven for 45 minutes. Yield: 6-8 servings.

Idy Bramlet
Niobrara Co. H.S., Lusk, Wyoming

TUNA CRUNCH CASSEROLE

1 can cream of mushroom soup
1/3 c. milk
1 7-oz. can tuna, drained and flaked
2 hard-cooked eggs, diced
1 c. cooked peas
1/2 c. crumbled potato chips

Blend soup and milk in 1-quart casserole; stir in tuna, eggs, and peas. Bake in preheated 350-degree oven for 25 minutes. Top with crumbled potato chips; return to oven until top is browned.

Kathryn G. Motsinger
Mount Tabor H.S., Winston-Salem, North Carolina

TUNA SANDWICH FONDUE

12 slices buttered bread, crusts removed
1 7-oz. can white chunk tuna
1/2 lb. Cheddar cheese, grated
1/4 c. chopped onion, sauteed

4 eggs
3 1/2 c. milk
1/2 tsp. salt
Dash of pepper
1 tsp. prepared mustard
1 10 1/2-oz. can cream of mushroom soup

Place 6 slices bread, buttered side up, in buttered 13 x 9 x 2-inch pan. Combine tuna, cheese and onion; spread over bread slices. Place remaining bread slices, buttered side up, on top. Beat eggs; add 3 cups milk, salt, pepper and mustard. Pour over casserole; let stand overnight in refrigerator. Bake in preheated 300-degree oven for 1 hour and 30 minutes. Combine soup and remaining milk in saucepan; heat until bubbly. Serve sauce with fondue. Yield: 6 servings.

Mrs. Irene Knudsen
Del Norte H.S., Crescent City, California

POTATO-COD CASSEROLE

1 lb. cod fillets
1 5 5/8-oz. package French's scalloped potatoes
4 slices bacon, chopped
1 tbsp. French's parsley flakes

Cut cod fillets into 1-inch cubes. Prepare scalloped potatoes according to package directions, placing in 2-quart casserole. Stir in cod, bacon and parsley flakes. Bake in preheated 400-degree oven for 35 to 40 minutes or until potatoes are tender; garnish with strips of cooked bacon, if desired. Yield: 6 servings.

Potato-Cod Casserole

CAPTAIN'S CASSEROLE

    1 1-lb. can whole tomatoes
    1 can cream of chicken soup
    1/2 c. milk
    2/3 c. shredded cheese
    1 2/3 c. Minute rice
    1/2 tsp. oregano
    1/8 tsp. pepper
    1 c. water
    1/2 sm. onion, thinly sliced
    2 cans tuna, drained
    1/2 c. crushed potato chips or
        bread crumbs

Drain tomatoes; reserve 1/2 cup juice. Reserve 1 tomato; cut remaining tomatoes into slices. Combine soup, milk and cheese in saucepan; heat until cheese is melted, stirring constantly. Combine rice, oregano and pepper in greased casserole; stir in reserved tomato juice and water. Arrange sliced tomatoes over rice; top with onion slices and tuna. Pour sauce over tuna; sprinkle with potato chips. Arrange reserved tomato on top. Bake in preheated 350-degree oven for 30 minutes. Yield: 6 servings.

Mrs. Kathleen Boeckstiegel
Detroit H.S., Detroit, Oregon

SALMON BAKE FOR A CROWD

    3/4 c. diced green pepper
    3 c. sliced celery
    1 c. chopped onions
    1/4 c. butter
    2 c. milk
    3 10 1/2-oz. cans cream of
        mushroom soup
    1 12-oz. package American cheese,
        cubed
    3 8-oz. packages med. noodles
    1/4 c. cooked diced carrots
    1 4-oz. can chopped pimento
    3 9 1/2-oz. cans red salmon,
        flaked

Combine green pepper, celery, onions and butter in a large skillet and saute for 10 minutes. Blend the milk and soup together in a large skillet; add onion mixture and heat through. Add cheese cubes; heat, stirring, until cheese melts. Cook noodles in boiling salted water until tender; drain. Combine noodles with 2 cups soup mixture, then toss to coat noodles. Turn into two 13 x 9 x 2-inch baking pans or one 18 x 12 x 2-inch pan. Combine remaining soup mixture with carrots, pimento and salmon. Pour over noodles; mix lightly. Bake in a preheated 375-degree oven for 40 minutes or until bubbly. Yield: 25 one-cup servings.

Judith A. Evans
Desert Elem. Sch., Wamsutter, Wyoming

SCALLOPED SALMON AND SPAGHETTI

    1 4-oz. package spaghetti
    1 7 3/4-oz. can salmon
    Milk
    1 10-oz. can cream of mushroom
        soup
    Dash of cayenne pepper
    3/4 c. grated process cheese
    3/4 c. frozen peas
    2 tbsp. slivered pimento
    2 c. 1/4-in. soft bread cubes
    3 tbsp. melted margarine

Break spaghetti into 2-inch pieces; cook in a large amount of boiling salted water for about 7 minutes or until just tender. Drain. Drain salmon, reserving liquid. Combine the reserved liquid with enough milk to make 2/3 cup liquid, then blend with soup in a medium saucepan. Sprinkle with cayenne pepper. Add cheese and heat, stirring, until cheese is melted. Stir in peas, pimento and spaghetti. Flake salmon and blend in lightly. Turn into a greased casserole. Toss bread cubes and margarine together until cubes are well coated. Sprinkle over top of casserole. Bake in a preheated 400-degree oven for about 15 minutes or until bread cubes are golden and salmon mixture is bubbly. Yield: 4 servings.

Mrs. Jane K. Marsh
Delta Sr. Sec. Sch.
Delta, British Columbia, Canada

EASY SALMON CASSEROLE

    1 lg. can salmon
    1 med. onion, diced
    3 slices bread, broken
    3 stalks celery, chopped
    3 tbsp. minced parsley
    3 eggs, beaten
    3 tbsp. Worcestershire sauce
    Pinch of thyme
    1/4 tsp. salt
    Dash of pepper
    1/2 c. milk
    Paprika

Preheat oven to 350 degrees. Break salmon into pieces; stir in onion, bread, celery, parsley, eggs, Worcestershire sauce, thyme, salt, pepper and milk. The mixture will be thin. Pour into buttered casserole; sprinkle with paprika. Bake for about 1 hour or until set.

Mrs. E. T. Charlesworth
North East H.S., Pasadena, Maryland

SALMON AND SPAGHETTI

1 c. elbow spaghetti or macaroni
1 sm. can salmon, flaked
1 can mushroom soup
1/2 c. cracker crumbs

Cook spaghetti according to package directions. Combine salmon, soup and spaghetti in buttered casserole; sprinkle with cracker crumbs. Bake in a preheated 350-degree oven for 30 to 40 minutes.

Mrs. Eleanor Weatherhead
Northridge Middle Sch., Dayton, Ohio

SALMON-ALMOND CASSEROLE DELUXE

1   7 3/4-oz. can salmon
Milk
1/2 c. chopped onion
2 tbsp. diced green pepper
2 tbsp. butter or other fat
1 c. cooked rice
1 can mushroom soup
1 tbsp. lemon juice
1 tsp. Worcestershire sauce
1 3/4 c. coarsely crushed potato
    chips
1/4 c. blanched slivered almonds

Preheat oven to 350 degrees. Drain salmon, reserving the juice; flake salmon and crush bones. Combine reserved juice and enough milk to measure 2/3 cup liquid. Cook onion and green pepper in butter until tender. Combine salmon, rice and onion mixture; combine soup, milk mixture, lemon juice and Worcestershire sauce. Place half the potato chips in a greased 1 1/2-quart casserole; spread salmon over top. Pour soup mixture over salmon; cover with remaining potato chips. Sprinkle with almonds. Bake, uncovered, for 20 to 30 minutes.

Mrs. Hilda B. Lye
Bloomfield Jr. H.S.
Halifax, Nova Scotia, Canada

SALMON PARISIENNE

1 sm. package frozen cut broccoli
1/4 c. butter
1/4 c. flour
1 to 1 1/2 c. milk
1/2 tsp. salt
1/8 tsp. Tabasco sauce
1 tsp. Worcestershire sauce
2 tsp. grated onion
1 c. cubed sharp cheese
1 can salmon or tuna
Paprika

Cook broccoli according to package directions; set aside. Melt butter in heavy saucepan; stir in flour to make a smooth paste. Add milk, stirring constantly. Stir in salt, Tabasco sauce, Worcestershire sauce, onion and cheese; cook until thick and well blended. Arrange broccoli in buttered casserole; cover with salmon chunks. Pour cheese sauce over top; sprinkle with paprika. Bake in preheated 325 to 350-degree oven for 30 minutes or until heated through and bubbly. Yield: 4 servings.

Kathryn D. Turpen
Edlorado H.S., Albuquerque, New Mexico

STUFFED SOLE ROLL-UPS

1   10 3/4-oz. can cheese soup
1/2 c. chopped cooked tomatoes
1/8 tsp. oregano, crushed
1/2 c. chopped celery
1   2-oz. can mushrooms, drained
1 med. clove of garlic, minced
2 tbsp. butter
2 c. dry bread cubes
1 1/2 lb. sole fillets
2 tbsp. minced onion
1 tbsp. chopped parsley

Combine soup, tomatoes and oregano. Saute celery, mushrooms and garlic in butter in a small pan until celery is tender; add 1/4 cup soup mixture and bread cubes. Spread fillets with bread mixture, then roll up; fasten rolls with toothpicks. Place in shallow baking dish. Add onion and parsley to remaining soup mixture; pour over roll-ups. Bake in a preheated 350-degree oven for 30 minutes. Yield: 6 servings.

Betty Lakey
Paris Gibson Jr. H.S., Great Falls, Montana

109

Louisiana Yam-Ham Casserole

Magic Pork Specialties

Pork is a favorite meat with budget-conscious home-makers who appreciate its delicious flavor as well as its versatility. It is no surprise that pork is so popular — creative cooks everywhere have found many new and exciting ways to adapt pork to casserole recipes of all types.

In this section, you will find favorite recipes for casse-roles using pork, ham, bacon and sausage. One appetite-pleasing recipe for Pork Polynesian combines pork and applesauce with just the right flavorings to produce a tantalizingly different casserole. It's sure to bring com-pliments from your appreciative family and guests at a summer patio party. Another recipe which is perfect for those crisp fall and winter meals is Harvest Casserole, featuring a delightful mixture of sausage, onions and bread stuffing. Delicious!

You'll also be pleased with the wide variety of ham recipes included in this section. The Broccoli and Ham Casserole is perfect for a prepare-ahead dinner — a great find for today's busy homemaker. "Eunie's Rice" com-bines rice and sausage for an interesting new taste treat with extra zest.

As you browse through the following recipes, you'll encounter many new and imaginative recipe ideas, some of which will be just right for a spur-of-the-moment party, while others are ideal for a planned-in-advance luncheon. Whatever the occasion, you're certain to find an appropriate pork casserole recipe to fit the menu.

HOLIDAY PORK CHOPS

6 strips bacon, chopped
1   14-oz. can sauerkraut
1   1-lb. can applesauce
1 tbsp. (packed) brown sugar
1/2 tsp. dry mustard
1/2 c. white wine
Paprika
Accent
4 to 6 pork chops

Saute bacon until crisp; drain on paper towel. Mix sauerkraut, applesauce, sugar, mustard and wine. Place half the sauerkraut mixture in a large casserole. Sprinkle with paprika. Sprinkle Accent on pork chops, then saute chops in bacon drippings until brown on both sides. Place 2 or 3 chops on top of sauerkraut mixture. Spoon remaining sauerkraut mixture on top of pork chops and sprinkle with paprika. Add remaining pork chops; cover. Bake in preheated 350-degree oven for 1 hour and 30 minutes. Yield: 4 servings.

Mrs. Ruth Pastula
Elderton H.S., Elderton, Pennsylvania

PORK AND APPLE CASSEROLE

1/2 c. sugar
2 tbsp. flour
1/2 tsp. cinnamon
1/8 tsp. nutmeg
4 c. peeled sliced tart apples
4 lean pork cutlets or pork chops

Mix sugar, flour, cinnamon and nutmeg; sprinkle over apples, tossing until well mixed. Place in a well-greased square baking dish. Place pork cutlets on top. Bake, uncovered, in preheated 400-degree oven for 50 minutes.

Carolyn Reif
Western Dubuque H.S., Epworth, Iowa

PORK AND SAUERKRAUT

Pork steaks or pork backbone, cut
   into individual servings
Flour
Salt
Freshly ground pepper

Oil
2 cans sauerkraut
3 onions, sliced
3 apples, pared and sliced
1 clove of garlic, minced
1/2 c. vermouth

Dredge pork with flour; sprinkle with salt and pepper. Fry pork in oil in skillet until brown on all sides. Place 1 can sauerkraut in greased casserole. Place layers of onions and apples over the sauerkraut; arrange pork over apples. Sprinkle with pepper and garlic. Add remaining onions, apples and sauerkraut in layers. Pour vermouth over top. Cover casserole. Bake in preheated 300-degree oven for about 3 hours.

Waunice A. Aldridge
Milton H.S., Alpharetta, Georgia

PORK CHOP-BAKED BEANS CASSEROLE

5 pork chops
Salt and pepper to taste
1   1-lb. 4-oz. can baked beans
1 c. chili sauce
1 tbsp. brown sugar
1 tsp. Worcestershire sauce
Green pepper rings

Trim excess fat from pork chops and fry in frying pan over medium heat until brown on both sides. Season with salt and pepper. Place in deep baking dish. Combine baked beans, chili sauce, brown sugar and Worcestershire sauce; mix well. Pour bean mixture over chops, then place green pepper rings on top. Bake in preheated 375-degree oven for 1 hour. Yield: 5 servings.

Rebecca B. Johnson
North Chattanooga Jr. H.S.
Chattanooga, Tennessee

PORK CHOPS WITH SAGE STUFFING

4 tbsp. butter
1/2 c. diced celery
1/2 c. finely minced onion
2 c. soft bread crumbs
Salt
Pepper
2 tsp. leaf sage
1 can chicken broth

4   1-in. thick rib pork chops
    with pocket
1 c. diced onion

Melt 3 tablespoons butter in small skillet; add celery. Cook until tender, stirring occasionally. Combine celery, onion, bread crumbs, 1/4 teaspoon salt, dash of pepper, sage and 3 tablespoons broth; toss with fork to mix well. Stuff pockets in chops loosely with stuffing mixture. Fasten pockets securely with wooden picks. Heat remaining butter in large skillet. Sprinkle chops with salt and pepper to taste; fry in butter in skillet until brown on both sides. Transfer to baking dish. Add onion to pan drippings; cook for 1 minute over medium heat. Add remaining broth; bring to a boil. Pour over chops. Bake in preheated 375-degree oven for 1 hour. Place chops on serving platter. Strain sauce over chops. Yield: 4 servings.

Mrs. Marion Price Elkin
Beulaville H.S., Beulaville, North Carolina

PORK POLYNESIAN

6 pork chops, trimmed
1 to 2 tbsp. Dijon mustard
1 c. applesauce
2 tbsp. Chinese duck sauce

Place pork chops in shallow casserole. Spread with mustard. Combine applesauce with duck sauce and spoon over pork chops. Bake in preheated 350-degree oven for about 1 hour or until pork chops are tender. Yield: 3-4 servings.

Mrs. Beverly Sachs
Westlake H.S., Thornwood, New York

GRANDMA'S PORK CHOPS

1 lg. onion
1 tbsp. shortening
1 tbsp. paprika
4 to 6 potatoes, peeled and sliced
1 med. can peas (opt.)
Salt and pepper to taste
4 to 6 pork chops

Chop onion and fry in shortening in skillet until tender. Remove from heat and stir in paprika. Place potatoes in large casserole or baking dish. Add onion mixture. Mix to coat potatoes. Drain peas; pour in casserole. Season with salt and pepper. Add enough cold water to reach top of potatoes; do not cover. Sprinkle pork chops with salt and pepper, then place on top of potatoes. Bake, uncovered, in preheated 350 to 375-degree oven until chops are brown. Turn chops; bake until brown and potatoes are tender. Yield: 2-3 servings.

Diane Panzone
L'Anse Creuse H.S., Mt. Clemens, Michigan

MOM'S PORK CHOP-POTATO BAKE

6 center cut pork chops
6 med. potatoes
2 cans cream of mushroom soup
Salt and pepper to taste

Place pork chops in frying pan; fry until brown on both sides. Peel and quarter each potato. Place potatoes in a 2-quart baking dish. Arrange pork chops over potatoes and pour soup over entire casserole. Season with salt and pepper; cover. Bake in preheated 350-degree oven for 1 hour. Yield: 6 servings.

Karen M. Russell
Greensville Co. Jr. H.S., Emporia, Virginia

PORK CHOP AND POTATO CASSEROLE

6 pork chops
8 med. potatoes, pared and sliced
1/4 c. minced onion
1/4 lb. mild cheese, diced
1 can cream of mushroom soup
1 c. milk
2 tsp. salt
Dash of pepper

Fry pork chops in skillet until brown, then trim off fat. Place layers of potatoes, onion and cheese in a greased casserole. Combine mushroom soup, milk and seasonings in bowl; blend well. Pour soup mixture over top. Top with pork chops; cover. Bake in preheated 350-degree oven for 1 hour and 15 minutes or until potatoes are done. Yield: 6 servings.

Mrs. Paula Calhoun
Fisher H.S., Fisher, Illinois

SOUTHERN PORK CHOP AND RICE CASSEROLE

2 c. rice
2 cans beef consomme
2 8-oz. cans mushrooms and liquid
1 lg. onion, chopped
6 to 8 pork chops
Salt and pepper to taste
Garlic salt to taste

Pour rice, beef consomme, mushrooms and onion in large casserole. Season pork chops with salt, pepper and garlic salt. Place pork chops on top of rice and cover. Bake in pre-heated 325-degree oven for 1 hour. Yield: 6-8 servings.

Mrs. Mavis Holley
Palatka Central H.S., Palatka, Florida

TASTY PORK CHOP CASSEROLE

6 pork chops
1/2 c. chopped onions

1 1/2 c. Uncle Ben's rice
1 can beef bouillon
1 can cream of mushroom soup
Salt and pepper to taste

Preheat oven to 350 degrees. Fry pork chops in heavy skillet until brown. Remove from skillet. Add onions and rice to skillet; cook until slightly browned. Place pork chops in baking dish; cover with rice mixture. Combine bouillon and soup; stir until well mixed. Pour over rice mixture, then sprinkle with salt and pepper. Bake, covered, for about 1 hour.

Mrs. Margaret W. Lyles
Westminster H.S., Westminster, South Carolina

GOURMET-STYLE PORK TENDERLOIN

1/2 c. flour
2 1/2 tsp. salt
1/2 tsp. paprika
12 pork tenderloin patties
1/4 c. butter
1/2 c. chopped onion

Gourmet-Style Pork Tenderloin

1/2 c. chopped green pepper
1   4-oz. can sliced mushrooms,
      drained
2 c. milk
3 tbsp. fresh lemon juice
1/4 tsp. pepper

Combine 1/4 cup flour, 1 1/2 teaspoons salt and paprika; dredge pork patties with flour mixture. Melt butter in large, heavy skillet over moderate heat; cook pork patties in butter until brown on both sides. Arrange patties in shallow 2-quart baking dish. Add onion, green pepper and mushrooms to pan drippings; cook over low heat until onion is tender. Add remaining flour; mix well. Stir in milk; cook, stirring constantly, until thickened. Stir in lemon juice, remaining salt and pepper; pour over patties. Cover. Bake in preheated 350-degree oven for about 1 hour or until pork is tender. Yield: 6 servings.

PORK CHOP-APPLE AND POTATO CASSEROLE

4 lean pork chops
Flour
Salt and pepper to taste
Shortening
2 or 3 Winesap apples
4 med. sweet potatoes
1 tbsp. sugar
1/4 c. water

Dredge pork chops in flour; season with salt and pepper. Cook in a small amount of shortening until browned, then place in a casserole. Pare and quarter apples and arrange over chops. Pare and slice potatoes 1/2 inch thick and place over apples. Sprinkle with salt and pepper, then add the sugar. Add water; cover. Bake in preheated 400-degree oven for 1 hour or until chops are tender.

Mrs. Raye L. Evers
Midway H.S., Waco, Texas

TANGY PORK CHOPS AND SWEET POTATOES

3 to 4 sweet potatoes
4 center cut pork chops
Salt and pepper to taste
Flour
2 tbsp. butter

1/2 c. currant jelly
1/2 c. orange juice
1 tbsp. lemon juice
Grated rind of lemon
1 tsp. dry mustard
1 tsp. paprika
1/2 tsp. ground ginger

Cook sweet potatoes in boiling salted water until tender; peel and slice. Season pork chops with salt and pepper; dredge in flour. Fry in fat until brown on both sides. Melt butter in small saucepan. Stir in jelly, juices and lemon rind. Add remaining ingredients, stirring to blend. Arrange potatoes and pork chops in casserole and cover with 3/4 of the jelly sauce. Bake, uncovered, in preheated 350-degree oven, basting occasionally with remaining sauce until pork chops are tender. Yield: 4 servings.

Mrs. Anne Beatty Ransing
Miami-Palmetto Sr. H.S., Miami, Florida

TOP HAT PORK CHOPS

6 pork loin chops, 1 in. thick
2 tbsp. oil
2 tart red apples
1 med. red onion, thinly sliced
1/2 c. golden raisins
2 tbsp. (firmly packed) brown
   sugar
1 tsp. salt
1/8 tsp. pepper
1/2 tsp. basil
1/4 tsp. nutmeg
1/8 tsp. cloves
1 c. water
1/4 c. red apple jelly

Fry pork chops in oil for about 5 minutes on each side. Transfer to baking dish. Core apples; cut in thick slices. Place layers of onion, apples and raisins over pork chops. Combine brown sugar, salt, pepper, basil and spices. Sprinkle over fruit. Pour water over top. Bake in preheated 325-degree oven for 45 minutes to 1 hour or until tender. Remove pork chops and fruit to serving dish. Add jelly to liquid remaining in baking dish; heat to melt. Pour sauce over chops. Yield: 6 servings.

Mrs. Barbara Goedicke
Lindsay Thurber Comp. H.S.
Red Deer, Alberta, Canada

POLISH MEATBALLS WITH SOUR CREAM SAUCE

1   6 1/2-oz. package instant mashed
    potatoes
2 lb. lean ground pork
1/2 c. chopped onion
1/2 c. packaged bread crumbs
1/2 c. milk
1 egg
1 1/2 tsp. salt
1/4 tsp. pepper
1/2 tsp. marjoram
1/2 tsp. oregano
4 tbsp. flour
2 tbsp. butter
1 beef bouillon cube
1 1/2 c. sour cream
1 tbsp. capers, drained
1/4 c. grated Parmesan cheese
Chopped parsley

Prepare potatoes according to package directions. Combine the ground pork, onion, bread crumbs, milk, egg, salt, pepper, marjoram and oregano in a large bowl; mix well. Shape into 1 1/2-inch meatballs. Roll meatballs in 2 tablespoons flour; saute in butter in skillet until brown. Remove meatballs as they are cooked to a 3-quart casserole, mounding in center. Pour off all pan drippings except 2 tablespoons; stir in remaining flour. Stir in 1 cup water and add bouillon cube. Bring to a boil, stirring until bouillon cube is dissolved. Add sour cream and capers, stirring. Simmer, uncovered, for 2 minutes. Spoon mashed potatoes around meatballs, then sprinkle with cheese. Pour sour cream sauce over meatballs. Bake, uncovered, in a preheated 350-degree oven for 1 hour. Sprinkle with parsley before serving. Yield: 6-8 servings.

Jean Searcy
Silver Lake H.S., Silver Lake, Kansas

TAMALE PIE

1 onion, chopped
1 clove of garlic, minced
3 tbsp. oil
2 lb. lean ground pork
Cumin seed to taste
Salt to taste
1/2 tsp. chili powder
1 tbsp. sugar
2 c. tomato sauce

2/3 c. flour
1 can white hominy
1 can yellow hominy
2 tbsp. melted shortening
3/4 c. olives

Saute onion and garlic in oil until browned. Add pork; saute until browned. Cover with water; cook for about 1 hour or until pork is tender. Stir in seasonings. Combine tomato sauce and 1/2 of the flour to make a smooth mixture; stir into pork mixture. Grind hominy; mix hominy, remaining flour and shortening together. Reserve a small amount of the hominy mixture; line casserole with remaining mixture. Pour pork mixture and olives into casserole; top with reserved hominy mixture. Bake in preheated 350-degree oven for 40 minutes.

Audrey E. Macedo
Rancho-Milpitas Sch., Milpitas, California

PORK AND POTATO CASSOULET

1 to 2 lb. boneless pork shoulder
1 c. chopped celery
1   5 5/8-oz. package French's
    scalloped potatoes
2 1/2 c. boiling water
1   4-oz. can pimentos
1 tbsp. butter
1/4 c. fine dry bread crumbs
1 tbsp. grated Parmesan cheese

Cut pork into cubes. Brown pork with celery in large skillet, stirring frequently; spoon into 2-quart casserole. Stir in potato slices and sea-

Pork and Potato Cassoulet

soning mix from package of scalloped potatoes, boiling water and pimentos; cover. Bake in preheated 350-degree oven for 40 minutes. Melt butter in small saucepan; stir in bread crumbs and cheese. Uncover casserole; sprinkle crumb mixture over potato mixture. Return casserole to oven. Increase oven temperature to 400 degrees; bake for 10 minutes longer or until browned. Yield: 5-6 servings.

FESTIVE HAM-BROCCOLI CASSEROLE

2 c. cubed ham
6 slices bread, broken
1/2 lb. Cheddar cheese, cubed
1 pkg. frozen chopped broccoli,
    cooked
1/4 c. margarine, melted
3 eggs, beaten
1/2 tsp. dry mustard
1/2 tsp. salt
2 c. milk

Arrange layers of ham, bread, cheese and broccoli in casserole; pour melted margarine over top. Combine eggs, mustard, salt and milk; mix well. Pour over casserole ingredients. Let set overnight in refrigerator. Bake in preheated 350-degree oven for 1 hour. Yield: 6 servings.

Mrs. Martha Jo Mims, Asst. Prof., Home Ec. Ed.
Mississippi State College for Women
Columbus, Mississippi

FRESH BROCCOLI AND HAM CASSEROLE

1 1/2 lb. fresh broccoli
Salt
1/2 c. chopped cooked ham or
    luncheon meat
1 1/2 c. medium white sauce
1/2 c. grated sharp Cheddar cheese
3/4 c. soft bread crumbs
2 tbsp. butter, melted

Wash broccoli; split large stems. Place in boiling salted water. Bring to boiling point, uncovered, and cook for 3 minutes. Cover; boil for 20 minutes or until just crisp-tender. Drain, if necessary. Place in a 6-cup casserole, then cover with ham. Spoon on white sauce and season with salt to taste. Combine cheese with bread crumbs and butter; sprinkle over top.

Bake in a preheated 350-degree oven for 25 minutes or until brown. Yield: 6 servings.

Elizabeth McClure
Greencastle H.S., Greencastle, Indiana

CHEESE-HAM SOUFFLE

16 slices thin-sliced bread
8 to 10 slices ham
Grated Cheddar cheese
Grated Swiss cheese
6 eggs
3 c. milk
1/2 tsp. dry mustard
1/2 tsp. onion salt
3 c. crushed corn flakes or
    Special K
1/4 tsp. melted butter

Remove crusts from bread slices. Place 8 slices in greased 9 x 12-inch baking dish. Top with half the ham and cheeses. Repeat layers. Combine eggs, milk, dry mustard and onion salt. Pour over bread layers, then let set in retrigerator overnight. Combine corn flakes and butter, tossing until mixed. Sprinkle over top. Bake in preheated 375-degree oven for 40 minutes. Yield: 8-10 servings.

Joan Joslin
Staley Jr. H.S., Rome, New York

HAM-TURKEY CASSEROLE

2 tbsp. chopped onion
1/8 tsp. leaf thyme
1 tbsp. butter
1 can cream of mushroom soup
1/2 c. milk
1   10-oz. package frozen French-style
    green beans
4 slices cooked ham
4 slices cooked turkey
1/3 c. shredded Cheddar cheese

Cook onion and thyme in butter in saucepan until onion is tender. Blend in soup; add milk. Cook and stir until heated through. Prepare green beans according to package directions, then arrange in shallow baking dish. Top with ham and turkey. Pour soup mixture over meat. Sprinkle with cheese. Bake in preheated 400-degree oven for 20 minutes or until hot and bubbly. Yield: 4 servings.

Mrs. Paula Calhoun
Fisher H.S., Fisher, Illinois

117

CANTONESE CASSEROLE

1 10-oz. package French-style
   green beans
1 tbsp. butter
1 tbsp. flour
3/4 c. milk
2 tbsp. soy sauce
1 5-oz. can water chestnuts
1 c. sour cream
2 c. cubed cooked ham
1 c. buttered soft bread crumbs
Paprika

Pour boiling water over beans to separate; drain well. Melt butter in saucepan; blend in flour. Stir in milk and soy sauce; cook and stir over medium heat until thick and bubbly. Drain water chestnuts and cut in thin slices. Add sour cream, ham, beans and water chestnuts to white sauce. Pour into greased 10 x 6 x 1 1/2-inch baking dish. Sprinkle crumbs over ham mixture; sprinkle with paprika. Bake in preheated 350-degree oven for 30 minutes or until hot. Yield: 6 servings.

Mrs. Dorothy M. Scanlon
North Sr. H.S., West Mifflin, Pennsylvania

SAUCY HAM AND GREEN BEAN CASSEROLE

1 10-oz. package frozen
   French-cut green beans
3 tbsp. butter
3 tbsp. regular all-purpose flour
1/2 tsp. salt
2/3 c. instant nonfat dry milk
2 c. chopped cooked ham
1 c. shredded Cheddar cheese
2 hard-cooked eggs, chopped
2 tbsp. chopped pimento
1 tbsp. chopped parsley
1 tsp. finely chopped onion
1/2 c. buttered bread crumbs

Preheat oven to 350 degrees. Cook green beans according to package directions; drain, reserving liquid. Add water to make 1 1/2 cups liquid. Melt butter in a 2-quart saucepan; stir in flour and salt. Remove from heat; stir in reserved liquid and dry milk gradually. Return to heat and cook, stirring constantly, until thickened. Cook for 2 minutes longer. Remove from heat; stir in ham, cheese, eggs, pimento, parsley and onion. Place beans in buttered 1 1/2-quart baking dish and cover

with ham mixture. Sprinkle crumbs over top. Bake for 20 to 25 minutes. Yield: 6-8 servings.

Mrs. Lois W. Gerald
Whiteville Sr. H.S., Whiteville, North Carolina

MOTHER'S HAM AND GREEN BEAN CASSEROLE

2 pkg. frozen French-cut green beans
2 tbsp. butter or margarine
1/2 c. chopped onion
2 tbsp. flour
1 1/2 c. milk
1 c. grated cheese
1/4 tsp. Worcestershire sauce
1 lb. cooked ham, diced

Preheat oven to 375 degrees. Cook beans according to package directions; drain. Melt butter in saucepan over medium heat. Add onion; cook for 1 minute. Stir in flour. Cook for 1 minute, stirring constantly. Add milk. Bring to a boil, stirring rapidly with wire whisk. Cook for 1 minute; remove from heat. Stir in cheese and Worcestershire sauce. Combine beans, ham and cheese sauce. Turn into a 2-quart baking dish. Bake for 15 to 20 minutes. Yield: 6 servings.

Mrs. Elizabeth B. Lengle
Warrior Run H.S., Turbotville, Pennsylvania

LOUISIANA YAM-HAM CASSEROLE

2 16-oz. cans Louisiana yams,
   drained
1 8-oz. jar sweetened applesauce
1/4 tsp. salt
1/2 tsp. ground coriander or ginger
4 tbsp. melted butter or margarine
1 1 1/2-lb. slice fully cooked ham
1/4 c. chopped walnuts
Parsley sprigs

Mash yams in large bowl, then whip until light and fluffy. Blend in applesauce, seasonings and 2 tablespoons butter. Place ham on heat-proof platter. Spoon yam mixture around ham; sprinkle yam mixture with walnuts. Spoon remaining butter over ham. Bake in preheated 350-degree oven for 35 minutes. Place platter under hot broiler briefly until yam mixture is golden brown, if desired. Garnish with parsley sprigs. Yield: 6 servings.

Photograph for this recipe on page 110.

HAM AND CHEESE CASSEROLE

6 lg. potatoes
1 can mushroom soup
1 c. chopped ham
1/2 c. chopped onion
1 8-oz. package American cheese
slices

Peel and cut potatoes in thin slices. Arrange 1/3 of the potato slices in a greased casserole. Spread 1/3 of the soup over potatoes, then add half the ham and onion. Arrange alternating layers of remaining potatoes, soup, ham and onion. Top with cheese slices. Cover with heavy-duty foil. Bake in preheated 375-degree oven for 1 hour and 15 minutes or until potatoes are tender.

Mrs. Mildred Marsh
Jones H.S., Orlando, Florida

HAM AND EGG CASSEROLE

1 1/2 c. ground or cubed ham
1 can mushrooms
12 hard-boiled eggs, sliced
1 can mushroom soup
Milk
Cracker crumbs

Arrange a layer of ham in a casserole. Spoon the mushrooms over the ham. Arrange the egg slices over the mushrooms. Combine the soup with a small amount of milk; mix well. Pour over top; top with cracker crumbs. Bake in a preheated 350-degree oven for about 20 minutes or until bubbly. Yield: 6-8 servings.

Gerry Smith
Waco H.S., Waco, Texas

HAM SURPRISE

1 thick slice ham
1 1/2 c. thinly sliced potatoes
2 c. milk
1/2 c. cubed sharp cheese
1/4 c. bread crumbs

Preheat oven to 350 degrees. Trim fat from ham. Place in casserole. Cover with potatoes. Add milk. Sprinkle with cheese and crumbs. Bake for 1 hour and 30 minutes to 2 hours.

Clara May Charlesworth
Northeast H.S., Pasadena, Maryland

HAM-VEGETABLE SCALLOP

1 can cream of mushroom or
cream of celery soup
1/2 c. milk
1/3 c. finely chopped onion
2 c. diced potatoes
1 c. sliced carrots
1 10-oz. package frozen lima beans,
thawed
1 1/2 c. cooked ham, cut in pieces
1/2 c. buttered soft bread crumbs

Combine soup and milk in saucepan; stir until blended. Bring to a boil, stirring, then remove from heat. Cook onion, potatoes, carrots and lima beans in small amount of boiling salted water for 5 minutes. Arrange layer of ham in greased 1 1/2-quart casserole; cover with vegetable mixture. Spoon remaining ham over vegetables. Spread bread crumbs over ham. Bake in preheated 350-degree oven for 1 hour and 30 minutes.

Betty Jane Mincemoyer
Mifflinburg Area H.S., Mifflinburg, Pennsylvania

SUPER EASY DINNER

1 pkg. macaroni and cheese
dinner
1 10-oz. package frozen peas
and carrots
2 c. cubed cooked ham
1 c. sour cream
1/4 c. chopped onion
2 tbsp. chopped pimento
1 tbsp. chopped parsley
1/2 tsp. salt
1/4 tsp. rosemary
Dash of pepper
Dash of hot pepper sauce

Prepare macaroni and cheese dinner according to package directions. Cook frozen vegetables according to package directions; drain. Combine macaroni and cheese dinner, vegetables, ham, sour cream, onion, pimento, parsley and seasonings in large bowl; toss until well mixed. Turn into greased baking dish; cover. Bake in preheated 350-degree oven for about 20 minutes or until heated through. Yield: 6 servings.

Mrs. Helen M. Godwin
Northwest Sr. H.S., Greensboro, North Carolina

PORK AND SWEETS

6 med. sweet potatoes
2 lb. pork shoulder, cubed
2 med. onions, sliced
3 apples, cored and cut into rings
2 tbsp. (firmly packed) brown sugar
2 tbsp. flour
2 tsp. salt
1 tsp. marjoram
2 1/2 c. apple juice

Pare and quarter sweet potatoes. Cook in boiling salted water for 20 minutes or until tender, then drain. Trim fat from pork; brown in small amount of fat in large skillet. Arrange sweet potatoes around edge of a 12-cup baking dish; place half the pork in middle. Top with layers of half the onions and half the apples. Sprinkle with brown sugar. Repeat layers and sprinkle with brown sugar. Drain all but 3 tablespoons of fat from skillet. Blend in flour, salt and marjoram. Stir in apple juice. Cook, stirring constantly, until thick. Pour over casserole; cover. Bake in preheated 350-degree oven for 2 hours. Yield: 6-8 servings.

Karen Hussong
Slayton H.S., Slayton, Minnesota

HARVEST CASSEROLE

1 lb. pork sausage
1 med. onion, chopped
4 c. dry bread cubes
2 eggs, slightly beaten
1/2 c. milk
1 tbsp. minced parsley
1/4 c. diced celery
2 tsp. poultry seasoning
1/2 tsp. monosodium glutamate
Salt and pepper to taste

Crumble sausage; mix with onion. Combine sausage mixture with bread cubes; blend in eggs and milk. Moisten with additional milk, if mixture is dry. Add remaining ingredients. Place in a well-greased 2-quart casserole or roaster; cover. Bake in preheated 350-degree oven for 1 hour and 15 minutes.

Patricia Shradel Mundy
Perry Jr. H.S., Perry, Iowa

POTATO-SAUSAGE SCALLOP

4 c. sliced potatoes
1 1/2 tsp. onion salt
1/2 tsp. salt
1/8 tsp. pepper
1 tbsp. flour
1/4 c. chopped stuffed olives
1 c. milk
1/2 c. bread crumbs
1 lb. pork sausage

Place the potatoes in a greased 1 1/2-quart casserole. Combine seasonings, flour and olives; toss to mix well. Sprinkle over potatoes. Pour milk over top; sprinkle with bread crumbs. Bake in preheated 400-degree oven for 45 minutes. Form sausage into small balls; panfry until browned. Place sausage on top and bake for 15 minutes longer. Yield: 6 servings.

Roby C. Reitz
Springhouse Jr. H.S., Allentown, Pennsylvania

SAUSAGE-POTATO SUPPER CASSEROLE

1 1/2 lb. sausage
5 to 6 slices dry bread, cubed
2 c. milk
1 1/2 tsp. salt
1 med. onion, chopped
1 tsp. thyme
4 med. potatoes, diced

Fry sausage in skillet until brown, then drain. Combine bread and milk in bowl; let soak for several minutes. Add sausage, salt, onion, thyme and potatoes; mix lightly. Turn into greased casserole; cover. Bake in preheated 325-degree oven for 1 hour and 30 minutes.

Lois J. Smeltzer
Eastern Lebanon Co. H.S.
Myerstown, Pennsylvania

CHINESE CASSEROLE

1 lb. bulk pork sausage
1/2 green pepper, diced
1 lg. onion, diced
1 1/2 c. diced celery
2 tbsp. butter or margarine
1/2 c. rice
4 c. water

2 pkg. dehydrated noodle soup
1/2 c. blanched slivered almonds

Crumble sausage in skillet. Fry and stir until brown; drain. Saute green pepper, onion and celery in butter until brown. Add vegetables and rice to sausage. Bring water to a boil in saucepan; add soup. Simmer for several minutes, then pour over sausage mixture. Add almonds; stir until well mixed. Spoon into casserole dish. Bake, covered, in preheated 375-degree oven for 40 minutes. Uncover; bake for 20 minutes longer.

Cathy R. Lobe
North Central H.S., Spokane, Washington

EUNIE'S SAUSAGE AND RICE

2 env. Lipton noodle soup
1 lb. bulk sausage
1 bunch celery, chopped
1 green pepper, chopped
1 onion, chopped
3/4 c. packaged precooked rice
3/4 c. water
1 c. slivered almonds

Prepare soup according to package directions. Remove from heat; set aside. Fry sausage in skillet, stirring to break up; pour off grease.

Add celery, pepper and onion; cook until slightly tender. Add the prepared soup mixture, rice, water and almonds. Spoon in greased casserole. Bake in preheated 350-degree oven for 45 minutes. Two pounds sausage may be used, if desired. Yield: 4 servings with 1 pound sausage or 6-8 servings with 2 pounds sausage.

Marilee Joyce
Lowpoint-Washburn H.S., Washburn, Illinois

SPUR-OF-THE-MOMENT SUPPER SKILLET

1 lg. red apple
1 lb. bulk pork sausage
1 med. onion, sliced
2 1/2 c. undrained sauerkraut
1/3 c. maple-blended syrup
1 tsp. caraway seed

Core apple; cut into thin wedges. Shape sausage into 1 1/2-inch balls. Place in large skillet; cook until brown on all sides. Add onion; saute for several minutes. Remove sausage and onion from skillet; drain off fat. Combine sauerkraut, syrup, caraway seed, sausage and onion in skillet. Arrange apple slices in sauerkraut mixture, skin side up; simmer for 5 minutes. Cover; simmer for 1 to 2 minutes longer. Yield: 4 servings.

Spur-Of-The-Moment Supper Skillet

Vegetables A La Espana

Money-Saving Vegetables

The vegetable connoisseurs in your family will be delighted with a hot, bubbly casserole comprised of tasty, nutritious garden vegetables. Even the more finicky eaters at your house (who ordinarily don't ask for second helpings of the vegetable course) will love these taste-tempting vegetable casseroles. That's because vegetables acquire a delightfully different flavor when combined with luscious sauces, soups and seasonings in mouth-watering casseroles.

In the following pages, you'll find many new recipes for vegetable casseroles, such as Peanut-Broccoli Casserole, an unusual combination of salted peanuts, broccoli, cream of chicken soup and chopped onions. Cauliflower has a magnificent flavor appeal when prepared in an Italian Cauliflower Casserole flavored with Parmesan cheese and garlic. Also in the following pages are the best recipes for old favorites like luscious Scalloped Potatoes, made with cream of celery soup, parsley and paper-thin potato slices.

The following selection of recipes will present many new ways to serve vegetables and give you some wonderful ideas for creating your own irresistible casseroles.

VEGETABLES A LA ESPANA

4 med. carrots
1   10 3/4-oz. can chicken broth
2 tbsp. lemon juice
1/3 c. olive or salad oil
1/4 tsp. pepper
1 clove of garlic, crushed
1 tsp. oregano leaves
1 c. celery, cut into 1-in. pieces
1 lg. green pepper, cut into 1-in.
   squares
2   10-oz. packages frozen cauliflower
1 lb. zucchini, cut into 3/4-in.
   slices
1 c. sliced lg. pimento-stuffed
   olives

Pare carrots; cut into 1/2-inch slices. Pour undiluted chicken broth into large saucepan; add lemon juice, oil, pepper, garlic and oregano. Bring to a boil. Add carrots, celery, green pepper, cauliflower and zucchini; bring to a boil again. Reduce heat; cover. Simmer for about 10 minutes or until vegetables are tender. Pour off liquid; stir in olives. Place in warm casserole. May be covered, chilled and served cold. Cooking liquid may be reserved, if desired. Chill liquid; use within 3 days for cooking other vegetables or in soups and stews. Yield: 8-10 servings.

Photograph for this recipe on page 122.

ASPARAGUS-PRETZEL QUEEN

1 can cream of mushroom soup
1/4 soup can milk
1/4 tsp. pepper
1   14 1/2-oz. can asparagus,
   drained
1   16-oz. can green peas, drained
4 hard-cooked eggs, sliced
1/2 c. grated cheese
3/4 c. crushed pretzels

Combine soup, milk and pepper in a bowl; stir until smooth. Arrange half the asparagus in a greased 1 1/2-quart casserole, then add layers of half the peas, eggs, cheese, soup mixture and pretzels. Repeat layers. Bake in a preheated 450-degree oven until bubbly.

Mrs. Ruth M. Wilson
MacArthur Jr. H.S., Beaumont, Texas

ASPARAGUS AU GRATIN

1 sm. can asparagus
Milk
1 hard-boiled egg, sliced
1/2 c. cracker crumbs
1 1/2 tbsp. butter
1 tbsp. flour
Dash of salt
1/2 c. grated cheese
Paprika

Drain asparagus, reserving liquid; add enough milk to make 1 cup liquid. Place asparagus in a buttered baking dish; top with egg slices. Sprinkle cracker crumbs evenly over egg. Melt butter in saucepan; add flour, stirring until blended. Add milk mixture and salt; cook and stir until thickened. Add cheese and mix until blended. Pour cheese sauce over asparagus mixture; sprinkle with paprika. Bake in preheated 350-degree oven for 30 minutes. Yield: 4 servings.

Mrs. Paul Bishop
Happy Valley H.S., Elizabethton, Tennessee

CASUAL ASPARAGUS-CHEESE CASSEROLE

4   14 1/2-oz. cans cut asparagus,
   well drained
Salt and pepper to taste
4 hard-cooked eggs, sliced
2   4-oz. cans sliced mushrooms,
   well drained
2 cans Cheddar cheese soup
10 crackers, crushed
3 oz. slivered almonds
1 c. grated Cheddar cheese
Paprika

Place half the asparagus in a greased large casserole. Season with salt and pepper. Arrange half the egg slices on top of asparagus, then add half the mushrooms. Beat cheese soup with a fork; spoon half the soup over mushrooms. Top with half the crackers; sprinkle almonds evenly over crackers. Repeat layers. Sprinkle cheese and paprika over all. Bake in preheated 350-degree oven for 45 minutes. Remove from oven and set aside for 15 minutes.

Mrs. John Griswold
Carrollton Comm. Unit H.S., Carrollton, Illinois

ASPARAGUS-EGG CASSEROLE

1 lg. can asparagus
1/4 lb. blanched almonds (opt.)
4 hard-boiled eggs, sliced
1 pimento, finely cut
2 cans mushroom soup
Ritz cheese crackers, crushed
Butter

Place a layer of asparagus in a buttered casserole. Add a layer each of almonds, sliced eggs, pimento, mushroom soup and cracker crumbs. Dot with butter. Bake in preheated 350-degree oven until brown.

Thelma Dilday
East Duplin H.S., Beulaville, North Carolina
Nettie C. Herring
Charity Jr. H.S., Rose Hill, North Carolina

ROLLED PANCAKE SUPPER DISH

4 eggs
1 c. cottage cheese, sieved
1/2 tsp. salt
1 c. instant nonfat dry milk
Flour
1 No. 2 can medium asparagus
   spears, drained
1/4 c. butter
Dash of pepper
2 2 1/2-oz. jars chipped beef
Grated Parmesan cheese or
   buttered bread crumbs

Place eggs in large bowl; beat well. Add cottage cheese; mix thoroughly. Stir in salt, 1/3 cup dry milk, 1/3 cup sifted flour and 2 tablespoons water. Pour 1/4 cup batter for each pancake onto hot, greased griddle; cook until golden brown. Turn; cook until golden brown. Divide asparagus spears into 8 portions. Roll each pancake around 1 asparagus spears portion; place side by side in shallow 7 1/2 x 12-inch casserole. Melt butter in saucepan; remove from heat. Blend 1/4 cup flour into butter. Mix remaining dry milk, pepper and 2 cups water; stir into flour mixture until well mixed. Cook over low heat until thickened, stirring constantly. Add chipped beef; mix well. Pour over pancakes; sprinkle with Parmesan cheese. Bake in preheated 350-degree oven for 20 to 25 minutes. Yield: 8 servings.

Rolled Pancake Supper Dish

125

ASPARAGUS-MUSHROOM CASSEROLE

1 No. 2 can green asparagus tips,
  drained
1 No. 2 can green peas, drained
3 hard-cooked eggs, chopped
1 can mushroom stems and pieces,
  drained
1 can cream of mushroom soup
Salt and pepper to taste
3/4 lb. American cheese, grated

Arrange alternate layers of asparagus, peas, eggs, mushrooms, soup, seasonings and cheese in large casserole. Bake in preheated 300-degree oven for 30 minutes. Yield: 8 servings.

Louise O. Gurley
Sun Valley H.S., Monroe, North Carolina

BEANS IN BARBECUE SAUCE CASSEROLE

1/2 lb. hamburger
1/2 c. chopped bacon
1 med. onion, chopped
1 can red kidney beans, drained
1 can pork and beans
1 can lima beans, drained
1/3 c. (firmly packed) brown sugar
1/3 c. sugar
1/4 c. barbecue sauce
1/4 c. catsup
1/2 tbsp. chili powder
1 tbsp. prepared mustard
Salt and pepper to taste

Fry hamburger in skillet, stirring to separate particles, until brown, then drain off fat. Fry bacon until crisp, then remove from skillet. Drain on paper towels. Add onion and fry until brown, then drain off bacon fat. Combine beans, hamburger, bacon and onion in casserole. Combine remaining ingredients in small bowl; mix thoroughly. Stir sauce into bean mixture. Bake in a preheated 350-degree oven for 1 hour.

Peggy Munter
Moore H.S., Moore, Oklahoma

HOME-BAKED BEANS

1 lb. navy beans
1 tsp. soda
1/4 lb. bacon or ham

2 tsp. salt
1/2 tsp. black pepper
1 tsp. (rounded) dry mustard
1 tsp. onion powder
1 c. sugar

Sort and wash beans. Place in large kettle; add enough water to cover and the soda. Boil for 10 to 15 minutes; drain and rinse with cold water. Return beans to kettle and cover with hot water. Add bacon, salt, pepper, mustard, onion powder and sugar. Cook for about 2 to 2 hours and 30 minutes. Place beans and juice into casserole. Bake in preheated 350-degree oven until liquid has almost evaporated.

Mrs. Hilda J. Finch
Fort Edward H.S., Fort Edward, New York

SAUCY BEAN CASSEROLE

1 can cut green beans
1 can red kidney beans
1 can baby lima beans
8 slices bacon
1/2 c. chopped onion
1 can B&M baked beans
1 tbsp. dry mustard
1 tbsp. Worcestershire sauce
1 tsp. salt
1/2 c. catsup
3 tbsp. vinegar
1/2 c. (firmly packed) brown sugar

Drain the green beans, kidney beans and lima beans. Dice bacon and fry until crisp, then drain. Cook onion in bacon drippings until brown. Combine the beans, bacon, onion and the baked beans; mix well. Place in large baking dish. Combine remaining ingredients and pour over bean mixture. Bake in a preheated 325-degree oven for 30 to 40 minutes.

Charlotte L. Skinner
Grant Jr. H.S., Littleton, Colorado

BACON-GREEN BEAN CASSEROLE

4 slices bacon
2 cans French-style seasoned green
  beans
1 tsp. salt
Pepper to taste
1 can mushroom soup

1/2 pkg. slivered almonds
1 tbsp. Worcestershire sauce

Fry bacon until crisp, then crumble. Drain beans; arrange beans in layer in greased casserole. Sprinkle with salt and pepper. Spread soup over beans. Sprinkle bacon and almonds over mixture. Add Worcestershire sauce. Bake in a preheated 350-degree oven until bubbling. May be made ahead, refrigerated and then baked. Yield: 8 servings.

Mrs. Barbara P. Bell
Andrew Lewis H.S., Salem, Virginia

DELICIOUS GREEN BEAN CASSEROLE

1 can French-style green beans,
   drained
1 can mushroom or celery soup
1 can French-fried onion rings

Place green beans in well-buttered casserole or baking dish. Spread soup evenly over beans, then arrange onion rings on top. Bake in a preheated 350-degree oven until bubbly. Two cups crushed potato chips may be substituted for onion rings, if desired. Yield: 4 servings.

Mrs. David L. Beveridge
East Carteret H.S., Beaufort, North Carolina

LIMA BEAN AND PEAR CASSEROLE

3   1-lb. cans lima beans
1   1-lb. 15-oz. can pears, cut
      in pieces
1/2 c. butter
3/4 c. (packed) brown sugar

Place alternating layers of 1/3 of the lima beans, pears, butter and brown sugar in casserole until all ingredients are used. Bake in a preheated 350-degree oven for 2 hours.

Linda Adams
Millersburg Area Schools
Millersburg, Pennsylvania

BAKED LIMA BEANS

2   1-lb. cans cooked dried lima beans
1/2 c. (firmly packed) brown sugar
1/2 tsp. dry mustard
1/2 tsp. molasses

1/2 c. sour cream
1/4 tsp. salt
1 1/2 tbsp. butter

Drain lima beans, then combine with brown sugar, mustard, molasses, sour cream, salt and butter in casserole; mix well. Bake, uncovered, in preheated 350-degree oven for 1 hour and 30 minutes, stirring occasionally.

Jenny L. Curtis
Orrville H.S., Orrville, Ohio

LIMA BEAN-BACON CASSEROLE

1 lb. dry lima beans
3 onions
1 lb. bacon, chopped
1 lb. brown sugar

Cover lima beans with cold water; let soak overnight, then drain. Cut 1 onion in quarters. Combine beans, onion and 1/2 cup bacon in large kettle; cover with water. Cook over low heat for 1 hour and 30 minutes. Drain and reserve liquid. Place beans in 2 1/2 or 3-quart casserole. Chop remaining onions; spoon evenly over beans. Arrange remaining bacon over onions. Spoon brown sugar over all. Pour reserved liquid to moisten all ingredients. Bake in preheated 300-degree oven for 3 hours.

Mrs. Karl Moos
Marion Steele H.S., Amherst, Ohio

RED BEANS AND RICE

1 egg
1 c. skim milk
1   15 1/2-oz. can kidney beans
1 clove of garlic, minced
1/2 c. chopped parsley
1 sm. onion
1 tsp. salt
2 c. cooked rice
1/4 c. grated cheese

Beat egg until light; add milk. Drain kidney beans. Combine all ingredients; mix well. Turn into oiled baking dish. Bake in preheated 350-degree oven for 30 minutes. Yield: 4 servings.

Mrs. Doris Wilcoxon Larke
Woodruff H.S., Peoria, Illinois

Sprout Vegetable Mix-Up

SPROUT VEGETABLE MIX-UP

1 lb. small new potatoes
1/2 lb. small white onions, peeled
1   10-oz. package frozen sliced
*   carrots*
2   10-oz. packages frozen Brussels
*   sprouts*
3/4 c. orange juice
1/4 c. dry sherry
4 tsp. cornstarch
1/4 tsp. nutmeg
1/4 tsp. salt
2 chicken bouillon cubes
1/3 c. butter or margarine

Wash and scrub unpeeled potatoes; cut each into quarters. Cook potatoes and onions in 3 cups boiling, salted water for 5 minutes. Add carrots and Brussels sprouts; simmer until all vegetables are tender. Drain; place in casserole. Keep warm. Mix orange juice, sherry, cornstarch, nutmeg and salt in bowl. Place chicken bouillon cubes and 1/2 cup water in medium saucepan; bring to a boil, stirring until cubes dissolve. Add butter; stir until melted. Stir in cornstarch mixture; simmer until thickened. Pour over vegetables; toss lightly until vegetables are coated. Yield: 6 servings.

BROCCOLI-CHEESE CASSEROLE

1 pkg. frozen broccoli spears,
*   chopped*

2 eggs
1/2 c. mayonnaise
1 can cream of mushroom soup
1/2 c. grated sharp cheese
1 tbsp. grated onion
Salt and pepper to taste
1/2 c. crushed cheese crackers

Cook broccoli according to package directions; drain. Place eggs in bowl; beat well. Stir in mayonnaise. Add broccoli and remaining ingredients except crumbs; mix well. Place in buttered casserole; top with crumbs. Bake in preheated 375-degree oven for 30 minutes.

Mrs. Stacie O. Houser
Sun Valley H.S., Monroe, North Carolina

BROCCOLI IN CHEESE SAUCE

2   10-oz. packages frozen broccoli
1 can Cheddar cheese soup
1/4 c. milk
1/4 c. buttered bread crumbs

Cook broccoli according to package directions; drain. Place broccoli in shallow baking dish. Blend soup and milk. Pour over broccoli; top with crumbs. Bake in preheated 350-degree oven for 30 minutes or until bubbly. Yield: 6-8 servings.

Mrs. Elizabeth B. Lengle
Warrior Run H.S., Turbotville, Pennsylvania

BROCCOLI-MUSHROOM CASSEROLE

1 to 1 1/2 lb. broccoli
1/2 lb. mushrooms, sliced
Butter
1 c. grated or cubed cheese
2 tbsp. chopped green pepper
2 c. medium white sauce
Paprika

Cook broccoli in boiling, salted water for 3 to 5 minutes or until crisp-tender; drain. Place in greased 9-inch square baking pan or 1-quart baking dish. Saute mushrooms in small amount of butter for 5 minutes. Reserve 1/4 cup cheese. Add remaining cheese, mushrooms and green pepper to sauce; mix well. Pour over broccoli. Sprinkle with reserved cheese, then with paprika. Bake in preheated 350-degree oven for 15 to 20 minutes or until brown.

Jeanne Scheinoha
Valders H.S., Valders, Wisconsin

EASY BROCCOLI CASSEROLE

1 c. garlic-flavored croutons
2 tbsp. melted butter or margarine
1   10-oz. package frozen chopped
    broccoli
1/2 c. water
1 tsp. salt
3/4 c. shredded Cheddar or American
    cheese
1/2 c. cream of mushroom soup

Toss croutons with melted butter; set aside. Place broccoli, water and salt in saucepan; bring to a boil. Separate broccoli pieces with fork. Remove from heat; drain well. Place cheese and soup in small saucepan; cook over medium heat until cheese is melted, stirring frequently. Add broccoli; mix gently. Pour into ungreased 1-quart baking dish; sprinkle croutons over top. Bake in preheated 350-degree oven for 20 minutes or until bubbly.

Mrs. Magdaline Dhuey
Luxemburg-Caseo Sr. H.S., Luxemburg, Wisconsin

PEANUT-BROCCOLI CASSEROLE

2   10-oz. packages frozen broccoli
1 can cream of chicken soup
2 tbsp. lemon juice
1 c. chopped salted peanuts
1/4 c. mayonnaise
1/4 c. chopped onions
2 eggs, beaten
1 c. grated sharp cheese

Prepare broccoli according to package directions; drain. Mix broccoli with remaining ingredients except cheese; pour into greased 1 1/2-quart casserole. Sprinkle cheese over broccoli mixture. Bake in preheated 350-degree oven for 30 minutes. Yield: 6 servings.

Mrs. Houston Banner
Castlewood H.S., Castlewood, Virginia

RITZY BROCCOLI CASSEROLE

3 pkg. frozen chopped broccoli
1/2 c. margarine
1/2 lb. Velveeta cheese, cut in cubes
1 stack pack Ritz crackers

Cook broccoli according to package directions; drain. Melt half the margarine with cheese in double boiler; add to hot broccoli. Crush crackers in blender. Add half the crumbs to broccoli; mix well. Place in 1 1/2-quart casserole. Melt remaining margarine; mix with remaining crumbs. Sprinkle over broccoli mixture. Bake in preheated 350-degree oven for 35 to 40 minutes.

Phyllis T. Krumrine
Susquehannock H.S., Glen Rock, Pennsylvania

BROCCOLI-RICE BAKE

1 pkg. frozen chopped broccoli,
    thawed
1/3 c. thinly sliced celery
1/4 c. chopped onion
1/4 c. melted margarine
1 can cream of mushroom soup
1 c. Minute rice
1/2 c. Cheez Whiz

Place broccoli in bowl. Add celery and onion; mix well. Add remaining ingredients; stir until mixed. Place in well-buttered casserole; cover. Bake in preheated 300-degree oven for 1 hour.

Mrs. Mary V. Watson
Sullivan West H.S., Kingsport, Tennessee

CREAMY BROCCOLI-RICE CASSEROLE

1 c. chopped onions
1 c. chopped celery
1 tbsp. cooking oil
2 pkg. frozen chopped broccoli
1 can cream of mushroom soup
1 can cream of chicken soup
1 8-oz. jar Cheez Whiz
2 c. cooked rice
1 tbsp. butter
Salt and pepper to taste

Saute onions and celery in oil in saucepan until tender. Cook broccoli according to package directions; drain well. Combine soups and Cheez Whiz in saucepan; heat until cheese is melted. Add broccoli, rice, butter, salt, pepper and onion mixture; mix well. Place in 3-quart casserole. Bake in preheated 350-degree oven for 30 minutes. Yield: 12 servings.

Mrs. Norma Shipman
Area Homemaking Consultant
Texas Education Agency
Sulphur Springs, Texas

HOT BROCCOLI-RICE CASSEROLE

1 1/2 c. chopped onions
1/4 c. butter
2 c. cooked rice
1 box frozen chopped broccoli,
    thawed
1 c. diced celery
1 can cream of chicken soup
1 sm. jar Cheez Whiz

Saute onions in butter in saucepan until tender. Add remaining ingredients; mix well. Place in greased casserole. Bake in preheated 350-degree oven for 1 hour. Sliced water chestnuts may be substituted for celery.

Junia M. Schlinkert
Willow Lake H.S., Willow Lake, South Dakota

QUICK BROCCOLI-CHEESE CASSEROLE

2 med. onions, chopped
1/4 c. margarine
1 pkg. frozen broccoli, thawed
2 c. Minute rice
1 can cream of mushroom soup
1 8-oz. jar Cheez Whiz

Saute onions in margarine in saucepan until tender. Cook broccoli and rice separately according to package directions; drain. Place broccoli and rice in bowl; add onions and remaining ingredients. Mix well. Place in 9 x 13-inch baking dish. Bake in preheated 350-degree oven for 1 hour.

Nancy Stearley
Bloomfield H.S., Bloomfield, Indiana

TEXAS BROCCOLI AND RICE CASSEROLE

1 c. chopped celery
1 c. chopped onions
2 tbsp. butter
1 can cream of chicken soup
1 lg. jar pimento Cheez Whiz
1 c. Minute rice
1 pkg. frozen chopped broccoli,
    partially thawed
Salt and pepper to taste

Saute celery and onions in butter in saucepan until tender. Combine soup, Cheez Whiz and rice. Break broccoli apart with fork; add to cheese mixture. Add salt, pepper and onion mixture; mix well. Place in buttered casserole; refrigerate for 12 hours. Bake in preheated 350-degree oven for 35 minutes.

Missy Davis
Penelope Sch., Penelope, Texas

CREAMY CABBAGE CASSEROLE

1 head of cabbage, coarsely chopped
1 can cream of celery soup
1 soup can milk
1/4 c. grated cheese
Cracker crumbs
2 tbsp. margarine

Cook cabbage in boiling salted water until tender. Drain; place in greased casserole. Combine soup and milk; stir until blended. Add cheese; cook over low heat, stirring constantly, until cheese is melted. Pour over cabbage. Sprinkle crumbs over top; dot with margarine. Bake in preheated 350-degree oven until heated through and bubbly.

Frances Steenbergen
Austin Tracy Sch., Lucas, Kentucky

SCALLOPED CABBAGE CASSEROLE

4 c. chopped cabbage
1 1/2 tbsp. water
1 1/2 c. grated American cheese
1 1/2 c. cracker crumbs
Salt and pepper to taste

Place cabbage in saucepan; add water and cover. Cook over low heat until just wilted. Place half the cabbage in buttered 9 x 13-inch baking dish; sprinkle with half the cheese and half the cracker crumbs. Season with salt and pepper. Repeat layers. Bake in preheated 350-degree oven for 30 minutes.

Nancy Stearley
Bloomfield H.S., Bloomfield, Indiana

CARROT PUDDING

3 eggs, separated
1/4 c. sugar
1 1/2 tbsp. cornstarch
1 c. milk
3 c. carrots, cooked and mashed
3 tbsp. butter
1 tsp. salt
1 c. fine bread crumbs
1 c. light cream
1/2 tsp. grated nutmeg
1/4 c. cream sherry

Beat egg yolks and sugar until light; set aside. Combine cornstarch with a small amount of the milk. Heat remaining milk. Add cornstarch mixture; cook until smooth and slightly thickened, stirring constantly. Stir a small amount of the hot cornstarch mixture into egg yolk mixture; stir egg yolk mixture into cornstarch mixture. Cook, stirring, over medium heat until smooth and thick. Add carrots, butter, salt and bread crumbs; blend well. Stir in cream, then add the nutmeg and sherry. Mix well. Beat egg whites until stiff peaks form; fold into carrot mixture. Pour into greased 2-quart casserole; place casserole in pan of hot water. Bake in preheated 300-degree oven for 30 minutes. Increase oven temperature to 350 degrees and bake for 45 minutes longer or until knife inserted in center comes out clean. Yield: 10-12 servings.

Mrs. Anne Beatty Ransing
Miami-Palmetto Sr. H.S., Miami, Florida

MARMALADE CARROTS

2 tbsp. butter or margarine
1/4 c. orange marmalade
1 lb. carrots, sliced and cooked

Melt butter and marmalade in casserole; stir in carrots just to coat. Bake in preheated 300-degree oven for 30 minutes. One large can sliced carrots may be substituted for fresh carrots.

Helen B. Boots
Lakeland Village Sch., Medical Lake, Washington

PEACHY CARROTS

2 c. sliced, diced or ripple cut
  carrots
1 can peach pie filling
1/2 tsp. salt
1/2 tsp. cinnamon
1 tbsp. butter

Cook carrots in a small amount of boiling salted water until crisp-tender. Drain; combine with pie filling, salt and cinnamon. Pour into a greased casserole; dot with butter. Bake, covered, in a preheated 350-degree oven for 25 minutes.

Helen C. Hollinger
Celina Jr. H.S., Celina, Ohio

SCALLOPED CARROT CASSEROLE

1 med. onion, chopped
Margarine
4 c. sliced cooked carrots
1 can cream of celery soup
1/2 tsp. salt
Dash of pepper
1/2 c. grated Cheddar cheese
3 c. Pepperidge Farm herb seasoned
  stuffing mix

Brown onion in 3 tablespoons margarine; combine with the carrots. Add soup, salt, pepper and cheese. Melt 1/2 cup margarine; toss with stuffing mix. Place 1/3 of the carrot mixture in a casserole; top with 1/3 of the stuffing mixture. Repeat layers, ending with stuffing mixture. Bake in preheated 350-degree oven for 45 minutes.

Lois J. Smeltzer
Eastern Lebanon Co. H.S.
Myerstown, Pennsylvania

COMPANY CAULIFLOWER

2 tsp. sesame seed
1 med. head cauliflower
Salt and pepper to taste
1 c. sour cream at room temperature
1 c. shredded Cheddar cheese

Place sesame seed in shallow pan; toast until brown. Rinse cauliflower; separate into small flowerets. Cook in 1-inch boiling salted water in covered saucepan for 8 to 10 minutes or until tender; drain well. Place half the cauliflower in casserole; season with salt and pepper. Spread 1/2 cup sour cream over the cauliflower; sprinkle with 1/2 cup shredded cheese. Top with 1 teaspoon sesame seed. Repeat layers. Bake in preheated 350-degree oven for about 20 minutes or until heated through.

Rebecca B. Johnson
North Chattanooga Jr. H.S., Chattanooga, Tennessee

ITALIAN CAULIFLOWER

1 cauliflower
3 eggs
1/2 c. Parmesan cheese
1/4 c. chopped parsley
3 tbsp. olive oil
2 cloves of garlic, minced

Separate cauliflower into flowerets; cook in small amount of boiling salted water until tender. Let cool. Beat eggs; stir in cheese. Add parsley and cauliflower. Heat oil in iron skillet. Add garlic; saute until golden. Pour garlic and oil into cauliflower mixture. Stir carefully; pour cauliflower mixture into skillet. Bake in preheated 300-degree oven for 45 minutes to 1 hour.

Waunice A. Aldridge
Milton H.S., Alpharetta, Georgia

CELERY PARMIGIANA

4 slices bacon
4 c. sliced celery
1/4 c. chopped onion
1/2 clove of garlic, minced
1 c. water
1 tsp. salt
2 tomatoes, peeled and chopped
1 c. grated Parmesan cheese

Cook bacon in large skillet until crisp; drain well on paper towels. Crumble bacon. Drain bacon fat from skillet. Add celery, onion, garlic, water and salt to skillet; cover. Simmer for 20 minutes or until celery is tender. Drain celery mixture; place in 1 1/2-quart casserole. Top with bacon and tomatoes; sprinkle with cheese. Bake in preheated 350-degree oven for 15 to 20 minutes. Yield: 6 servings.

Celery Parmigiana

CELERY CUSTARD

2 c. diced celery
2 sm. onions, chopped
2 c. milk
1 tsp. salt
1/8 tsp. pepper
4 eggs, slightly beaten

Cook celery and onions in milk for about 5 minutes or until partially tender. Add salt and pepper; stir into beaten eggs. Pour into buttered casserole; place casserole in pan of water. Bake in a preheated 350-degree oven for 1 hour or until firm. May be baked in a ring mold; serve with harvard beets in center, if desired. Yield: 8-10 servings.

Mrs. Emely Sundbeck
Manor H.S., Manor, Texas

CELERY-WATER CHESTNUT CASSEROLE

4 c. celery, cut in 2-in. pieces
1 can cream of chicken soup
1/2 c. sour cream
1/2 c. slivered almonds
1 4-oz. can water chestnuts,
    drained and sliced
Buttered soft bread crumbs

Cook celery in small amount of boiling, salted water until crisp-tender; drain well. Combine celery, soup, sour cream, almonds and water chestnuts; place in shallow 2-quart baking dish. Sprinkle crumbs over top. Bake in a preheated 350-degree oven for 30 minutes.

Mrs. Magdaline Dhuey
Luxemburg-Caseo Sr. H.S.
Luxemburg, Wisconsin

DELICIOUS CELERY CASSEROLE

4 c. 1-inch pieces of celery
1/2 c. water
1 tsp. salt
1 can cream of chicken soup
1 c. sliced water chestnuts
1/2 c. slivered almonds
Buttered bread crumbs

Combine celery, water and salt in saucepan. Cook until just tender; drain. Place in but-

tered casserole; pour soup over celery. Sprinkle with water chestnuts; top with almonds and bread crumbs. Bake in preheated 350-degree oven until brown.

Mrs. Mary V. Watson
Sullivan West Sch., Kingsport, Tennessee

FAR EAST CELERY CASSEROLE

4 c. 1-inch pieces of celery
1 5-oz. can water chestnuts, sliced
1/4 c. diced pimento
1 c. cream of chicken soup
1 c. bread crumbs
1/4 c. toasted almonds
4 tbsp. melted butter

Cook celery in small amount of boiling salted water for 8 minutes or until crisp-tender. Drain, then add water chestnuts, pimento and soup. Spoon into lightly greased casserole. Top with bread crumbs and almonds; drizzle with butter. Bake in a preheated 350-degree oven for 30 minutes. Yield: 6 servings.

Mrs. Ruth L. DeFriese
Young H.S., Knoxville, Tennessee

COMPANY CORN CASSEROLE

1 lg. onion, chopped
6 tbsp. margarine
2 cans cream-style corn
1 lg. bell pepper, chopped
1 med. can pimento, chopped
1 sm. box Minute rice, cooked
3 tbsp. sugar
1/2 tsp. salt
Dash of pepper
1 egg, beaten
Grated Cheddar cheese
Paprika

Saute onion in margarine until lightly browned. Combine all ingredients except cheese and paprika; pour into greased casserole. Bake in preheated 350-degree oven for 20 minutes. Cover top thickly with cheese; sprinkle with paprika. Bake for 15 minutes longer.

Mrs. Juanita Pitts
Linden-Kildare H.S., Linden, Texas

MINCED CRANBERRY PIE

3 c. Ocean Spray fresh cranberries
2 c. chopped tart apples
1/4 c. currants
1/2 c. raisins
1/4 c. chopped suet
1/4 c. finely chopped citron
1 tbsp. grated orange rind
1/4 c. molasses
1 1/4 c. sugar
1/2 tsp. cinnamon
1/2 tsp. mace
1/2 tsp. ground cloves
1/4 tsp. salt
1/2 c. cider
1/3 c. dark rum (opt.)
Pastry for 2-crust pie

Rinse and drain cranberries. Combine cranberries, apples, currants, raisins, suet, citron, orange rind, molasses, sugar, spices, salt and cider in saucepan; bring to a simmer. Cover; simmer for 30 minutes. Cool. Add rum; mix well. Line 9-inch pie pan with half the pastry. Pour in cranberry filling; cover with top crust. Flute edge; cut several slits in top crust. Place 2-inch strip of foil around rim of pie to prevent overbrowning. Place pie on lowest shelf of oven. Bake at 425 degrees for 50 to 55 minutes, removing foil 5 minutes before removing pie from oven. Garnish with additional cranberries, if desired. Serve warm.

CRANBERRY BAKED ALASKA

1   18 1/2-oz. package yellow cake mix
1 c. Ocean Spray fresh or frozen-fresh
    cranberries, chopped
1 3/4 c. sugar
1   13-oz. can evaporated skim milk
2 1/3 c. heavy cream
4 eggs, separated
2 tsp. vanilla extract
Frosted cranberries (opt.)

Prepare and bake cake mix according to package directions, using 9-inch square pan. Cool and remove from pan. Mix cranberries with 1/4 cup sugar; place in freezer. Combine skim milk, cream, egg yolks, 3/4 cup sugar and vanilla; beat until sugar is dissolved. Pour into freezer container; freeze until half frozen. Scrape ice cream into bowl: beat with electric mixer until doubled in bulk. Fold in cranberry mixture; pour into 9-inch square pan. Cover and freeze. Place cake on wooden board or heatproof platter. Unmold ice cream; place on top of cake. Place in freezer. Beat egg whites until stiff; beat in remaining sugar, 1 tablespoon at a time, until mixture is glossy. Remove ice cream-covered cake from freezer; spread meringue on sides and top of cake and ice cream until completely covered, sealing all edges. Bake in a preheated 400-degree oven for 5 to 6 minutes or until lightly browned. Garnish with frosted cranberries. Cut into slices; serve at once. Yield: 10-12 servings.

CRANBERRY CRUNCH

1 c. quick-cooking oatmeal
1/2 c. all-purpose flour
1 c. (firmly packed) brown sugar
1/2 c. butter or margarine
1 c. sugar
1 c. water
2 c. fresh cranberries

Combine oatmeal, flour and brown sugar in bowl; cut in butter until mixture is crumbly. Press 1/2 of the crumbs evenly into bottom of greased 8 x 8 x 2-inch baking pan. Place sugar and water in a saucepan; stir until mixed. Bring to a boil; boil for 5 minutes. Add cranberries; cook for about 5 minutes or until skins pop. Spoon cranberry sauce evenly over crumb layer. Sprinkle remaining crumbs in an even layer over cranberry sauce. Bake in a preheated 325-degree oven for 40 to 45 minutes or until well browned. Cool thoroughly in pan; cut into squares. Serve topped with vanilla ice cream or sweetened whipped cream, if desired. One and three-fourths cups Ocean Spray whole berry cranberry sauce, mashed, may be substituted for fresh cranberry sauce. Yield: 6-8 servings.

Photograph for these recipes on page 135.

FROSTED CRANBERRY-CAKE ROLL

3 eggs
2 c. sugar
3/4 c. water
1 tsp. vanilla
1 c. all-purpose flour
1 tsp. baking powder
1/4 tsp. salt
Confectioners' sugar
3 c. Ocean Spray fresh or
*   frozen-fresh cranberries*
2 tbsp. cornstarch
1 can vanilla buttercream frosting
Green food coloring
Spearmint gum leaves
Lemon jelly slices
Candy flowers

Beat eggs in bowl until thick; beat in 1 cup sugar gradually. Add 1/4 cup water and vanilla, beating constantly. Sift flour, baking powder and salt together; fold into egg mixture gently. Pour into foil-lined and greased 15 x 10 x 1-inch jelly roll pan. Bake in a preheated 350-degree oven for 15 minutes or until cake is lightly browned. Turn out onto a towel sprinkled with confectioners' sugar; remove foil. Roll up cake, starting at 10-inch side and rolling towel up into cake. Place on flat surface, seam side down; cool thoroughly. Combine cranberries and remaining sugar in saucepan. Mix remaining water and cornstarch; stir into cranberry mixture. Cook, stirring, until sauce bubbles and thickens; cool. Unroll cake carefully; remove towel. Spread filling over cake; reroll. Place cake roll on a platter. Tint frosting with food coloring; spread on cake roll. Decorate with gum leaves, jelly slices and flowers.

CHICKEN AND PINEAPPLE CASSEROLE

2 broiler-fryer chickens
2 tsp. salt
1 tbsp. melted butter or margarine
1   1-lb. 4-oz. can sliced pineapple
*   in syrup*
2   1-lb. 1-oz. cans yams in syrup
3 tbsp. cornstarch
1/4 c. lemon juice
1/2 tsp. dry mustard
1/2 tsp. ginger
2 tsp. instant minced onion

Photograph for these recipes on page 136.

1/2 c. currant jelly
8 maraschino cherries with stems

Cut chickens into quarters; sprinkle with 1 1/2 teaspoons salt. Place, skin side up, in shallow 3-quart casserole; brush with butter. Bake in 375-degree oven for 45 minutes. Prepare sauce while chicken is baking. Drain syrup from pineapple and yams into saucepan. Add cornstarch, lemon juice, remaining salt, mustard, ginger and onion; stir until well blended. Add jelly. Cook, stirring constantly, until mixture comes to a boil and thickens; remove from heat. Remove chicken from oven; add pineapple and yams. Pour sauce over all. Return to oven; bake for 20 minutes longer or until chicken is tender. Garnish with maraschino cherries. Yield: 8 servings.

COCONUT SOUFFLE

2 env. unflavored gelatin
3/4 c. sugar
1/4 tsp. salt
6 eggs, separated
2 1/2 c. milk
1   3 1/2-oz. can flaked coconut
1/2 c. chopped blanched almonds
1 tsp. vanilla
1/2 tsp. almond extract
1 c. heavy cream, whipped

Fold strip of aluminum foil long enough to go around 1 1/2-quart souffle dish with generous overlap into 4 thicknesses to make strip 3 inches wide. Wrap around outside of souffle dish so that strip extends 2 inches above rim of dish; attach securely with tape. Mix gelatin, 1/4 cup sugar and salt in saucepan. Beat egg yolks with milk; stir into gelatin mixture. Place over low heat; stir constantly for 5 to 8 minutes or until gelatin dissolves and mixture thickens slightly. Remove from heat; stir in coconut, almonds, vanilla and almond extract. Chill, stirring occasionally, until mixture mounds slightly when dropped from a spoon. Beat egg whites until stiff, but not dry. Add remaining sugar gradually; beat until very stiff. Fold into gelatin mixture; fold in whipped cream. Turn coconut mixture into prepared souffle dish; chill for several hours or overnight. Remove foil collar; garnish souffle with additional whipped cream and pink-tinted coconut. Yield: 10-12 servings.

Olive-Corn Pudding

OLIVE-CORN PUDDING

1 1/2 c. fine cracker crumbs
1/2 c. melted butter or margarine
2 tbsp. butter or margarine
1 1/4 c. milk
2 c. cut fresh corn
1/2 tsp. salt
1/2 tsp. onion salt
2 tbsp. flour
2 eggs, beaten
1/2 c. sliced pimento-stuffed olives

Mix cracker crumbs with melted butter. Reserve 1/2 cup crumb mixture; press remaining crumb mixture over bottom and sides of 9-inch pie plate. Combine butter, 1 cup milk, corn, salt and onion salt in saucepan. Bring to a boil; reduce heat. Simmer for 3 minutes. Blend flour with remaining milk; stir into corn mixture. Cook for 2 minutes longer; stir into eggs gradually. Add olives; pour into pie shell. Sprinkle reserved crumb mixture on top. Bake in preheated 400-degree oven for 25 minutes or until knife inserted in center comes out clean. Serve warm. Canned or frozen whole kernel corn, lightly chopped, may be used instead of fresh corn. Yield: 6 servings.

CORN AND CHEESE SCALLOP

1   17-oz. can cream-style corn
2 eggs, beaten
1/2 c. crushed crackers
1/4 c. melted butter
1/4 c. milk
1/4 c. finely shredded carrot
1 tbsp. chopped celery
1 tsp. chopped onion
6 drops of Tabasco sauce
1/2 tsp. sugar
1/2 tsp. salt
1/2 c. shredded Cheddar cheese

Combine all ingredients except cheese; mix well. Turn into greased 8-inch square baking dish. Top with shredded cheese. Bake in preheated 350-degree oven for 30 to 35 minutes or until corn mixture is set and cheese golden brown. Yield: 8 servings.

Doris Everson
Havre Jr. H.S., Havre, Montana

CORN PUDDING

1 can cream-style corn
1/2 tsp. salt
1 tsp. sugar
2 tbsp. melted butter
2 eggs, well beaten
1 c. milk

Stir corn, salt, sugar and melted butter together. Combine eggs and milk; stir into corn mixture. Pour into greased baking dish. Bake in preheated 300-degree oven for 25 minutes. One pint frozen corn may be substituted for cream-style corn, if desired. Yield: 6 servings.

Mrs. Dorothy Ray
East Yancey H.S., Burnsville, North Carolina

LUNCHEON CASSEROLE

1 green pepper, chopped
1 onion, chopped
1 can cream-style corn
1 lg. can tomatoes, cut up
1 c. yellow cornmeal
1 c. grated Cheddar cheese
1 lg. can evaporated milk
2 eggs, beaten

Combine green pepper, onion, corn, tomatoes, cornmeal and cheese; let stand in refrigerator overnight. Stir in milk and eggs; pour in casserole. Bake in preheated 350-degree oven for about 1 hour or until firm. May be served with creamed chicken or chipped beef, if desired.

Elnor Alkio
Pendleton Sr. H.S., Pendleton, Oregon

FESTIVE CORN-CARROT BAKE

1 1-lb. can cream-style corn
1 c. diced cooked carrots
1/4 c. finely chopped onion
1/4 c. chopped green pepper
1/4 c. sliced pitted ripe olives
2 eggs, beaten
1 tsp. salt
Dash of pepper
Dash of hot pepper sauce
1 3/4 c. soft bread crumbs
1 tbsp. melted butter or margarine

Combine corn, carrots, onion, green pepper and olives in bowl. Add eggs, salt, pepper, hot sauce and 1 cup bread crumbs; place in 1-quart greased casserole. Toss remaining crumbs with melted butter; sprinkle over corn mixture. Bake in preheated 350-degree oven for 50 minutes. Remove from oven; let stand for 5 minutes before serving. Garnish with ripe olive wedges, if desired. Yield: 6 servings.

Mrs. R. Bruce Wheelwright
Melba H.S., Melba, Idaho

BAKED EGGPLANT

1 med. eggplant, peeled and diced
3 slices fresh bread
2 eggs, beaten
2 tbsp. chopped onion
2/3 c. grated longhorn cheese
Salt to taste
2 tbsp. butter
1 to 1 1/2 c. milk

Cook eggplant in boiling salted water until tender; drain. Tear bread into small pieces; add to eggplant. Add eggs, onion, cheese and salt. Melt butter in hot milk, then beat into eggplant mixture until mixture is thin. Pour into buttered casserole. Bake in preheated 350-degree oven for 45 minutes to 1 hour.

Mrs. Carol Mapes
Pella Community Middle Sch., Pella, Iowa

DOUBLE EGG CASSEROLE

1 sm. eggplant
1 egg, beaten
3 tbsp. evaporated milk
Salt
1/2 c. cornmeal
1/8 tsp. pepper
1/2 c. oil
2 tbsp. butter
Oregano to taste
Onion salt to taste
1/2 can tomato sauce
1/2 c. shredded Cheddar or American
    cheese

Peel and slice eggplant lengthwise into 1/8-inch slices. Combine egg, milk and 1/8 teaspoon salt in a shallow bowl. Combine cornmeal, 1/2 teaspoon salt and pepper. Dip eggplant slices into egg mixture, then coat with cornmeal mixture. Brown the slices on both sides in hot oil in a heavy skillet. Melt butter in square 2-inch deep casserole. Place layer of eggplant in casserole; sprinkle with oregano and onion salt. Spread half the tomato sauce and cheese over eggplant. Repeat layers. Pour any remaining egg mixture over top. Bake in preheated 350-degree oven for about 10 minutes or until the egg is set and cheese melted. Strips of cheese may be placed over top of casserole to form spokes, if desired.

Mrs. Gertrude Payton
North Division H.S., Milwaukee, Wisconsin

EGGPLANT-TOMATO CASSEROLE

1 lg. eggplant
2 c. tomatoes
1 med. onion, chopped
1 sm. green pepper, chopped
1 tsp. salt
1/2 tsp. pepper
1/2 tsp. oregano
1/2 c. bread crumbs
1 4-oz. can mushrooms
6 slices cheese

Wash and cube eggplant. Combine tomatoes, onion, green pepper, salt, pepper and oregano in saucepan; simmer for 15 minutes. Arrange layer of eggplant in greased 2-quart casserole; sprinkle with 2 tablespoons bread crumbs. Add layer of mushrooms and sauce. Repeat layers, ending with eggplant and sauce. Bake in preheated 350-degree oven for 45 minutes. Place cheese slices on top; return to oven for 5 minutes or until cheese is melted. Yield: 4 servings.

Rosemarie Sullivan
Saugerties Sr. H.S., Saugerties, New York

EGGPLANT-CLAM CASSEROLE

1 lg. eggplant
2 tbsp. lemon juice
1/2 tsp. salt
2 c. thick white sauce
1 can minced clams
1 c. cracker crumbs
Buttered crumbs

Peel and dice eggplant; place in saucepan. Add lemon juice, salt and enough water to cover. Cook until tender; drain. Add to white sauce. Add clams and cracker crumbs; mix well. Place in buttered casserole; top with buttered crumbs. Bake in preheated 325-degree oven for 40 minutes.

Mrs. H. B. Watson
St. Edward Pub. Sch., Saint Edward, Nebraska

GOLDEN EGGPLANT CASSEROLE

2 1/2 c. cubed peeled eggplant
1 c. milk
1/2 c. grated Cheddar cheese
1/2 c. chopped celery
2 tbsp. chopped pimento or
* green pepper*
1 or 2 tbsp. melted margarine
1/2 tsp. salt
Dash of pepper

Cook eggplant in salted water for 10 minutes; drain. Pour milk into saucepan; bring just to boiling point. Add eggplant, cheese, celery, pimento, margarine, salt and pepper; mix well. Place in 1-quart casserole. Bake in preheated 350-degree oven for about 45 minutes.

Lorene L. Arent
Wausa Pub. Schools, Wausa, Nebraska

EGGPLANT PARMESAN

1 lg. eggplant
1 egg, slightly beaten
1/4 c. dry white wine
1 c. cracker crumbs
1 clove of garlic, minced
1/4 c. olive oil
2 c. tomato juice
2 tbsp. minced parsley
1/4 tsp. basil
1/4 tsp. oregano
1 bay leaf, crumbled
1 tsp. salt
1/4 c. grated Parmesan cheese
1/4 lb. mozzarella cheese, sliced

Peel eggplant; cut crosswise into 1/4-inch slices. Beat egg with wine. Dip eggplant in egg mixture, then in cracker crumbs. Saute garlic in oil for 5 minutes. Add eggplant to garlic oil and saute for 10 minutes or until golden brown. Remove eggplant and keep warm in oven. Add tomato juice, parsley, basil, oregano, bay leaf and salt to skillet; simmer for 15 minutes, stirring frequently. Arrange alternate layers of eggplant, Parmesan cheese, mozzarella cheese and sauce in casserole. Bake in preheated 350-degree oven for 30 minutes.

Mrs. Tomoe Nimori
Reedley H.S., Reedley, California

HERB-SEASONED EGGPLANT CASSEROLE

3 med. eggplant
1 1/4 lb. ground meat
2 onions, chopped
1 bell pepper, chopped
5 cloves of garlic, crushed
1 tsp. salt
Dash of pepper
Dash of chili powder
1 tbsp. Worcestershire sauce
1 egg, well beaten
3/4 c. Pepperidge Farm herb-seasoned
* stuffing mix*

Peel and dice eggplant; place in saucepan. Cover with boiling salted water; cook until tender. Drain and reserve 1/2 cup liquid. Brown meat in skillet; add onions, bell pepper and garlic. Cook until onions are tender. Add salt, pepper, chili powder and Worcestershire sauce. Simmer for several minutes; add eggplant. Cook for about 10 to 15 minutes longer. Add reserved eggplant liquid; cook for 10 minutes longer until mixture thickens. Let cool for 10 minutes, then add egg and 1/2 cup stuffing mix. Pour into well-buttered casserole. Cover with remaining herb stuffing mix. Bake in preheated 375-degree oven for 25 to 30 minutes.

Susan Dorsey
Hogg Jr. H.S., Houston, Texas

EASY EGGPLANT CASSEROLE

1 med. eggplant, peeled and sliced
3 tbsp. margarine
3 fresh tomatoes, peeled and sliced
1 lg. onion, cut into rings
6 slices processed cheese

Saute eggplant slices in margarine until tender. Place 2 or 3 slices eggplant in casserole; add 2 or 3 slices tomatoes, layer of onion, then 2 slices cheese. Repeat layers, ending with cheese. Cover. Bake in preheated 350-degree oven for 30 minutes. Yield: 6 servings.

Karen Hussong
Slayton H.S., Slayton, Minnesota

EGGPLANT CALIFORNIA

3 tbsp. butter
1 med. yellow onion, coarsely
   chopped
1 lg. eggplant
1/2 c. beef broth or bouillon
2 med. firm tomatoes, peeled
1 tsp. seasoned salt
1 tsp. pepper
1 c. sour cream
1/2 tsp. oregano
2 tsp. chopped chives
2/3 c. soft bread crumbs

Melt 2 tablespoons butter in skillet over medium heat. Add onion; saute until onion is tender, but not brown. Peel eggplant; cut into 1-inch cubes. Add to onion, stirring to blend; cook for several minutes. Add broth; mix lightly. Spoon half the eggplant mixture into buttered 2-quart shallow baking dish or casserole; cover with half the tomatoes. Sprinkle with half the seasoned salt and pepper. Spread half the sour cream over tomatoes; sprinkle with all the oregano and 1 teaspoon chives. Repeat layers. Melt remaining butter in small saucepan. Add bread crumbs; mix well. Sprinkle over sour cream. Bake in preheated 350-degree oven for 20 to 25 minutes or until bubbly and brown. Yield: 6 servings.

OKRA-TOMATO CASSEROLE

1 to 2 lb. okra, sliced
1 No. 303 can tomatoes
1 bell pepper, cubed
1 med. onion, cubed
4 slices toast, crumbled
Bacon slices

Combine all ingredients except bacon; turn into greased baking dish. Cover with bacon. Bake in preheated 300-degree oven for 40 minutes or until okra is tender and bacon is crisp.

Joanne Snider
Dimmitt H.S., Dimmitt, Texas

Eggplant California

GREEN VEGETABLE CASSEROLE

1 10-oz. package frozen chopped
   broccoli
1 10-oz. package frozen green peas
1 10-oz. package frozen spinach
Shredded cheese to taste
Slivered almonds or bread crumbs

Cook broccoli, peas and spinach together according to package directions; drain well. Place half the vegetables in 9 x 13-inch baking pan; cover with cheese. Add remaining vegetables; cover with slivered almonds. Bake in preheated 350-degree oven for 30 minutes or until bubbly.

Mrs. Larry Clark
Cowley Co. Comm. Jr. College
Arkansas City, Kansas

LETTIE ANN'S VEGETABLE CASSEROLE

2 c. diced celery
2 c. diced carrots
1 pkg. frozen green beans
1 pkg. frozen lima beans
1 pkg. frozen cauliflower
1 can cream of chicken soup
1 can cream of mushroom soup
1/4 lb. Old English cheese, diced
Buttered crumbs

Cook celery and carrots separately in boiling, salted water until crisp-tender. Cook frozen vegetables separately according to package directions until just tender; drain. Mix soups in a saucepan. Add cheese; heat until cheese is melted. Layer vegetables in large casserole; pour soup mixture over top. Cover with buttered crumbs. Bake in preheated 350-degree oven for 1 hour.

Mrs. William Boggs
Orrville Sr. H.S., Orrville, Ohio

MONEY-SAVING VEGETABLE CASSEROLE

2 c. chopped celery
2 c. chopped carrots
2 c. cut green beans
1/2 c. chopped onion
2 c. canned tomatoes, drained
2 1/2 tsp. salt
Pepper to taste
3 tbsp. Minute tapioca
1 tbsp. sugar
1/4 c. butter

Combine all ingredients except butter; place in large, greased casserole. Dot with butter; cover. Bake in preheated 350-degree oven for 1 hour and 30 minutes.

Mrs. Betty Anderson
Laurel Public Sch., Laurel, Nebraska

ONIONS AND CLAMS

1 6 1/2-oz. can minced clams
3 med. onions, cut into lg. pieces
1/2 c. margarine
2 tsp. sugar
4 tbsp. flour
1/4 tsp. salt
1/8 tsp. white pepper
1/2 c. milk
1 tbsp. Worcestershire sauce
1/2 tsp. hot sauce
1/3 c. corn flake crumbs

Drain clams; reserve liquid. Saute onions in margarine in saucepan until crisp-tender. Add sugar; stir until dissolved. Add flour, salt and pepper. Add milk and reserved liquid gradually, stirring constantly; stir in Worcestershire sauce and hot sauce. Cook over low heat, stirring constantly, until thickened. Add clams; heat through. Place in eight 3-ounce souffle dishes or large shells; sprinkle with crumbs. Bake in preheated 325-degree oven for 15 to 20 minutes.

Mrs. Patricia A. Gannon
Ben Franklin Jr. H.S., Kenmore, New York

PARTY ONIONS

2 lb. small onions
5 tbsp. butter or margarine
3 tbsp. all-purpose flour
1 c. water
1 tbsp. brown sugar
1 tsp. salt
1 tsp. Worcestershire sauce
Dash of pepper
1/4 tsp. paprika
2 tbsp. toasted slivered almonds

Cook onions, covered, in small amount of boiling, salted water for 10 to 15 minutes or until tender; drain well. Arrange in 1-quart casserole. Melt butter in saucepan; blend in flour. Stir in water, brown sugar, salt, Worcestershire sauce and pepper; cook, stirring, until thickened. Pour over onions; sprinkle with paprika. Cover. Bake in preheated 375-degree oven for 20 minutes; sprinkle with almonds. Two pounds medium onions, quartered, may be substituted for small onions. Yield: 6 servings.

Mrs. Willetta R. Wallace
Whiteville Sr. H.S., Whiteville, North Carolina

ONIONS AU GRATIN

2 lb. small onions
1 c. sharp grated cheese
1 can cream of mushroom soup
1 tbsp. Lea and Perrins sauce
Dash of Tabasco sauce
Croutons

Peel onions; cook in boiling, salted water until tender. Drain in colander for about 30 minutes. Arrange onions in buttered baking dish; sprinkle with cheese. Mix soup and sauces; pour over cheese. Cover top with croutons. Bake in preheated 350-degree oven until brown and bubbly.

Mrs. Norma Francis Bachschmid
Hurst Jr. H.S., Hurst, Texas

SCALLOPED PEAS

1 can cream of mushroom soup
1/4 c. milk
1 can med. green peas, drained
1 can Chinese noodles
2 hard-boiled eggs, diced
2 tbsp. diced pimento
1/4 c. chopped pecans
1/2 c. buttered bread crumbs

Mix soup, milk, peas, noodles, eggs, pimento and pecans; place in buttered casserole. Top with bread crumbs. Bake in preheated 375-degree oven for 20 minutes; serve warm. Yield: 6 servings.

Mrs. Lila Akes
Central Decatur Comm. H.S., Leon, Iowa

ENGLISH PEA CASSEROLE

1/2 can water chestnuts
2 No. 2 cans English peas, drained
1 can cream of chicken soup
1   4-oz. can mushroom stems and
*   pieces, drained*
3 tbsp. finely chopped onion
Bread crumbs
Butter

Drain water chestnuts; chop fine. Add remaining ingredients except bread crumbs and butter; mix well. Place in greased baking dish. Cover generously with bread crumbs; dot generously with butter. Bake in preheated 350-degree oven for 45 minutes to 1 hour or until crumbs are golden brown. Cut green beans may be substituted for English peas, if desired.

Mrs. H. M. Thomas
Breckenridge H.S., Breckenridge, Texas

GRATED POTATO CASSEROLE

1/2 c. milk
3 eggs
1/2 tsp. salt
1/8 tsp. pepper
1 c. cubed sharp American cheese
2 tbsp. butter or margarine, softened
1/2 sm. onion, cut in pieces
3 med. potatoes, pared and cubed

Place milk, eggs, salt, pepper, cheese, butter, onion and cubed potatoes in blender container in order listed. Cover blender. Blend on high speed just until all potatoes are grated. Do not overblend. Pour into greased 10 x 6 x 1 1/2-inch baking dish. Bake in preheated 375-degree oven for 35 to 40 minutes. Garnish with green pepper rings, if desired.

Mrs. Virginia Claypool
Marshall H.S., Marshall, Illinois

WINTER CASSEROLE

2 potatoes
3 apples
1 onion
3/4 tsp. salt
4 strips bacon

Peel and cut potatoes and apples in thick slices. Peel and cut onion in thin slices. Place alternating layers of potatoes, apples and onion into a well-buttered 6-inch casserole. Sprinkle each layer lightly with salt, then place strips of bacon over the top. Bake, covered, in a preheated 400-degree oven for 15 minutes. Remove cover and bake for 10 minutes longer or until brown. Serve hot. Yield: 6 servings.

Linda L. Bingham
Cascade Jr. H.S., Vancouver, Washington

FLAVORFUL POTATO CASSEROLE

1 can Cheddar cheese soup
1/2 c. milk
4 c. thinly sliced potatoes
1 sm. onion, thinly sliced
1 tbsp. butter or margarine
Paprika

Stir soup until smooth; add milk gradually, stirring until blended. Arrange alternate layers of potatoes, onion and sauce in buttered 1 1/2-quart casserole. Dot top with butter, then sprinkle with paprika. Bake, covered, in preheated 375-degree oven for 1 hour. Uncover; bake for 15 minutes longer. One cup grated cheese and the milk may be heated together until cheese is melted and substituted for the soup. Yield: 4 to 6 servings.

Mrs. Grace Caperton
Mississippi College, Clinton, Mississippi

MAKE-AHEAD POTATO CASSEROLE

1 qt. cooked cubed potatoes
1 can cream of chicken soup
1 c. shredded process cheese
1/4 c. minced onion
1 tbsp. onion juice
2 tbsp. finely cut pimento (opt.)
Salt and pepper to taste
1/2 c. buttered bread crumbs

Place layer of potatoes in greased 8 x 4 x 2 1/2-inch loaf pan. Combine soup, cheese, onion, onion juice, pimento and seasonings. Spread a layer of cheese mixture over potatoes. Repeat layers, ending with potatoes. Cover with crumbs. Bake in preheated 350-degree oven for about 30 minutes. Casserole may be made a day ahead and refrigerated or frozen well in advance. Yield: 6-8 servings.

Mrs. Cheryl Assenheimer
Troy Jr. H.S., Avon Lake, Ohio

P-T CASSEROLE

7 slices bacon
4 c. diced potatoes
3 c. canned tomatoes
1 tsp. salt
1/2 tsp. pepper
1/2 tsp. oregano
3 sm. onions, sliced thin

Fry 3 slices of bacon until partially cooked, but not crisp; drain. Cut remaining bacon into small pieces. Place half the potatoes, tomatoes, uncooked bacon pieces, seasonings and sliced onions in layers in a greased 2-quart casserole. Repeat layers, then top with the partially cooked bacon. Bake in preheated 350-degree oven for 1 hour and 30 minutes or until tender. Yield: 6-8 servings.

Charwynne Schultz
Rio Vista H.S., Rio Vista, Texas

TASTY SCALLOPED POTATOES

5 or 6 med. potatoes, sliced thin
1 sm. onion, finely chopped
3 tbsp. flour
1 tbsp. parsley flakes
Salt and pepper to taste
3 tbsp. butter or margarine
1 can cream of celery soup
1/2 c. milk

Arrange 1/3 of the potatoes in a buttered and floured 2-quart casserole. Sprinkle with half the onion, flour, parsley flakes, salt and pepper. Dot with butter. Combine soup and milk. Pour 1/3 of the soup mixture over ingredients in casserole and repeat layers. Bake, covered, in preheated 400-degree oven for 1 hour or until potatoes are tender. Remove cover during last 10 minutes of baking if a browned top is desired. Yield: 6 servings.

Mrs. A. A. Luyben
Carroll H.S., Fort Wayne, Indiana

SCALLOPED POTATOES WITH PIMENTOS

4 c. diced potatoes
2 chopped pimentos
1 green bell pepper, chopped
Salt and pepper to taste
2 tbsp. margarine
2 tbsp. flour
1 c. milk
1/2 c. grated cheese

Cook potatoes in boiling salted water for 10 minutes, then drain. Combine potatoes, pimentos, green pepper, salt and pepper; turn into well-oiled baking dish. Melt margarine in saucepan, then blend in flour. Add milk, stirring until smooth. Cook and stir until thickened. Remove from heat; stir in cheese until melted. Pour cheese sauce over potato mixture. Bake in preheated 350-degree oven for about 50 minutes. Yield: 6-8 servings.

Mrs. Mildred Sanders
Clint H.S., Clint, Texas

CREOLE POTATO PUFF

3 c. frozen southern-style hashed
   brown potatoes, thawed
1 c. finely chopped onions
1/2 c. finely chopped green pepper
Margarine
6 eggs, separated
1 tsp. salt
1 med. tomato, finely chopped
1 tsp. leaf oregano
1 tsp. basil leaves
2 tbsp. grated Parmesan cheese

Saute potatoes, onions and green pepper in a small amount of margarine until potatoes are soft and onions are translucent. Beat egg yolks until thick and lemon colored; beat egg whites and salt together until stiff but not dry. Fold yolks and whites together, then fold in potato mixture, tomato, oregano and basil. Turn into buttered 2-quart casserole; sprinkle with cheese. Bake in preheated 350-degree oven for 30 minutes or until a knife inserted near center comes out clean. Yield: 4 servings.

Mrs. Charlotte VanArum
Greece Olympia H.S., Rochester, New York

BAKED BARBECUED POTATOES

4 slices bacon, diced
1 tbsp. flour
1 1/2 tsp. salt
1/8 tsp. pepper
4 c. thinly sliced potatoes
1/2 c. chopped onion
1 c. shredded pasteurized American
   process cheese
1/3 c. catsup
1 tsp. Worcestershire sauce
3 drops of spicy hot sauce
1 1/2 c. scalded milk
2 tbsp. butter

Fry bacon until crisp; drain on paper toweling. Combine flour, salt and pepper. Arrange potatoes, onion, flour mixture and 1/2 of the cheese in layers in shallow 2-quart casserole. Combine catsup, Worcestershire sauce, hot sauce and milk, mixing well. Pour over potato mixture; dot with butter. Cover. Bake in preheated 375-degree oven for 45 minutes. Uncover; stir. Bake for 15 to 20 minutes longer or until potatoes are tender. Sprinkle with bacon and remaining cheese; serve at once. Yield: 4-6 servings.

Baked Barbecued Potatoes

POTATO-ONION CASSEROLE

3 med. potatoes
1 tsp. seasoned salt
1/2 c. sour cream
1/2 c. Cheez Whiz
1/2 can French-fried onion rings

Cook potatoes in skins in boiling water to cover for about 45 minutes or until tender. Drain; remove skins quickly. Add seasoned salt, sour cream, Cheez Whiz and mash, then whip until fluffy. Place potato mixture in greased casserole. Bake in preheated 350-degree oven for about 20 minutes or until hot and bubbly. Remove from oven and top with onion rings. Return to oven; bake for about 4 minutes longer or until onions are toasted.

Sarah A. McCreight
Oak Hill Jr. H.S., Morganton, North Carolina

TINA'S ITALIAN POTATOES

2 to 4 potatoes
2 to 4 carrots
1 lg. onion, chopped
1/4 c. olive oil
2 tsp. oregano
3 sprigs fresh parsley, chopped
Garlic salt and pepper to taste

Peel potatoes and carrots. Cut in strips as for French fries. Place potatoes, carrots and chopped onion in baking dish. Add olive oil, oregano, parsley, garlic salt and pepper; mix well. Bake, covered, in preheated 350-degree oven for 1 hour to 1 hour and 30 minutes or until vegetables are tender. Yield: 2-4 servings.

Diane Panzone
L'Anse Creuse H.S., Mt. Clemens, Michigan

NOODLE AND SPINACH CASSEROLE

1 8-oz. package narrow noodles
1 10-oz. package frozen chopped spinach
1 c. sliced mushrooms
2 tbsp. butter
2 tbsp. melted butter
Salt and pepper to taste
1 1/2 c. diced cooked meat
1 1/2 c. sour cream
1 c. buttered bread crumbs

Cook noodles and spinach separately according to package directions; drain. Saute mushrooms in butter until tender. Mix noodles with melted butter, salt and pepper. Mix spinach with mushrooms; combine meat with sour cream. Arrange half the noodles in greased 2-quart casserole; add meat mixture. Add spinach. Top with remaining noodles; sprinkle with crumbs. Bake in preheated 350-degree oven for 30 minutes. Yield: 6 servings.

Mrs. Doris Malo
Mountain View H.S., Mountain View, California

SPINACH CASSEROLE JALAPENO

2 pkg. frozen spinach
1 6-oz. roll jalapeno cheese
1/4 c. butter
2 tbsp. flour
2 tbsp. chopped onion
1/2 c. evaporated milk
1/2 tsp. pepper
3/4 tsp. celery salt
3/4 tsp. garlic salt
1/2 tsp. salt
1 tsp. Worcestershire sauce
Buttered crumbs

Cook spinach according to package directions. Drain; reserve liquid. Cut cheese into small pieces. Melt butter in saucepan. Add flour; mix until smooth. Add onion; cook over low heat until soft, but not brown. Add reserved liquid and milk slowly; cook, stirring, until thick. Add seasonings and cheese; cook, stirring, until smooth. Add spinach; mix well. Place in casserole; cover with crumbs. Bake in preheated 350-degree oven until bubbly; may be frozen.

Gerry Smith
Waco H.S., Waco, Texas

SPINACH-CHEESE CASSEROLE

1 sm. carton cottage cheese
1/4 lb. Cheddar cheese, grated
1/2 c. margarine
3 eggs, beaten
3 tbsp. flour
1 pkg. frozen chopped spinach, thawed

Mix all ingredients; place in buttered casserole. Bake in preheated 350-degree oven for 45 minutes.

Flora Mae Doville
Southside H.S., Fort Smith, Arkansas

SPINACH-MACARONI AND CHEESE CASSEROLE

3 c. shell macaroni, cooked and
    drained
2 pkg. frozen spinach, cooked and
    drained
1   16-oz. jar Cheez Whiz
1 lg. onion, chopped

Combine all ingredients in 2-quart casserole. Bake in preheated 325-degree oven until heated through. Yield: 8 servings.

Mrs. Diane Yakos
Versailles H.S., Versailles, Ohio

PEPPERY VEGETABLE MEDLEY

1 pkg. frozen French-style green
    beans
1 pkg. frozen lima beans
1 pkg. frozen English peas
3 green peppers, cut julienne-style
1 pt. heavy cream, whipped
1 pt. mayonnaise
3 tbsp. grated Parmesan cheese

Cook green beans, lima beans and peas together according to package directions until almost done. Add green pepper strips; cook until beans and peas are tender. Drain. Arrange half the vegetables in greased casserole. Combine whipped cream, mayonnaise and cheese; spread half the cream mixture over vegetables. Repeat layers. Bake in preheated 350-degree oven until heated through and brown. Do not substitute salad dressing for mayonnaise.

Mrs. Emely Sundbeck
Manor H.S., Manor, Texas

CRUMB-TOPPED SQUASH CASSEROLE

4 c. cooked squash
1 med. onion, sliced
1 can cream of mushroom soup
1 c. grated sharp cheese
1/2 c. bread crumbs

Place squash in casserole; arrange onion slices over squash. Spoon undiluted mushroom soup over onion; sprinkle cheese over soup. Sprinkle bread crumbs over cheese. Bake in preheated 400-degree oven for 20 to 30 minutes or until brown and bubbly. Asparagus or broccoli may be used instead of squash.

Evelyn W. Knowles
Charles L. Coon Jr. H.S., Wilson, North Carolina

EASY SQUASH CASSEROLE

2 lb. squash
2 eggs
1/2 c. mayonnaise
1 tsp. salt
1/4 c. chopped green pepper
3 tbsp. chopped onion
Ritz cheese cracker crumbs

Cook squash in small amount of water until tender; drain and mash. Beat eggs in bowl; add mayonnaise, salt, green pepper and onion. Stir in squash; place in buttered casserole. Cover with crumbs. Bake in preheated 325-degree oven for 30 minutes. Yield: 6 servings.

Clarise Garner
West Montgomery Sch., Mt. Gilead, North Carolina

SQUASH AND SHRIMP CASSEROLE

2 lb. yellow squash
2 lg. onions, thinly sliced
2 tbsp. butter
1/2 lb. boiled shrimp, peeled
    and deveined
Salt to taste
3/4 tsp. pepper
2 eggs, well beaten
1/4 c. bread crumbs

Cook squash in small amount of water until tender; drain well and mash. Saute onions in 1 tablespoon butter until soft; stir in squash, shrimp, salt, pepper and eggs until well blended. Turn into greased 1-quart casserole. Sprinkle with bread crumbs; dot with remaining butter. Bake in preheated 350-degree oven for 45 minutes or until puffed and brown. Yield: 6 servings.

Bernadette Varnado
Pine View Jr. H.S., Covington, Louisiana

Cheese And Squash Bake

CHEESE AND SQUASH BAKE

Salt
8 c. cubed squash
Pepper
1/4 c. Borden Danish flavor
   margarine, melted
1 8-oz. package Borden Eagle Brand
   Neufchatel or cream cheese, softened
1/4 c. Borden homogenized milk
1 tbsp. flour
Chopped peanuts (opt.)
Green pepper rings (opt.)

Pour 2 cups water into large saucepan. Add 1 teaspoon salt; bring to a boil. Add squash; bring to a boil again. Reduce heat; cover. Cook for 10 to 15 minutes or until squash is just tender; drain. Turn into greased shallow 10 x 6 1/2 x 2-inch baking dish. Sprinkle with salt and pepper to taste. Pour margarine over squash. Blend cheese until smooth. Add milk and flour; mix well. Spread over squash. Bake in preheated 375-degree oven for about 20 minutes or until topping is set. Garnish with peanuts and pepper rings. Yield: 4-6 servings.

SCALLOPED SQUASH WITH CHEESE TOPPING

1/3 c. milk
1 can cream of mushroom soup
1 egg, slightly beaten
4 c. cooked squash, drained
1/2 c. chopped onion

3/4 c. herb-seasoned stuffing mix
1 recipe Cheese Topping

Mix milk with soup. Add egg; mix well. Add squash, onion and stuffing mix; toss lightly to mix. Turn into greased 10 x 6 x 1 1/2-inch casserole. Add Cheese Topping. Bake in preheated 350-degree oven for 20 minutes. Eggplant may be substituted for squash.

Cheese Topping

1/2 c. herb-seasoned stuffing mix,
   finely crushed
2 tbsp. melted butter or margarine
1 c. grated sharp cheese

Combine stuffing mix and butter; sprinkle over casserole. Top with cheese.

Mrs. Mildred Green
Central Cabarrus H.S., Concord, North Carolina

SUMMER SQUASH CASSEROLE

4 med. yellow squash
1 1/2 tsp. salt
1 tsp. sugar
1 1/2 tbsp. butter
3 tbsp. flour
1 1/2 c. milk
1/4 tsp. pepper
1/2 c. chopped onion
1 c. shredded Cheddar cheese
1 c. soda cracker crumbs

Wash squash; cut into 1/2-inch slices. Cook in 1 inch of boiling water with 1 teaspoon salt and sugar for about 10 minutes or until tender; drain. Melt butter in small saucepan; stir in remaining salt and flour. Stir in milk gradually; cook over medium heat, stirring constantly, until thickened. Place half the squash in ungreased casserole; sprinkle with half the pepper. Arrange half the onion over squash; pour half the sauce over onion. Add half the cheese, then half the cracker crumbs; repeat layers. Bake in preheated 350-degree oven for about 30 minutes or until golden brown and bubbly.

Vicki Sommers
Roosevelt Jr. H.S., Coffeyville, Kansas

EASY ZUCCHINI CASSEROLE

2 med. onions, diced
2 to 3 tbsp. margarine

1 lg. zucchini
1/2 tsp. oregano
1/2 c. grated Cheddar cheese
1 1/2 c. tomato sauce
Salt and pepper to taste

Partially cook onions in margarine and set aside. Peel zucchini and remove seeds. Cut into 1-inch strips about 4 inches long. Drop zucchini strips into boiling water for 4 to 5 minutes. Remove and drain. Place zucchini strips in ungreased casserole; spoon onions evenly over zucchini. Sprinkle with oregano and cover with cheese. Spoon the tomato sauce over the cheese. Season with salt and pepper. Bake in preheated 350-degree oven for about 30 minutes. May be frozen.

Mrs. Sally T. Ninos
Benjamin Franklin Jr. H.S., Kenmore, New York

FAVORITE ZUCCHINI

1 med. zucchini
3 med. onions
2 tbsp. margarine
1 can spaghetti sauce
1/2 c. grated Parmesan cheese
Garlic powder to taste
1/2 tsp. oregano

Wash zucchini, but do not peel. Slice zucchini and onions thin. Saute onions in margarine in skillet. Place half the zucchini, onions, spaghetti sauce and cheese in layers in casserole. Sprinkle garlic powder and oregano over each layer. Repeat layers; cover. Bake in preheated 350-degree oven for 1 hour.

Mrs. Eleanor Weatherhead
Northridge Middle Sch., Dayton, Ohio

HEARTY ZUCCHINI CASSEROLE

6 sm. zucchini, cut in 1/2-in. cubes
1 c. grated soft processed cheese
1 c. crushed oyster crackers or
    saltines
2 eggs
1 1/2 c. milk
2 tbsp. grated onion or 1 tsp. onion
    powder
3/4 tsp. salt
1/2 tsp. pepper

Place zucchini in saucepan; cover with water. Bring to a boil and simmer for 5 minutes, then drain. Add half the cheese to the squash and stir until cheese is melted. Add crackers and mix. Beat eggs slightly; add milk, onion, salt, and pepper. Combine with squash mixture. Turn into a greased 1 1/2-quart casserole. Place the remaining cheese on top. Bake in preheated 350-degree oven for 45 minutes or until set. Yield: 6 servings.

Phyllis Fry
Orrville H.S., Orrville, Ohio

PUFFED-UP ZUCCHINI

4 c. chopped zucchini
1 c. chopped onions
5 tbsp. butter
1/2 tsp. salt
Dash of pepper
1 tbsp. horseradish
1 egg, beaten
1 c. cracker crumbs

Cook zucchini and onions in 1/4 cup boiling water in saucepan for about 15 minutes or until tender; drain and mash. Add 2 tablespoons butter, salt, pepper and horseradish; mix well. Cool. Add egg; mix well. Pour into greased baking dish. Cook crumbs in remaining butter until brown; sprinkle over zucchini mixture. Bake in preheated 350-degree oven for 30 minutes. Yield: 6 servings.

Mrs. Mary R. Abney
Bay Springs H.S., Bay Springs, Mississippi

ZUCCHINI-CHEESE CASSEROLE

3 zucchini
1 lg. onion, chopped
1 1/2 c. grated sharp cheese
1 c. bread crumbs
Salt and pepper to taste

Pare and cube zucchini. Combine zucchini and onion in saucepan; add small amount of water. Bring to a boil, then cover and cook for 5 to 10 minutes. Arrange layers of half the squash mixture, cheese, crumbs and seasonings in casserole. Repeat layers. Bake in preheated 350-degree oven for 30 minutes. Yield: 6 servings.

Mrs. Mary Ada Parks
Anna-Jonesboro Comm. H.S., Anna, Illinois

Macaroni-Zucchini Casserole

MACARONI-ZUCCHINI CASSEROLE

Salt
1   8-oz. package elbow macaroni
4 tbsp. butter or margarine
2 tbsp. flour
1/8 tsp. white pepper
2 c. milk
1 c. cubed Cheddar cheese
1 c. cubed Swiss cheese
1 1/2 lb. zucchini, sliced and
   cooked
1/2 c. fine dry bread crumbs
Nutmeg (opt.)

Add 1 tablespoon salt to 3 quarts rapidly boiling water; add macaroni gradually so that water continues to boil. Cook, stirring occasionally, until tender; drain in colander. Melt 2 tablespoons butter in saucepan; blend in flour, 1 teaspoon salt and pepper. Add milk gradually; cook, stirring constantly, until sauce comes to a boil. Boil for 1 minute. Reduce heat. Add cheeses; cook, stirring, until cheeses melt. Spread half the macaroni over bottom of 3-quart casserole; top with half the zucchini, then half the sauce. Repeat layers. Melt remaining butter; mix with bread crumbs. Sprinkle over sauce. Sprinkle with nutmeg. Bake in preheated 350-degree oven for 30 minutes. Macaroni and zucchini may be arranged as shown in the photograph, if desired. Yield: 6 servings.

ZUCCHINI-STUFFING CASSEROLE

4 med. zucchini, sliced 1/2 in. thick
3/4 c. shredded carrots

1/2 c. chopped onion
6 tbsp. butter or margarine
2 1/4 c. herbed stuffing cubes
1 can cream of chicken soup
1/2 c. sour cream

Cook zucchini in small amount of boiling, salted water until tender; drain. Cook carrots and onion in 4 tablespoons butter in saucepan until tender. Remove from heat; stir in 1 1/2 cups stuffing cubes, soup and sour cream. Stir in zucchini gently; turn into 1 1/2-quart casserole. Melt remaining butter; add remaining stuffing cubes. Toss gently; sprinkle over casserole. Bake in preheated 350-degree oven for 30 to 40 minutes. Yield: 6-8 servings.

Gertrude Rohr
South Campus Sch., Waukesha, Wisconsin

ZUCCHINI SUPREME

2 lb. zucchini
3 eggs, beaten
1 c. grated Cheddar cheese or
   process cheese
1 tsp. grated onion
1/2 tsp. salt
1/2 c. crushed Ritz crackers

Wash zucchini and cut crosswise in 1/2-inch slices. Cook zucchini in small amount of boiling salted water until barely tender and drain. Combine zucchini, eggs, cheese, onion and salt; mix carefully. Place in greased casserole. Sprinkle crackers over top. Bake in preheated 350-degree oven for 25 minutes. Yield: 6 servings.

Mrs. M. Judelle Jones
Turlock H.S., Turlock, California

SUNDAY COMPANY CASSEROLE

1 pkg. frozen green peas
1 can water chestnuts
2   4-oz. cans mushroom stems
   and pieces
1 can bean sprouts, drained
1 can cream of mushroom soup
1/2 lb. Cheddar cheese, grated
1 can French-fried onion rings

Cook peas according to package directions; drain. Drain water chestnuts; slice. Drain mushrooms; reserve liquid. Place peas, bean sprouts, mushrooms and water chestnuts in 9-inch casserole. Mix some of the reserved mushroom liquid with soup in saucepan; heat through. Add to peas mixture; mix well. Sprinkle with cheese; cover. Bake in preheated 350-degree oven for 30 minutes. Remove from oven; uncover. Place onion rings on top; bake for 15 minutes longer.

Mrs. Irvin Lepien
Clayton H.S., Clayton, Wisconsin

SPECIAL SWEET POTATO CASSEROLE

Margarine
3 c. mashed sweet potatoes
3/4 c. sugar
1/2 tsp. salt
2 eggs, beaten
1/2 c. milk
1/2 tsp. vanilla
1 c. (packed) brown sugar
1/3 c. all-purpose flour
1 c. coconut or chopped pecans

Melt 1/2 cup margarine; pour into mixing bowl. Add sweet potatoes, sugar, salt, eggs, milk and vanilla. Mix well. Pour into casserole. Combine 3 tablespoons margarine and remaining ingredients in mixing bowl; place over sweet potato mixture. Bake in preheated 350-degree oven for 35 minutes.

Emily Rickman, Asst. Supvr.
Home Economics Ed. Services, State Dept. of Ed.
Richmond, Virginia

SWEET POTATO-PINEAPPLE CASSEROLE

4 sweet potatoes
1/4 c. melted margarine
Brown sugar
1 egg
1/2 c. raisins
1 sm. can crushed pineapple
1/8 tsp. salt
1/4 tsp. nutmeg
1/4 tsp. cinnamon
1 sm. bag miniature marshmallows

Cook sweet potatoes in boiling salted water. Remove peelings and place potatoes in mixing bowl. Beat with electric mixer, adding margarine and 1/4 cup brown sugar. Add egg, raisins, pineapple and salt. Beat until well mixed. Pour into greased casserole; sprinkle with nutmeg, cinnamon and 3 tablespoons brown sugar. Arrange marshmallows over top. Bake in preheated 275-degree oven until brown.

Avis Burge
South Central H.S., Union Mills, Indiana

APRICOT-ORANGE SAUCE WITH YAMS

6 med. cooked Louisiana yams
1/3 c. (firmly packed) light brown
*   sugar*
4 tsp. cornstarch
1/4 tsp. cinnamon
Dash of salt
1 c. dry sauterne
1/2 c. orange juice
1 tbsp. butter or margarine
1 c. dried apricots
1/4 c. seedless raisins

Peel and quarter yams; place in casserole. Mix sugar, cornstarch, cinnamon and salt in saucepan. Add sauterne and orange juice gradually; cook, stirring constantly, until sauce comes to a boil. Boil for 30 seconds. Add butter, apricots and raisins; cook, stirring, until butter melts. Pour over yams. Bake in preheated 350-degree oven for 10 minutes or until heated through. Three 16-ounce cans Louisiana yams, drained, may be used instead of fresh potatoes. Yield: 6 servings.

Apricot-Orange Sauce With Yams

SCALLOPED SWEET POTATOES AND APPLES

2 c. sliced boiled sweet potatoes
1 1/2 c. thinly sliced sour apples
1/2 c. (packed) brown sugar
1/4 c. butter
1 tsp. salt

Place half the potatoes in buttered baking dish, cover with half the apples. Sprinkle with half the sugar; dot with half the butter. Sprinkle with half the salt; repeat layers. Bake in preheated 350-degree oven for 1 hour.

Mrs. Mary Irish
Shawano H.S., Shawano, Wisconsin

GREEN TOMATO CASSEROLE

4 green tomatoes, sliced
1 tsp. salt
1/2 tsp. pepper
2 tsp. butter
1 c. grated cheese
1 c. cracker crumbs

Place layer of tomatoes in lightly greased casserole. Sprinkle with salt and pepper; dot with butter. Add 1/3 of the cheese. Repeat layers 2 times; cover. Bake in preheated 350-degree oven for 30 to 40 minutes. Remove from oven; sprinkle cracker crumbs over top. Dot with additional butter. Return to oven for about 5 minutes or until lightly browned. Yield: 4 servings.

Sarah A. McCreight
Oak Hill Jr. H.S., Morganton, North Carolina

MAKE-AHEAD SPINACH-TOPPED TOMATOES

1 med. onion, minced
1 lg. garlic clove, minced
1/4 c. butter
2 10-oz. packages frozen chopped
    spinach
1 c. dry bread crumbs
2 eggs, beaten
2 tsp. salt
4 lg. tomatoes, cut in half

Saute onion and garlic in butter in 10-inch skillet over medium heat for about 5 minutes or until onion is tender. Add spinach; cook for 8 minutes, separating spinach with spoon and stirring occasionally. Remove from heat; stir in bread crumbs, eggs and salt. Place tomatoes, cut side up, in greased 13 x 9-inch baking dish; may need to cut thin slice from bottom of halves to stand upright. Mound scant 1/2 cup spinach mixture on each tomato half. Cover; refrigerate. Remove from refrigerator 45 minutes before baking; uncover. Bake in preheated 350-degree oven for 35 minutes or until heated through. Yield: 8 servings.

Margaret Bruce
Redwood H.S., Larkspur, California

TOMATO SURPRISE

3/4 c. melted butter or margarine
3 c. (lightly packed) bread cubes
1 15-oz. can tomato puree
1 1/2 c. (packed) brown sugar
Juice of 1 lemon

Pour butter over bread cubes; toss lightly. Combine tomato puree, brown sugar and lemon juice in saucepan; simmer for 5 minutes. Combine all ingredients; pour into greased 9 x 13 x 2-inch casserole. Bake in preheated 350-degree oven for 45 minutes.

Dorothy E. Perryman
Alpine H.S., Alpine, Texas

TOMATO-ZUCCHINI CASSEROLE

Butter or margarine
3 zucchini, sliced
1 lg. onion, sliced
3 lg. tomatoes, sliced
1 tsp. salt
2 tsp. basil
1/4 c. grated Parmesan cheese

Grease shallow, oblong casserole with butter. Place half the zucchini in prepared casserole; add half the onion. Add half the tomatoes, then season with half the salt and basil. Sprinkle with half the Parmesan cheese; dot with butter. Repeat layers. Bake in preheated 350-degree oven for 45 minutes.

Clara Rena Stringer
Steubenville H.S., Steubenville, Ohio

EASY TOMATO CASSEROLE

2 c. canned tomatoes
1/4 tsp. salt
5 tbsp. brown sugar

3 slices bread
1/4 c. melted margarine

Place tomatoes in greased casserole; sprinkle with salt and sugar. Crumble bread over top; drizzle margarine evenly over bread. Bake in preheated 350-degree oven for 30 to 40 minutes or until puffy and light brown.

Evelyn Blake
Andrew Lewis Sch., Salem, Virginia

CREAMY TURNIP CASSEROLE

6 med. white or yellow turnips
1/4 tsp. caraway seed
3 tbsp. butter
1/2 c. sour cream, seasoned with salt
Dash of cayenne pepper
1/4 tsp. powdered sweet basil
1 tsp. grated lemon rind
1/3 c. buttered bread crumbs

Wash turnips; peel and quarter. Place in saucepan; add caraway seed and cover with boiling salted water. Cook, uncovered, for about 15 to 20 minutes or until tender. Drain well; turn into generously buttered casserole. Heat sour cream; pour over turnips. Sprinkle with cayenne pepper, basil and lemon rind. Top with bread crumbs. Bake in preheated 400-degree oven for 10 to 12 minutes.

Sister Alphonsa Masterson
St. Francis H.S., Nevada, Missouri

TURNIP SOUFFLE

2 lb. turnips, cubed
1 onion, chopped
3 tbsp. butter
1 can cream of mushroom soup
3/4 tsp. salt
1/2 tsp. pepper
3 well-beaten eggs
Bread crumbs
Parmesan cheese

Cook turnips and onion in small amount of water until tender. Drain and mash. Add remaining ingredients except crumbs and cheese. Pour into buttered casserole; sprinkle top with bread crumbs and Parmesan cheese. Bake in preheated 350-degree oven for 30 minutes.

Mrs. Agnes Foster, Home Ec. Supvr.
State Dept. of Ed., Frankfort, Kentucky

VEGETABLE CASSEROLE ROYALE

1 1/3 c. Minute rice
1/2 tsp. salt
1 1/3 c. boiling water
1   10-oz. package frozen chopped
    broccoli
3 tbsp. slivered almonds
3 tbsp. butter
2 tomatoes, sliced
Salt and pepper to taste
Melted butter
1 egg white
3/4 c. mayonnaise

Add Minute rice and salt to boiling water in saucepan; mix just to moisten all rice. Cover; remove from heat. Let stand for 5 minutes. Cook broccoli according to package directions; drain. Saute almonds in butter until golden brown. Add rice; mix lightly with a fork. Add broccoli; mix well. Spoon into greased 1 1/2-quart casserole; arrange tomatoes over top. Season tomatoes with salt and pepper; brush with melted butter. Broil for 8 to 10 minutes. Beat egg white until soft peaks form. Add mayonnaise; blend well. Spread over tomatoes. Broil for 2 minutes longer.

Mrs. Dorothy M. Scanlon
North Sr. H.S., West Mifflin, Pennsylvania

ZUCCHINI AND TOMATO BAKE

2 tbsp. butter
1/2 c. chopped green pepper
1/4 c. chopped onion
2 c. zucchini, sliced 1/2 in. thick
1/2 c. soft bread crumbs
1/4 c. grated Parmesan cheese
1 tsp. salt
Dash of pepper
2 med. tomatoes, cut in wedges
1/2 c. shredded Monterey Jack
    cheese

Melt butter in small saucepan. Add green pepper and onion; saute until tender. Add zucchini, bread crumbs, Parmesan cheese, salt and pepper; mix well. Place in 1-quart casserole; cover. Bake in preheated 375-degree oven for 20 minutes. Add tomatoes; bake for 10 minutes longer. Remove from oven; sprinkle Monterey Jack cheese over top. Yield: 6 servings.

Robby Effron
Miller Jr. H.S., San Jose, California

Skillet Fettucine

Grain, Pasta, Egg 'n Cheese Casseroles

Cereal, pasta, egg and cheese casseroles are important assets in the culinary repertory of today's budget-minded homemaker. Low in cost, they are high in the nutritional values essential to a well-balanced diet. The interesting and delicious flavor combinations are certain to please family and guests. The wide range of ingredients used in these dishes make them appropriate for inclusion in virtually any type menu. There is a fluffy, mild-flavored Grits Souffle, rich with Gruyere and Parmesan cheese — it's perfect as an accompaniment for roast ham or sausage. Speaking of sausage, why not try the Sausage and Egg Casserole? It's good for breakfast, naturally, but it would also be ideal for a leisurely Sunday night supper!

Among the "spicier" offerings is the Green Chili Enchilada Casserole featuring corn tortillas, green chilies and cream of chicken soup. Great with homemade tacos, this delicious dish can be prepared ahead and served as party fare for casual entertaining. The Rich Chile Verde is a quick and easy casserole combining rice, cottage cheese, green chilies and Cheddar cheese. It's piquant flavor is guaranteed to draw raves from those in your family who are fond of Mexican food.

One of the more unusual recipes included in this section is the Deviled Eggs and Shrimp casserole — spicy with curry, mustard, garlic and just the right tang of lemon juice — what could be better to include on a buffet menu? There are, of course, many more interesting and delicious recipes besides these. Your only problem will be deciding which one to try first!

SKILLET FETTUCINE

1   8-oz. package egg noodles
6 slices bacon
1/2 c. coarsely chopped green
     pepper
1   1 1/2-oz. envelope French's
     spaghetti sauce mix
1   6-oz. can tomato paste
1 3/4 c. water
3 or 4 slices American process
     cheese

Cook noodles according to package directions; drain. Cook bacon in large skillet until crisp. Remove bacon; drain on paper toweling. Crumble bacon. Drain off all except 1 table-spoon drippings from skillet. Add green pepper to drippings; cook until tender, but not brown. Add spaghetti sauce mix, tomato paste and water; bring to a boil, stirring occasionally. Reduce heat; simmer for 10 minutes. Stir in noodles and bacon; simmer for 5 to 10 minutes longer. Cut cheese into strips; arrange over noodles. Yield: 4 servings.

Photograph for this recipe on page 154.

DEVILED EGGS AND SHRIMP

12 med. hard-cooked eggs
1 tbsp. parsley flakes
2 tbsp. mayonnaise
2 tsp. lemon juice
1/8 tsp. garlic powder
1/8 tsp. curry powder
2 tbsp. melted butter
3 tbsp. flour
2 tsp. prepared mustard
3/4 c. milk
Salt and pepper to taste
1 lb. frozen cooked and cleaned
     shrimp, thawed

Cut the eggs in half lengthwise, then remove yolks. Mash yolks. Add parsley, mayonnaise, lemon juice, garlic powder, curry powder, butter, flour and mustard. Mix well. Add milk, salt and pepper; mix until smooth. Place egg whites, cavity sides up, in single layer in greased 10-inch square casserole. Place a shrimp in the center of each egg white; tuck remaining shrimp around whites. Spoon yolk mixture over top. Bake, covered, in preheated 350-degree oven for about 30 minutes. Yield: 12 servings.

Mrs. Cora E. Fagre
Centaurus H.S., Lafayette, Colorado

PUFFY EGG CASSEROLE

2 tbsp. butter
4 slices bread
1 c. milk
Salt and pepper to taste
1 c. grated cheese
4 eggs, separated

Spread butter on bread; cut in 1-inch squares. Combine bread, milk, salt, pepper and cheese in mixing bowl. Beat egg yolks until light and fluffy; stir into cheese mixture. Fold in stiffly beaten egg whites. Turn into 9-inch square pan. Bake, uncovered, in preheated 325-degree oven for 30 to 35 minutes.

Opal Pruitt
Western H.S., Buda, Illinois

DEVILED EGGS AND RICE

1/2 c. minced onion
1/4 c. minced green pepper
2 tbsp. margarine
1/2 c. milk
1 can mushroom soup
2 c. cooked rice
1 c. diced cooked ham or Spam
7 Deviled Eggs
3/4 c. grated American cheese
1 c. soft buttered bread crumbs

Cook onion and green pepper in margarine in saucepan until onion is tender. Combine milk and soup in bowl. Mix rice and ham with 3/4 of the soup mixture. Add onion mixture; mix well. Place in greased casserole; top with Deviled Eggs. Pour remaining soup mixture over eggs; sprinkle with cheese, then with crumbs. Bake in preheated 350-degree oven for 30 minutes.

Deviled Eggs

7 hard-boiled eggs
1/2 tsp. salt
1/8 tsp. pepper
1 tsp. prepared mustard
1 tsp. prepared horseradish
1 tsp. minced parsley
1/4 c. mayonnaise

Cut eggs in half lengthwise. Remove egg yolks from egg whites; place yolks in bowl. Mash well. Add salt, pepper, mustard, horseradish and parsley; mix well. Add mayonnaise; stir until combined. Fill egg whites with yolk mixture.

Jolinda Willis
Northern Burlington Co. Reg. H.S.
Columbus, New Jersey

Crunchy Baked Eggs Au Gratin

CRUNCHY BAKED EGGS AU GRATIN

 3 tbsp. shortening
 1/4 c. flour
 1/8 tsp. paprika
 1 tsp. salt
 2 c. milk
 2 tsp. Angostura aromatic bitters
 2 tbsp. chopped green pepper
 1/2 c. grated American cheese
 3 c. toasted bread cubes
 6 hard-cooked eggs, halved

Melt shortening in a saucepan; stir in flour, paprika and salt. Stir in milk gradually; cook over low heat, stirring constantly, until smooth and thick. Add bitters, green pepper and cheese; stir until cheese has melted. Fold in 2 cups bread cubes. Arrange eggs in well-greased 1 1/2-quart casserole or deep skillet; pour cheese sauce over eggs. Top sauce with remaining bread cubes. Bake in preheated 350-degree oven for 20 minutes or until heated through. Yield: 6 servings.

BUBBLY BRUNCH EGGS

 Margarine
 1/4 c. flour
 1/4 tsp. salt
 1/8 tsp. pepper
 1 1/4 tsp. dry mustard
 2 c. milk
 1 c. grated American cheese
 1 c. cooked cubed ham
 1 2 1/2-oz. jar sliced mushrooms,
    drained
 6 hard-cooked eggs, sliced
 1 1/2 c. Special K cereal

Melt 1/4 cup margarine in medium-sized saucepan over low heat; stir in flour and seasonings. Remove from heat. Add milk gradually, stirring until smooth. Return to medium heat and cook, stirring constantly, until bubbly and thickened. Add cheese; mix until blended. Remove from heat. Place equal portions of ham, mushrooms and eggs evenly into 6 well-buttered 10-ounce casseroles. Pour about 1/2 cup sauce over each portion. Place dishes on baking sheet. Bake in preheated 350-degree oven for about 20 minutes or until thoroughly heated and bubbly. Melt 1 tablespoon margarine in medium frypan about 10 minutes before serving. Add cereal; stir to coat. Remove casseroles from oven. Sprinkle 2 rounded measuring tablespoons of warm cereal in a ring around the top edge of each casserole just before serving. Yield: 6 servings.

Mrs. Alice Sheppard
South Jr. H.S., Grand Forks, North Dakota

CREAMY DEVILED EGG AND MUSHROOM CASSEROLE

6 hard-boiled eggs
1/2 tsp. salt
1/2 tsp. pepper
1/2 tsp. dry mustard
Dash of Worcestershire sauce
1 sm. can chopped mushrooms,
   drained
Mayonnaise
2 c. white sauce
Bread crumbs
1 c. grated sharp cheese
Paprika

Cut eggs in half lengthwise. Remove egg yolks from egg whites; place yolks in bowl. Mash until smooth. Add seasonings, mushrooms and enough mayonnaise to moisten; mix well. Fill egg whites with yolk mixture. Arrange half the eggs in casserole; pour half the white sauce over eggs. Repeat layers. Cover with bread crumbs; add cheese. Bake in preheated 350-degree oven until heated through and cheese is melted; sprinkle with paprika.

Mrs. Norman Sands
Ware Co. H.S., Waycross, Georgia

CURRIED EGG AND SHRIMP CASSEROLE

8 hard-boiled eggs
1/3 c. mayonnaise or salad dressing
1/4 tsp. curry powder
Paprika
Salt and pepper to taste
1 c. rice, cooked
2 tbsp. butter
2 tbsp. flour
1 c. milk
1/2 c. grated cheese
1   10-oz. can cream of shrimp soup

Cut the eggs in half lengthwise, then remove yolks and mash. Mix yolks with mayonnaise, curry, paprika, salt and pepper, then fill egg whites. Place the rice in a baking dish; arrange stuffed eggs on top. Melt butter in saucepan; stir in flour until smooth. Add milk gradually, stirring constantly until thick and smooth. Stir in cheese and soup; heat through. Pour over eggs. Bake in preheated 350-degree oven until heated through and bubbly.

Mrs. Marilyn Fritch
Hawthorne Jr. H.S., Wauwatosa, Wisconsin

EGG BREAKFAST

6 eggs
3 c. milk
3/4 tsp. dry mustard
Dash of salt
1/4 tsp. onion salt
2 tbsp. parsley
1 sm. onion, chopped
2 c. shredded cheese
1/2 green pepper, diced
Chopped cooked ham or bacon
   to taste
10 slices dry bread, cubed

Combine eggs, milk, mustard, salt, onion salt and parsley; beat until blended. Add onion, cheese, green pepper and ham. Stir in bread. Pour into greased 13 x 9-inch baking pan. Bake in preheated 350-degree oven for 20 minutes. Reduce oven temperature to 325 degrees; bake for 25 minutes longer.

Suzanne Reed
Shawnee Mission East H.S.
Shawnee Mission, Kansas

CHEESE AND EGG CASSEROLE

2 c. cracker crumbs
1 lb. cheese, coarsely grated
6 hard-cooked eggs, coarsely chopped
3 tbsp. chopped parsley
3 c. milk
3/4 tsp. Worcestershire sauce
1/2 tsp. dry mustard
Juice of 1 lemon
Salt and pepper to taste
2 eggs, well beaten

Arrange alternate layers of cracker crumbs, cheese, eggs and parsley in baking dish or casserole. Heat milk in saucepan until lukewarm. Add Worcestershire sauce, mustard, lemon juice, salt and pepper; mix well. Add the eggs slowly, stirring constantly. Pour over layers in casserole; shake gently to distribute liquid evenly. Bake in preheated 350-degree oven for 40 to 45 minutes. Yield: 6 servings.

Magdalene Beekler
Mount Saint Benedict Acad., Crookston, Minnesota

EGGS AU GRATIN

1/4 c. butter
6 tbsp. flour
3 c. milk
1 tsp. salt

1/4 tsp. pepper
1/4 tsp. celery salt
2 tbsp. chopped green pepper
2 tbsp. chopped parsley
2/3 c. pimento cheese
6 hard-cooked eggs, sliced
1/2 c. cracker crumbs
3 tbsp. melted butter

Melt butter in a saucepan, then blend in flour. Add milk gradually, stirring constantly. Cook and stir until thickened. Add salt, pepper, celery salt, green pepper, parsley and cheese; mix well. Add eggs to sauce, then spoon into a baking dish. Combine crumbs and melted butter; sprinkle over egg mixture. Bake in preheated 350-degree oven for 20 minutes or until browned.

Mrs. Frances Detmer
Weeping Water H.S., Weeping Water, Nebraska

PECAN ROAST

3/4 c. chopped onions
2 c. chopped celery
3 tbsp. minced parsley
1/2 c. butter
1 pt. cottage cheese
4 c. ground pecans
2 c. bread crumbs
3 tsp. salt
10 eggs, beaten
1 qt. milk

Saute onions, celery and parsley in butter. Add remaining ingredients; mix well. Pour into 9 x 13 x 2-inch casserole. Bake in preheated 350-degree oven for 45 minutes to 1 hour.

Gravy

1/2 c. butter
1/2 c. sifted flour
1 1/2 tsp. salt
4 lg. cans mushrooms, drained and
    juice reserved
Milk or half and half
Paprika to taste
1/2 tsp. garlic salt
1/2 tsp. onion salt
Spice Islands seasoning salt
    to taste
1 env. spaghetti sauce mix

Melt butter in a large saucepan; stir in flour and salt to make a smooth paste. Add part of the reserved mushroom juice and enough milk to make a thick gravy, stirring constantly. Stir in seasonings, sauce mix and mushrooms; cook until well blended and bubbly. Serve over roast.

Gloria Taylor
Laurelwood Adventist H.S., Gaston, Oregon

CHEESE FONDUE CASSEROLE

2 c. milk
3 eggs
1 tsp. salt
1 tsp. dry mustard
10 slices thin bread, buttered
1/2 c. cubed Cheddar cheese
1 can cream of chicken soup
1 can cream of mushroom soup

Combine milk, eggs, salt and mustard with wire whip until blended. Cut crusts from bread slices, then cut each slice into 9 pieces. Arrange alternate layers of bread and cheese in buttered 1 1/2-quart casserole, beginning and ending with bread. Pour milk mixture over bread. Lift around edge with fork. Place casserole in pan of water. Bake in preheated 350-degree oven for 1 hour. Combine soups in saucepan, then heat through. Serve as a sauce.

Mrs. Linda Anderson
Somonauk H.S., Somonauk, Illinois

DELICIOUS HOT SANDWICH CASSEROLE

12 slices bread
1 12-oz. package Cheddar cheese
    slices
3 tbsp. prepared mustard
6 eggs
1 tbsp. Worcestershire sauce
1/8 tsp. garlic salt
1 tsp. salt
1/4 tsp. dry mustard
5 c. milk

Remove crust from bread; place 6 slices in a shallow buttered baking dish. Place cheese over bread; spread with prepared mustard. Cover with remaining bread. Beat eggs until thick and foamy; beat in seasonings. Add milk; pour over sandwiches. Refrigerate for at least 2 hours. Remove from refrigerator 30 minutes before baking. Bake in preheated 325-degree oven for 1 hour or until fluffy and browned. Serve hot.

Elsie Klassen
Geores P. Vanier Sch., Donnelly, Alberta, Canada

BAKED EGGS IN CASSEROLE

5 oz. boiled ham, thinly sliced
6 hard-cooked eggs, sliced
Salt to taste
1 1/2 c. cream of chicken soup
2 tbsp. bread crumbs
1/2 c. grated Swiss cheese
Dash of paprika

Cut ham into thin strips. Arrange layers of ham and eggs in 1 1/2-quart casserole. Season with salt, then pour in soup. Sprinkle with bread crumbs, Swiss cheese and paprika. Bake in preheated 375-degree oven for 12 to 15 minutes or until cheese is bubbly and golden brown. Yield: 4 servings.

Mrs. Anne Beatty Ransing
Miami-Palmetto Sr. H.S., Miami, Florida

BRUNCH SAUSAGE AND EGGS

1 lb. sausage
1/3 c. (about) catsup
6 eggs
Vinegar
Salt and pepper to taste

Cut sausage in 1-inch lengths. Fry sausage in skillet until brown, then place in casserole. Spread catsup generously over sausage. Break eggs carefully on top of catsup. Sprinkle vinegar on egg whites. Season with salt and pepper. Bake in preheated 325-degree oven until eggs are cooked to desired doneness. Yield: 4-6 servings.

Mrs. Dorothy J. Hemenway
W. Boylston Jr.-Sr. H.S.
W. Boylston, Massachusetts

SWISS CHEESE-EGG BAKE

2 c. bread cubes
1 c. milk
8 eggs
1/2 tsp. salt
1/4 c. butter
8 slices cooked bacon, crumbled
3/4 to 1 lb. Swiss cheese, grated
  or shredded
1 c. bread crumbs

Soak bread cubes in milk. Place eggs and salt in blender container; process until well beaten. Melt butter in skillet. Add eggs; cook over low heat, stirring, until eggs are just set. Drain bread cubes; mix with eggs. Remove from heat; place in large, buttered casserole. May be refrigerated and baked later, if desired. Sprinkle bacon over egg mixture, then sprinkle with cheese. Sprinkle with bread crumbs. Bake in preheated 350-degree oven for 20 to 25 minutes. May be baked at 400 degrees for 15 minutes, if desired.

Mrs. Jean McOmber
Spring Lake H.S., Spring Lake, Michigan

EGG AND VEGETABLE CASSEROLE

2 c. canned mixed vegetables, drained
6 hard-cooked eggs, coarsely chopped
1/3 c. finely chopped onion
1/2 c. sliced olives
1/4 c. chopped pimento
1   10 1/2-oz. can cream of mushroom
  soup
1/2 tsp. salt
1/4 c. crushed Shredded Wheat
1/4 c. shredded Cheddar cheese

Combine mixed vegetables, eggs, onion, olives, pimento, soup and salt; place in greased 1-quart casserole. Mix Shredded Wheat and cheese; sprinkle over egg mixture. Bake in preheated 350-degree oven until bubbly. Yield: 6 servings.

Mrs. Paula Calhoun
Fisher H.S., Fisher, Illinois

GREEN CHILI-ENCHILADA CASSEROLE

3 cans cream of chicken soup
1 can evaporated milk
Salt to taste
1 c. sour cream
1   7-oz. can green chilies, diced
24 corn tortillas, cut in eighths
1 lb. sharp Cheddar cheese,
  shredded
1 med. onion, finely chopped

Combine soup, milk, salt, sour cream and chilies in large saucepan. Heat to just under boiling point. Spread layers of sauce, tortillas, sauce, cheese and onion in well-greased 4-quart casserole. Continue layers until all ingredients are used. Bake, uncovered, in preheated 350-degree oven for about 45 minutes or until hot and bubbly. Yield: 12 servings.

Mrs. Carolyn K. Simpson
Burbank Sr. H.S., Burbank, California

STRATA

8 slices day-old bread
1   8-oz. package Cheddar cheese
    slices
4 eggs, beaten
2 1/2 c. milk
1 tbsp. minced onion
1 1/2 tsp. salt
1/2 tsp. prepared mustard

Trim crust from 5 slices bread; cut in half diagonally. Place trim and remaining 3 slices of bread in 8 or 9-inch square baking dish. Top with cheese. Arrange the 10 trimmed triangles in 2 rows on top of cheese. Points should overlap bases. Blend eggs with the milk, onion, salt and mustard. Pour over the bread and cheese. Cover with foil. Let stand for 1 hour at room temperature or for several hours in refrigerator. Remove foil. Bake in preheated 325-degree oven for 1 hour or until knife inserted in center comes out clean.

Mrs. Margaret Morgan
Austin H.S., Austin, Minnesota

BACK-TO-SCHOOL CASSEROLE

4 tbsp. butter
3 tbsp. flour
1 1/4 tsp. salt
2 c. milk
2 tsp. prepared mustard
1 c. shredded pasteurized American
    process cheese
3 c. cooked rice
6 slices crisp-cooked bacon,
    crumbled
6 tomato slices

Melt 3 tablespoons butter in saucepan; blend in flour and 1 teaspoon salt. Stir in milk; cook, stirring, until smooth and thickened. Add mustard and cheese; stir until melted. Stir in rice and bacon; pour into buttered 1 1/2-quart shallow casserole. Bake in preheated 375-degree oven for 20 minutes. Arrange tomato slices on rice mixture; dot with remaining butter. Sprinkle with remaining salt; bake for 5 minutes longer. Yield: 6 servings.

Back-To-School Casserole

GRITS AND CHEESE

1/2 tsp. salt
2 1/2 c. water
1/2 c. grits
1/2 c. cubed sharp cheese
1/2 c. margarine
1 tbsp. Tabasco sauce
2 tbsp. Worcestershire sauce
2 cloves of garlic, minced
1 egg, beaten

Combine salt and water in medium saucepan; bring to a boil. Add grits, stirring constantly. Reduce heat; cook, stirring frequently, for about 15 minutes or until thick. Add cheese cubes, margarine, sauces, garlic and egg; mix well. Turn into greased baking dish. Bake in preheated 350-degree oven for about 50 minutes or until set.

Mrs. Emely Sundbeck
Manor H.S., Manor, Texas

GRITS SOUFFLE

4 c. milk
1 pkg. Gruyere cheese
1/2 c. butter
1 tsp. salt
1/8 tsp. pepper
1 c. instant grits
1/3 c. Parmesan cheese
1/3 c. melted butter

Pour milk in a double boiler; bring to a boil. Add Gruyere cheese, butter, salt and pepper; bring to a boil. Add grits slowly, stirring constantly. Cook until soft. Beat grits mixture with electric mixer until smooth. Pour into baking dish and sprinkle with Parmesan cheese. Pour melted butter over top; place in pan of water. Bake in preheated 350-degree oven for 30 minutes.

Pat Speakes
Bryan Station Sr. H.S., Lexington, Kentucky

COTTAGE CHEESE-OATMEAL ROAST

1 c. cottage cheese
1 c. quick-cooking oatmeal
2 eggs, beaten
1 1/4 tsp. savory
1 pkg. George Washington broth
2 tbsp. onion, chopped
1 tbsp. parsley leaves

1/2 tsp. sage
1/2 tsp. salt
1 can mushroom soup

Mix all ingredients together; pour into a greased casserole. Bake in a preheated 350-degree oven for 45 minutes.

Darlene Ehman
Laurelwood Acad., Gaston, Oregon

MEXICAN HOMINY CASSEROLE

1 can yellow hominy
1 med. onion, chopped
3/4 c. grated Cheddar cheese
1 tbsp. margarine
1 tbsp. flour
1 tbsp. chili powder
1 tsp. salt

Drain hominy, reserving the liquid. Place hominy, onion and 1/2 cup grated cheese in 1 1/2-quart casserole. Blend reserved liquid, margarine, flour, chili powder and salt in saucepan; cook, stirring constantly, over medium heat until slightly thickened. Pour over hominy mixture and top with remaining cheese. Bake in preheated 300-degree oven for 15 to 20 minutes.

Beth Cozart
Ballinger H.S., Ballinger, Texas

CHILI-HOMINY CASSEROLE

1 1-lb. 13-oz. can hominy,
  drained
2 tbsp. bacon drippings
Salt and pepper to taste
1 2-oz. jar pimentos
1 c. grated processed cheese
1 c. coarsely chopped onions
1 19-oz. can chili
Sliced olives

Fry hominy in bacon drippings in skillet for several minutes. Add salt, pepper and pimentos. Place hominy in a greased baking dish. Sprinkle a layer of cheese and onions on the hominy. Spread the chili over the cheese. Add remaining cheese and onions to the top. Garnish with sliced olives. Bake in preheated 350-degree oven for about 20 minutes or until heated through. Do not overcook; onions should be crisp. Yield: 4-6 servings.

Ella Jo Adams
Allen Sr. H.S., Allen, Texas

Macaroni-Nut Casserole

MACARONI-NUT CASSEROLE

Salt
1 8-oz. package elbow macaroni
2 tbsp. salad oil
1/4 c. sesame seed
4 eggs
1/3 c. chopped onion
1 1/2 c. chopped celery
1 c. chopped cashew nuts
1 c. chopped walnuts
1 lb. creamed cottage cheese
2 tbsp. chopped chives
1/4 c. chopped parsley
1 1/2 tsp. sea salt or kosher salt
1/4 tsp. pepper
1/2 tsp. crushed thyme leaves
1/4 c. wheat germ

Add 1 tablespoon salt to 3 quarts rapidly boiling water; add macaroni gradually so that water continues to boil. Cook, stirring occasionally, until macaroni is just tender; drain in colander. Heat oil in small skillet. Add sesame seed; cook, stirring, until brown. Beat eggs in large bowl. Add macaroni, sesame seed and oil, salt to taste and remaining ingredients; toss lightly until combined. Spoon into 2-quart casserole. Bake in preheated 375-degree oven for 50 to 55 minutes or until set. Garnish with parsley sprigs. Yield: 8 servings.

CREAMY MACARONI AND CHEESE

3 c. macaroni
1 tsp. salt

6 c. boiling water
2 1/4 c. grated sharp American cheese
2 c. medium white sauce
1/2 c. buttered bread crumbs

Stir macaroni and salt in boiling water; cook until tender. Drain well. Add 2 cups cheese to white sauce; stir until cheese is melted. Mix macaroni and cheese sauce together; pour into medium-sized casserole. Top with bread crumbs and remaining cheese. Bake in preheated 375-degree oven for 25 minutes.

Mildred T. Marsh
Jones H.S., Orlando, Florida

DOUBLE-GOOD MANICOTTI

1 c. chopped onion
1 clove of garlic, minced
2 tbsp. margarine
1 tbsp. Italian seasoning
2 1/2 tsp. salt
1 tsp. sugar
4 8-oz. cans tomato sauce
1 1-lb. can tomatoes
1 12-oz. package manicotti noodles
1 lb. ground beef
1/2 c. chopped walnuts
2 eggs
1 pkg. frozen chopped spinach, thawed and drained
1 1/2 c. cream-style cottage cheese
1 3-oz. package cream cheese
1 8-oz. package sliced mozzarella cheese

Saute onion and garlic in margarine until soft. Add Italian seasoning, 1 teaspoon salt, sugar, tomato sauce and tomatoes; simmer for 15 minutes. Cook noodles according to package directions; place in pan of cold water. Saute beef until brown; stir in 1 teaspoon salt, walnuts, 1 egg and half the spinach. Combine cottage cheese, cream cheese, 1/2 teaspoon salt, remaining egg and remaining spinach. Drain noodles. Fill half the noodles with beef mixture; fill remaining noodles with cheese mixture. Spoon 2 cups tomato sauce in 13 x 9 x 2-inch baking dish. Arrange noodles on top; spoon remaining sauce over noodles. Bake, covered, in preheated 350-degree oven for 30 minutes. Uncover; arrange mozzarella cheese over top. Bake for 10 minutes longer.

Betty Lakey
Paris Gibson Jr. H.S., Great Falls, Montana

CRUSTY MACARONI AND CHEESE

1 c. macaroni
1 1/2 tsp. butter or margarine
1 1/2 tbsp. flour
1/2 tsp. salt
1/8 tsp. pepper
1 1/2 c. milk
1 1/3 c. grated Cheddar cheese
1/4 c. bread crumbs
Margarine

Cook macaroni according to package directions; drain and rinse. Melt butter over low heat. Add flour; blend thoroughly. Add salt and pepper. Add milk all at once. Cook over moderate heat, stirring constantly, until thickened. Add 1 cup cheese to hot white sauce. Stir until blended. Combine macaroni and cheese sauce. Sprinkle a layer of crumbs in a well-greased shallow 1-quart baking dish. Add macaroni mixture. Top with remaining cheese and crumbs. Dot with margarine. Bake in preheated 400-degree oven for 30 minutes or until bubbly and brown. Chunks of cooked ham or chicken may be added to the macaroni before baking. Yield: 4 servings.

Sandra Adkins
Mogadore H.S., Mogadore, Ohio

CHEESE-MUSHROOM CASSEROLE

1 pkg. macaroni
1/2 c. chopped green pepper
1/2 c. chopped onion
1 can cream of mushroom soup
1/2 c. sliced mushrooms (opt.)
1 c. mayonnaise
1 lb. hoop cheese, grated
1/2 c. chopped pimento
Crushed crackers

Cook macaroni in boiling salted water until tender; drain. Cook green pepper and onion in small amount of fat in skillet until tender. Combine all ingredients except crackers in large mixing bowl, then pour into 2 buttered medium casseroles or 1 large casserole. Top with crushed crackers. Bake in preheated 350-degree oven for 20 minutes or until cheese melts and cracker crumbs are browned. Yield: 12 servings.

Mildred H. Morris
Reeltown H.S., Notasulga, Alabama

LINDA'S MACARONI AND CHEESE BAKE

4 c. cooked macaroni
1/2 lb. sliced sharp Cheddar cheese
1 1/2 stack packs saltine crackers
1 med. onion, finely chopped
1 tsp. salt
1/4 tsp. pepper
3 c. milk
Butter

Grease 2-quart casserole. Arrange 2 cups macaroni in casserole; spread 1/2 of the cheese over macaroni. Cover with 1/2 of the crackers; spoon onion over crackers. Add remaining macaroni; cover with remaining cheese. Sprinkle seasonings over cheese; place remaining crackers over cheese. Pour milk carefully around edges of crackers; dot with butter. Bake in preheated 400-degree oven for 1 hour. Yield: 4-6 servings.

Linda B. Wilbur
North Middle Sch., Westford, Massachusetts

ROAST LENTIL CASSEROLE

2 1/2 c. cooked lentils
2 eggs, beaten
1 c. ground nuts
1 onion, grated
1 c. evaporated milk
1 1/2 c. bread crumbs
1/2 tsp. sage
1/2 c. oil
1/2 tsp. Accent
1/2 tsp. salt

Combine lentils, eggs, nuts, onion, milk, bread crumbs, sage, oil, Accent and salt in a large bowl; mix well. Pour into a greased casserole. Bake in preheated 350-degree oven for 45 minutes or until firm. Serve with cranberry sauce.

Helen B. Boots
Lakeland Village Sch., Medical Lake, Washington

BAGDAD

1/2 c. chopped onions
1/2 c. chopped celery
1 sm. can mushrooms
2 tbsp. oil
2 tbsp. flour
1 can mushroom soup
1/4 c. milk

1 No. 303 can Chinese noodles
1/4 to 1/2 c. roasted cashews

Saute onions, celery and mushrooms in oil until golden. Stir in flour, mushroom soup and milk; cook until thick, stirring constantly. Add noodles and cashews; pour into casserole. Bake in preheated 375-degree oven for 30 minutes or until bubbly.

Darlene Ehman
Laurelwood Acad., Gaston, Oregon

NOODLE CARNIVAL

Salt
1 8-oz. package medium noodles
2 c. grated sharp Cheddar cheese
1/3 c. chopped pimentos
1/4 c. finely chopped green pepper
1/4 c. finely chopped onion
Pepper to taste
Paprika

Add 1 tablespoon salt to 3 quarts rapidly boiling water; add noodles gradually so that water continues to boil. Cook, uncovered, until tender, stirring occasionally. Drain in colander. Combine noodles and all remaining ingredients except paprika; mix well. Turn into greased 1 1/2-quart casserole; sprinkle with paprika. Bake, covered, in preheated 350-degree oven for 20 minutes. Yield: 4-6 servings.

Sister Mary Rosario, SC
Archbishop Alter H.S., Kettering, Ohio

FOUR-WAY DAIRY CASSEROLE

1 6-oz. package wide egg noodles
1 carton cottage cheese
1 carton sour cream
1/4 c. milk
1 c. cubed Cheddar cheese
1 tbsp. chopped pimento
1/4 tsp. Worcestershire sauce
1/4 tsp. salt
Olives

Cook noodles according to package directions; drain. Combine noodles, cottage cheese, sour cream, milk, cheese, pimento, Worcestershire sauce and salt; toss until well mixed. Turn into a buttered casserole. Bake in a preheated 325-degree oven for 20 to 30 minutes. Garnish with olives.

Patricia Johnson
Disque Jr. H.S., Gadsden, Alabama

BROWN RICE

1/4 lb. margarine
2 med. onions, thinly sliced
1 1/2 c. packaged precooked rice
2 cans beef consomme
Blanched sliced almonds (opt.)

Melt margarine in skillet; add onions. Cook until brown. Spoon onions and margarine in casserole. Sprinkle rice over onion mixture. Pour consomme over all. Bake in preheated 350-degree oven until slightly dry. Sprinkle almonds over top of rice mixture. Broil until almonds are brown.

Evelyn W. Knowles
Charles L. Coon Jr. H.S., Wilson, North Carolina

SPINACH-RICE BAKE

1 10-oz. package frozen chopped
  spinach
2 eggs, slightly beaten
2 c. milk
3/4 c. packaged precooked rice
1/3 c. finely chopped onion
1 c. shredded sharp American
  cheese
1/2 tsp. garlic salt

Cook spinach according to package directions, then drain. Combine eggs and milk. Add rice, onion, spinach, cheese and garlic salt. Pour into 10 x 6 x 1 1/2-inch baking dish. Bake in preheated 325-degree oven for 35 to 40 minutes or until firm. Yield: 4-6 servings.

Mrs. Mary Johnson
Deshler Pub. Sch., Deshler, Nebraska

ARKANSAS RICE CASSEROLE

1/2 c. margarine
1 c. rice
1 can cream of mushroom soup
1 can onion soup
2 chicken bouillon cubes

Melt margarine in a skillet. Add rice; cook and stir until brown. Add soups. Dissolve bouillon cubes in 1 soup can boiling water; add to rice mixture. Turn into buttered casserole. Bake in preheated 350-degree oven for 1 hour. Yield: 6-8 servings.

Blanche Young
Northeast H.S., North Little Rock, Arkansas

WILD RICE AND MUSHROOM CASSEROLE

1 c. wild rice
1/4 tsp. salt
1/4 tsp. pepper
1/4 tsp. sage
1/8 tsp. thyme
1 tsp. grated onion
2 tbsp. melted butter
1/4 c. slivered almonds
1 can mushroom stems and pieces

Wash rice thoroughly. Cover with salted water; bring to a boil. Cook without stirring for 30 minutes or until tender. Drain; dry and fluff by shaking pan over very low heat for 10 to 15 minutes. Add remaining ingredients and pile into greased 2-quart casserole. Bake, covered, in preheated 325-degree oven for 1 hour.

Susan Ehli
Bloomington, Minnesota

RICE-CHEESE RISOTTO

1 c. chopped onion
Margarine
1 c. rice
1 1/2 c. water
1   3-oz. can sliced mushrooms
Dash of pepper
2 c. tomatoes
2 chicken bouillon cubes
1 tsp. salt
8 oz. Cheddar cheese, shredded

Cook onion in margarine in skillet. Stir in rice; cook until lightly browned. Add remaining ingredients except cheese. Bring to a boil, stirring until bouillon cubes are dissolved. Combine rice mixture and 1 1/2 cups cheese in 1 1/2-quart casserole. Bake in preheated 350-degree oven for 45 minutes. Sprinkle with remaining cheese; bake until cheese melts. Yield: 8 servings.

Mrs. Barbara Goedicke
Lindsay Thurber Comp. H.S.
Red Deer, Alberta, Canada

RICE CHILI VERDE

1 c. sour cream
1 c. cottage cheese
2 tbsp. seeded chopped canned
*   green chilies*

3 c. cooked rice
2/3 lb. Monterey Jack cheese, cut
*   into thin slices*
1/2 c. shredded Cheddar cheese

Combine sour cream, cottage cheese and chilies. Arrange layers of rice, sour cream mixture and cheese slices in buttered 2-quart casserole, ending with rice. Bake, uncovered, in preheated 300-degree oven for about 30 minutes. Remove from oven; sprinkle with Cheddar cheese. Bake for 5 minutes longer.

Barsha Elzey
Terra Linda H.S., San Rafael, California

RICE AND BROCCOLI CASSEROLE

1 c. cooked rice
1/2 c. chopped onion
1/2 c. chopped celery
Butter
2 pkg. frozen chopped broccoli
1 can cream of chicken soup
1 can cream of mushroom soup
1 sm. jar Cheez Whiz
Grated Parmesan cheese

Form rice into crust in a greased large casserole. Saute onion and celery in small amount of butter in skillet. Cook broccoli according to package directions. Combine onion mixture, broccoli, soups and Cheez Whiz. Pour over rice. Sprinkle with Parmesan cheese. Bake in preheated 350-degree oven for 10 to 20 minutes or until bubbly and lightly browned.

Susan Knopfle
Edison Jr. H.S., Sioux Falls, South Dakota

HEARTY RICE CASSEROLE

3 c. cooked rice
1 can Spam or Treet, cubed
1 sm. can stewed tomatoes
1 sm. onion, chopped
Salt and pepper to taste
6 slices American cheese

Combine the rice, Spam, tomatoes, onion, salt and pepper in a large bowl; toss until well mixed. Place in 2-quart casserole. Place cheese slices on top. Bake, uncovered, in preheated 325-degree oven for 25 minutes.

Mrs. Goldie Thompson
Lake Orion Jr. H.S. West, Lake Orion, Michigan

RICE AND MUSHROOM CASSEROLE

3 onions, sliced
1/2 c. butter
2 c. fresh or canned mushrooms
1 can consomme
1 consomme can water
1 c. converted rice
Salt and pepper to taste

Saute onions in butter in skillet. Slice mushrooms; saute for 3 to 4 minutes. Combine consomme and water in saucepan; heat and stir until well mixed. Combine onions, mushrooms, consomme, rice, salt and pepper; turn into greased 1 1/2-quart casserole. Bake in preheated 350-degree oven for 45 minutes to 1 hour, stirring frequently. Yield: 5-6 servings.

Mrs. Ruth K. Ockman
Maplewood Jr. H.S., Maplewood, New Jersey

BAYTOWN GREEN RICE

2 c. rice
1 1/2 c. milk
1/2 c. salad oil
1 c. chopped parsley
1 c. chopped green onion tops
1 c. chopped green peppers
2 cloves of garlic, crushed
Seasoned salt to taste
1 lb. grated Cheddar cheese

Cook rice according to package directions; let cool. Add milk, salad oil, parsley, onions, peppers and garlic. Season with seasoned salt. Add cheese and mix well. Pour in a 8 x 12 x 2-inch casserole. Bake in preheated 300-degree oven for 1 hour. Yield: 15 servings.

Mrs. Elizabeth Muennink
Cedar Bayou Jr. H.S., Baytown, Texas

GREEN CHILI-RICE CASSEROLE

3/4 lb. Monterey Jack cheese
2 c. sour cream
1 can green chilies, chopped
4 c. cooked rice
Salt and pepper to taste
1/2 c. grated Cheddar cheese

Cut Monterey Jack cheese into strips. Combine sour cream and green chilies; mix well.

Arrange alternate layers of rice, cheese strips and sour cream mixture in buttered casserole. Season with salt and pepper. Bake in preheated 350-degree oven for 15 minutes. Remove from oven; sprinkle grated cheese on top. Bake for 15 minutes longer. Yield: 8-10 servings.

Kathryn Turpen
Eldorado H.S., Albuquerque, New Mexico

GOLDEN RICE BAKE

2 c. cooked rice
3 c. shredded carrots
2 eggs, well beaten
1 1/2 tsp. salt
1/2 c. milk
1/4 tsp. pepper
2 tbsp. minced onion
2 c. grated sharp processed cheese

Combine rice, carrots, eggs, salt, milk, pepper, onion and 1 1/2 cups cheese in a buttered 10 x 7 x 2-inch casserole. Bake in a preheated 350-degree oven for 30 minutes. Sprinkle top with remaining cheese; bake for 15 minutes longer.

Mrs. Leah K. Massey
Smithville Middle Sch., Smithville, Indiana

PARSLIED RICE

2 c. packaged precooked rice
2 3/4 c. boiling water
2 eggs, beaten
2/3 c. salad oil
1 sm. can evaporated milk
3 c. grated sharp cheese
2 cans mushroom soup
2 cans mushrooms
1 lg. onion, chopped
2 c. chopped parsley

Place rice in large bowl. Pour water over rice and let stand for 13 minutes. Combine eggs and oil, then add egg mixture, milk, cheese, soup, mushrooms, onion and parsley to rice. Spoon into shallow baking dishes. Bake in preheated 350-degree oven for 40 minutes. Yield: 10 servings.

Mrs. Mildred Blackwell
Lakeview H.S., Winter Garden, Florida

One-Pot Spaghetti Supper

Skillet Meals In-A-Dish

What a convenience it is for modern homemakers to combine foods and seasonings in one skillet and prepare a delicious meal. These one-dish favorites are an excellent way to stretch meat servings, and give new delightful flavor to meat and vegetable leftovers.

When somehow you manage to have not only your own, but also many of the neighborhood children for supper and you suddenly have to stretch your supply of ground beef, serve Goulash made with ground beef, kidney beans and canned spaghetti, or Chili Con Carne made with ground beef, chopped onion, chili powder and tomatoes. For a quick and nutritious family meal, prepare a Five-Decker Dinner made with ground beef, potatoes, carrots, onions and bacon. For the seafood lovers in your family, serve Shrimp Jambalaya made with shrimp, sweet pepper, mushrooms and Worcestershire sauce.

The following selection of skillet dishes offers a wealth of ideas for preparing easy, nutritious, one-dish meals which are sure to become favorites with your family.

CORNED BEEF AND CABBAGE

1 med. head cabbage, sliced
3 med. potatoes, thinly sliced
3 med. onions, thinly sliced
1 can corned beef, crumbled
1 can cream of mushroom soup
1 soup can water

Arrange cabbage, potatoes and onions in layers in Dutch oven or large kettle. Place corned beef over onions. Stir soup and water together; pour over corned beef. Cook slowly for 45 minutes. Yield: 5 servings.

Mrs. Robin A. Moore
Breckenridge H.S., Breckenridge, Texas

EB-STYLE BEEF STEW

1 lb. beef stew meat
1 onion, diced
1 lg. clove of garlic, minced
1/4 c. chopped parsley
1 can tomato sauce
1 bay leaf
3/4 tsp. minced oregano
3/4 tsp. minced rosemary
1/2 tsp. allspice
Pinch of Accent
Pinch of sugar
Salt and pepper to taste
1/4 c. Burgundy
3 potatoes, quartered
2 carrots, quartered
1 stalk celery, quartered
1 onion, quartered
1 bell pepper, quartered
1/2 pkg. green peas
1/2 c. flour

Saute beef in hot fat until browned. Add diced onion and garlic; saute until golden. Stir in parsley, tomato sauce, seasonings and Burgundy; add water to cover. Simmer for 2 hours or until beef is tender. Stir in quartered vegetables; cook until carrots are almost tender. Add peas; cook until tender. Mix flour with 1 cup water to make a smooth paste; stir into stew. Cook until stew is slightly thickened, stirring frequently. Add more salt and pepper, if needed. Serve over steamed rice, if desired. The stew base can be frozen.

Eileen Silva
Escalon H.S., Escalon, California

PEPPER STEW

6 slices bacon
1 lb. beef stew meat
4 potatoes, cut up
4 green peppers, sliced
2 lg. onions, sliced
1 sm. bottle catsup

Arrange bacon slices in a heavy saucepan. Place beef, potatoes, green peppers and onions in layers over bacon; pour catsup over top. Simmer, covered, for 1 hour and 30 minutes.

Mrs. Eleanor Greenberg
Palisades Park Jr.-Sr. H.S.
Palisades Park, New Jersey

CHICKEN SPAGHETTI

1 3-lb. chicken
2 tbsp. butter
1/2 c. chopped green peppers
1 sm. jar pimento
1 c. chopped celery
1 sm. can mushrooms
1 c. tomato sauce
1 tsp. salt
1 tsp. chili powder
1 lb. spaghetti, cooked

Cook chicken in boiling, salted water to cover until tender. Remove chicken from broth, reserving broth. Remove chicken from bone. Melt butter in heavy saucepan. Add peppers, pimento, celery and mushrooms; saute until tender. Add tomato sauce and seasonings; simmer for 15 minutes. Add 2 cups chicken broth and simmer for 30 minutes longer. Add spaghetti and chicken; cover. Simmer for 30 minutes longer. Stir occasionally to prevent sticking to bottom of pan. Cheese may be sprinkled over chicken mixture after placing in serving dish.

Mrs. Ann McDonald
Jane Long Jr. H.S., Houston, Texas

CHINESE CHICKEN

6 chicken breasts, skinned and
*   boned*
1/4 c. butter
1 c. diced water chestnuts
1 c. bamboo shoots
2 c. diced celery

1 c. frozen Italian green beans
3 c. chicken broth
1/4 c. soy sauce
2 tsp. salt
2 tsp. monosodium glutamate
1 tsp. sugar
1/4 tsp. pepper
2 tbsp. cornstarch

Cut chicken in small pieces; saute in butter until brown. Add water chestnuts, bamboo shoots, celery and green beans; pour in chicken broth. Add soy sauce and seasonings. Cover; let steam for 5 minutes. Combine cornstarch with small amount of water; stir into chicken mixture. Cook until transparent and thick. Serve over rice.

Vicki Sommers
Roosevelt Jr. H.S., Coffeyville, Kansas

BEEF AND CABBAGE DISH

1 lb. ground beef
1 head cabbage, shredded
1 No. 2 1/2 can sauerkraut
1 16-oz. bottle ginger ale
1 10-oz. bottle catsup

Cook ground beef in skillet until brown; drain fat. Place layer of cabbage, sauerkraut and ground beef in 5-quart Dutch oven. Add another layer of cabbage and top with sauerkraut. Combine ginger ale and catsup and pour over ingredients. Cover and simmer for about 2 hours, stirring occasionally. Ground beef may be made into small meatballs and cooked until brown, if desired.

Mrs. Frances A. Feltham
Stroudsburg H.S., Stroudsburg, Pennsylvania

BOUNTIFUL SUMMER CASSEROLE

1 lb. ground beef
2 med. potatoes, diced
1 lg. onion, chopped
1 c. chopped celery
1 c. sliced carrots
1 med. head cabbage
1 lg. green pepper, chopped
2 c. sliced zucchini
1 c. broken pole beans
Salt, pepper and garlic salt
*   to taste*

Cook ground beef in skillet until brown. Add potatoes, onion, celery, carrots, cabbage and green pepper. Cover and simmer for 15 to 20 minutes. Add zucchini and beans and simmer for another 10 to 15 minutes or until vegetables are tender crisp. Season with salt, pepper and garlic salt. Yield: 4-6 servings.

Carolyn S. Heimbuch
Howard D. Crull Intermediate Sch.
Port Huron, Michigan

CHILI CON CARNE

2 tbsp. bacon fat
3/4 c. chopped onions
1 or 2 garlic cloves, minced
1 lb. ground beef
1 tbsp. flour
1/2 tsp. salt
1/2 tsp. pepper
2 to 3 tbsp. chili powder
1 No. 2 can kidney beans, drained
1 No. 2 1/2 can tomatoes
1 6 1/2-oz. can tomato puree

Heat fat in deep large skillet. Add chopped onions and garlic; cook until lightly browned. Add ground beef and sprinkle with flour, salt, pepper and chili powder; cook until brown. Add beans, tomatoes and tomato puree to ground beef mixture. Simmer, covered, for 1 hour.

Mrs. A. S. Rinehardt
Trinity Sr. H.S., Trinity, North Carolina

GROUND BEEF AND CARROTS

1 lb. ground beef
1/2 med. onion, sliced
1 can sliced carrots
1/2 tsp. salt
1/4 tsp. pepper
1/4 to 1/2 tsp. garlic powder
1 tbsp. parsley flakes
2 tbsp. Worcestershire sauce
2 tbsp. soy sauce
2 to 4 drops of Tabasco sauce (opt.)
2 c. cooked rice

Cook ground beef and onion in skillet until brown, then drain. Add carrots and seasonings and simmer for 15 to 20 minutes. Serve over hot rice. Yield: 4-6 servings.

Mrs. Beverly J. LeCompte
Chaparral Jr. H.S., Alamogordo, New Mexico

POOR MAN'S HOT DISH

1 lb. ground beef
1 sm. onion, chopped
Salt and pepper to taste
1 can tomato soup
1 head cabbage, cut in chunks

Cook and stir ground beef and onion in skillet until brown; season with salt and pepper. Add soup; stir until blended. Add cabbage chunks; toss lightly. Cook over low heat for 30 to 40 minutes or until cabbage is tender. Yield: 4-6 servings.

Judith Evans
Desert Elem. Sch., Wamsutter, Wyoming

AMERICAN GOULASH

1 lb. ground beef
3/4 c. chopped mushrooms (opt.)
1 tsp. onion powder
1/4 tsp. garlic powder
3 1/2 c. canned tomatoes
1 tbsp. minced parsley
1 tbsp. salt
1/8 tsp. pepper
1/2 lb. hot partially cooked
   elbow macaroni or spaghetti

Brown beef and mushrooms in large skillet or kettle; add onion powder, garlic powder and tomatoes. Add parsley, salt and pepper; simmer for about 45 minutes. Add macaroni; simmer for about 15 minutes. Serve immediately. Yield: 6-8 servings.

Mrs. Hilda J. Finch
Fort Edward H.S., Fort Edward, New York

BUSY DAY CASSEROLE

3/4 lb. ground beef
1 c. macaroni or spaghetti pieces
1   29-oz. can whole tomatoes
1/2 c. catsup
1/3 c. finely chopped onion
1/3 c. finely chopped green pepper
1 tsp. salt
1/4 tsp. pepper

Brown beef in a 10-inch skillet; add remaining ingredients. Cover and cook for 25 minutes or until macaroni is tender. Yield: 6 servings.

Mrs. Brenda Brandt
Paw Paw H.S., Paw Paw, Michigan

MACARONI-HAMBURGER DISH

1 lb. ground beef
1 med. onion, chopped
2 stalks celery, diced
1   10 1/2-oz. can tomato soup
Salt and pepper to taste
1 pkg. macaroni and cheese mix

Brown ground beef in skillet; add onion, celery, soup, salt and pepper. Simmer for 15 to 20 minutes. Prepare macaroni and cheese mix according to package directions; add to skillet mixture. Simmer until heated through, stirring frequently.

Linda Zylstra
Willapa Valley H.S., Menlo, Washington

SLUMGULLION

2 med. onions, sliced
4 med. stalks celery, finely
   chopped
2 tbsp. cooking oil
1 lb. ground beef
Salt and pepper to taste
1 pkg. large shell macaroni
1   8-oz. can tomato sauce
1 No. 2 can whole tomatoes,
   chopped
1 to 2 c. water
Oregano to taste

Saute onions and celery in oil until soft. Add beef in small pieces and brown. Add salt and pepper. Cook the macaroni according to package directions; drain. Combine onions, celery, beef and macaroni in large pot. Stir, then add tomato sauce, tomatoes, water and oregano. Simmer for several minutes, stirring occasionally. Serve steaming with buttered French bread.

Sister Mary Roselina, B.V.M.
Bellarmine-Jefferson H.S., Burbank, California

EASY SKILLET BEEF CASSEROLE

1 1/2 lb. ground beef
1/2 c. minced onion
1/2 lb. macaroni
1/2 c. chopped green pepper
2   8-oz. cans Spanish-style
   tomato sauce
1 c. water

1 tsp. salt
1/4 tsp. pepper
1 1/2 tbsp. Worcestershire sauce

Brown beef lightly in large skillet, then remove beef from skillet with slotted spoon. Add onion, macaroni and green pepper to drippings and cook until macaroni is yellow. Return beef to skillet; add tomato sauce, water, salt, pepper and Worcestershire sauce. Cover; simmer for 25 minutes or until macaroni is tender.

Betty Ambrose
Lee H.S., Midland, Texas

CHILI MAC

1 lb. ground beef
1 med. onion, chopped
1 med. green pepper, chopped
1 8-oz. package elbow macaroni
1 1-lb. can kidney beans and
   liquid
2 8-oz. cans tomato sauce
1 c. water
1 tsp. chili powder
1 tsp. salt
1 c. shredded Cheddar cheese

Place ground beef, onion and green pepper in large skillet; cook, stirring frequently, until browned. Add remaining ingredients except cheese. Cover; simmer, stirring occasionally, for 15 minutes or until macaroni is tender. Sprinkle cheese over top; heat until cheese is melted. Yield: 4-6 servings.

Sandra Adkins
Mogadore H.S., Mogadore, Ohio

TOMATO-HAMBURGER CASSEROLE

3/4 lb. hamburger
1/4 tsp. pepper
1/2 tsp. chili powder
1 tsp. salt
1 tbsp. steak sauce
1 tbsp. Worcestershire sauce
1 16-oz. can tomatoes
1 c. macaroni

Brown hamburger in skillet; drain off grease. Add pepper, chili powder, salt, steak sauce,

Worcestershire sauce and tomatoes. Simmer while preparing macaroni. Cook macaroni according to package directions; drain. Add to hamburger mixture; simmer for 20 minutes, adding water, if needed. Mixture is better if made a day ahead and reheated. May be served over bread, if desired. Yield: 4-6 servings.

Mrs. Barbara P. Bell
Andrew Lewis H.S., Salem, Virginia

EASY HAMBURGER-NOODLE CASSEROLE

1 lb. hamburger
2 tbsp. finely chopped green
   pepper
1 tbsp. finely chopped onion
1 pkg. sloppy joe seasoning mix
2 c. tomato juice or sauce
2 c. noodles

Cook hamburger in skillet until brown. Add green pepper and onion; cook and stir until tender. Stir in seasoning mix, tomato juice and noodles. Cover and simmer for 10 minutes or until noodles are tender. Yield: 4-6 servings.

Mrs. Margaret Paulus
Ridgewood Jr. H.S., Arnold, Missouri

FAVORITE ALL-PURPOSE DISH

1 lb. ground beef
2 onions, chopped
1/2 c. chopped pimento
1 c. chopped ripe or green olives
2 c. canned tomatoes
4 c. cooked noodles
1 1/2 c. grated cheese
1 6-oz. can mushrooms
Salt and pepper to taste

Cook ground beef in a small amount of fat in skillet until lightly browned, then add onions and pimento. Add olives and tomatoes and simmer for 3 minutes. Add noodles, cheese, mushrooms, salt and pepper and cook, covered, for 30 minutes. Remove cover and cook for 20 minutes longer.

Mrs. Sue Stilley
Forestburg H.S., Forestburg, Texas

LASAGNA WITH A DIFFERENCE

1 lb. ground beef
1/2 med. onion, chopped
1 clove of garlic, minced
2 tsp. oregano
1 tsp. salt
2 8-oz. cans tomato sauce
3/4 c. water
1 4-oz. package wide noodles
1/4 c. cottage cheese
1/4 c. Parmesan cheese
2 tbsp. (about) milk

Saute ground beef in skillet until brown; drain off fat. Add onion and garlic; cook until tender. Stir in seasonings, tomato sauce and water; add noodles. Simmer, covered, for about 15 minutes or until noodles are tender, stirring occasionally. Add more water, if needed. Mix remaining ingredients together in a small bowl; drop by spoonfuls onto ground beef mixture. Simmer, covered, for 2 to 3 minutes or until cheese mixture is heated through. Yield: 6 servings.

Mrs. Jane Bower
Del Norte H.S., Crescent City, California

QUICK TOP OF STOVE BEEF CASSEROLE

1 lb. ground beef
1 sm. onion, chopped
1/2 tsp. salt
1/8 tsp. pepper
1/2 lb. American cheese slices
1/2 c. sliced ripe olives
1 c. chopped celery
2 c. fine noodles
1 lg. can tomatoes

Saute beef and onion until browned. Season with salt and pepper. Place cheese slices on beef; add a layer of ripe olives and a layer of celery. Sprinkle noodles over olives; pour tomatoes on top. Cover; simmer for 30 minutes. Yield: 3-4 servings.

Barbara Gaylor, Supervisor
Home Ec. Spec. Projects
Co-op and Work Study Unit
Michigan Dept. of Ed., Lansing, Michigan

TALLOPERINA

2 lb. ground beef
2 lg. onions, chopped

2 lg. bell peppers, chopped
2 lg. cloves of garlic, chopped
2 cans whole tomatoes
2 cans tomato puree
2 cans whole kernel corn,
   drained
1 4-oz. can mushrooms,
   drained
2 tsp. hot sauce
1 3/4 tsp. chili powder
2 tbsp. sugar
1/2 lb. grated cheese
Salt and pepper to taste
2 c. egg noodles, cooked

Saute beef, onions, bell peppers and garlic until browned. Add tomatoes, tomato puree, corn, mushrooms, hot sauce, chili powder, sugar, cheese, salt and pepper. Stir noodles into beef mixture; simmer for about 2 hours or until thick, stirring occasionally.

Mrs. Linda Herring
Lafayette H.S., Oxford, Mississippi

SAILOR'S SUPPER

2 lb. ground beef
2 tsp. salt
1/2 tsp. pepper
1 lg. onion, sliced thin
1 No. 2 1/2 can tomatoes
1 No. 303 can whole kernel corn
1 15-oz. can tomato sauce
1 tbsp. chili powder
2 c. fine noodles

Season ground beef with salt and pepper. Saute beef and onion together until beef loses red color. Add tomatoes, corn, tomato sauce, chili powder and noodles and stir until well mixed. Cover and simmer for 20 minutes. Remove cover and cook for 10 minutes longer. Yield: 8 servings.

Mrs. Diane Yakos
Versailles H.S., Versailles, Ohio

FAMILY GOULASH

1 4-oz. package fine noodles
Salt
1 lb. ground beef
1/2 c. chopped onion

Cheese Meatballs With Noodles

2 c. sliced celery
1/2 c. catsup
1   2 1/2-oz. jar sliced mushrooms
1   14 1/2-oz. can tomatoes
1/4 tsp. pepper

Add noodles and 1 1/2 teaspoons salt to 1 1/2 quarts boiling water; cook until tender. Drain well. Cook ground beef and onion in large skillet until beef is brown and onion is tender, stirring frequently. Drain off fat. Stir in noodles, celery, catsup, mushrooms with liquid, tomatoes, 2 teaspoons salt and pepper. Simmer, covered, for 30 to 45 minutes. Yield: 4 servings.

Sister M. Josepha Book
Forest Park H.S., Ferdinand, Indiana

CHEESE MEATBALLS WITH NOODLES

1 egg
1/2 tsp. ground nutmeg
1 1/4 tsp. salt
1/2 tsp. pepper
1 tbsp. finely chopped parsley
1 1/2 lb. ground beef chuck
1/3 c. dry bread crumbs
6 oz. Swiss cheese, cut in 1/2-in.
   cubes
2 tbsp. salad oil
3 med. onions, chopped
1   46-oz. can tomato juice
1   8-oz. package med. egg noodles
1/4 tsp. thyme leaves
Parsley sprigs (opt.)

Place egg, nutmeg, salt and 1/4 teaspoon pepper in large bowl; beat well. Add parsley, beef and bread crumbs; mix thoroughly. Roll 2 tablespoons beef mixture around a cheese cube for each hamburger ball. Heat oil in 4-quart saucepan; brown half the meatballs at a time in saucepan. Remove meatballs; set aside. Saute onions in pan drippings until golden brown. Add tomato juice; bring to a boil. Add uncooked noodles gradually so that liquid continues to boil. Stir in meatballs, thyme and remaining pepper; cover. Simmer for 10 minutes, stirring occasionally. Turn into serving bowl; garnish with parsley sprigs, if desired. Serve immediately. Yield: 6 servings.

THIRTY-MINUTE NOODLE DINNER

1 lb. ground beef
1 onion, chopped
1 6-oz. package medium noodles
1 10-oz. can mushroom soup
1 soup can water

Saute beef and onion in electric skillet at about 350 degrees until browned. Arrange noodles over the beef mixture. Combine soup and water; pour over the noodles. Do not stir. Reduce skillet temperature to simmer. Cook until noodles are tender, stirring carefully. Add more water, if needed. Yield: 4-5 servings.

Carolyn Rose
Marion Steele H.S., Amherst, Ohio

TENNESSEE GOULASH

1 tbsp. fat
1/2 med. onion, sliced
1 lb. ground beef
1 tsp. chili powder
1 tsp. salt
1/4 tsp. pepper
1 can kidney beans
1 can Franco-American spaghetti

Melt fat in a skillet, then add onion and cook until clear. Add ground beef and cook until brown. Add chili powder, salt, pepper, beans and spaghetti. Mix and simmer for about 30 minutes, stirring occasionally. Yield: 6 servings.

Mrs. Paul Bishop
Happy Valley H.S., Elizabethton, Tennessee

ONE-POT SPAGHETTI SUPPER

1 lb. ground beef
1 med. onion, chopped
1 clove of garlic, minced
1 1/2 tsp. salt
1/4 tsp. ground allspice
1/2 tsp. dry mustard
1/4 tsp. pepper
1 6-oz. package spaghetti, broken
   into fourths
1 c. water
2 1/2 c. tomato juice
Grated Parmesan cheese

Brown beef with onion and garlic in Dutch oven; add seasonings. Arrange uncooked spaghetti on top; pour water and tomato juice over spaghetti, moistening all the spaghetti. Cover. Bring to a boil; reduce heat. Simmer for about 15 minutes or until spaghetti is tender, stirring occasionally. Serve with Parmesan cheese. Add 1/3 cup sliced pimento-stuffed and/or black olives, with salt reduced to 3/4 teaspoon, or chopped parsley to beef mixture just before serving, if desired. Yield: 4-6 servings.

Photograph for this recipe on page 168.

SOPA DE FIDEO

2 tbsp. shortening
1/2 lb. vermicelli, broken in
   1-inch pieces
1 lb. ground beef
1 tsp. garlic powder
2 med. onions, chopped
1 No. 2 1/2 can tomatoes and
   juice
1/2 c. boiling water
1 green pepper, chopped
4 celery stalks, chopped
1/2 c. whole kernel corn, drained
1 tbsp. salt
1 tbsp. chili powder
1 tsp. pepper
1/2 lb. sharp cheese, sliced

Preheat electric skillet to 325 degrees. Melt shortening in skillet, then add vermicelli and cook until golden. Add ground beef and cook, stirring occasionally, until brown. Add remaining ingredients except cheese. Add enough hot water or tomato juice to just cover ingredients and reduce temperature to 200 degrees. Cover and cook for 20 minutes. Place cheese slices on top; cover. Cook for 5 minutes longer or until cheese melts.

Mrs. Fred Yost
Cairo Central Sch., Cairo, New York

MACARONI-BACON SAUTE

8 slices bacon
2 c. uncooked elbow macaroni
1/2 c. chopped onion
1/2 c. chopped green pepper

1 clove of garlic,minced,or
dash of garlic salt
3 c. V-8 juice
1 tsp. salt
1/2 tsp. pepper
2 tbsp. Worcestershire sauce

Fry bacon in electric skillet at 325 degrees; remove to paper toweling to drain. Add macaroni, onion, green pepper and garlic to bacon fat; saute for about 5 minutes or until macaroni is golden. Add V-8 juice and seasonings; cover skillet. Cook at 225 degrees for 20 minutes. Remove cover; sprinkle fried bacon bits over macaroni to garnish.

Jennie Lee Chastain
Bedford Jr. H.S., Bedford, Indiana

MACARONI-TOMATO SAUTE

1/3 c. margarine
1 10-oz. package elbow macaroni
1/2 c. chopped onion
1/2 c. chopped green pepper
1 clove of garlic, chopped
3 c. tomato juice
1 tsp. salt
1/4 tsp. pepper
2 tbsp. Worcestershire sauce

Melt margarine in frypan or electric skillet. Add macaroni, onion, green pepper and garlic; saute for about 10 minutes or until macaroni browns lightly. Stir in tomato juice, salt, pepper and Worcestershire sauce; bring to boil. Reduce heat to simmer, then cover. Cook, without stirring, for 20 minutes.

Connie Granato
Escobar Jr. H.S., San Antonio, Texas

Spicy Orange Yams And Chops

HAM SKILLET MEDLEY

1 1/2 c. sliced celery
1/2 c. sliced green onions
3 tbsp. butter or margarine
1 tbsp. flour
1/3 c. frozen pineapple-orange
juice concentrate, thawed
1/3 c. water
3 c. cooked noodles
2 c. diced cooked ham
1 2-oz. jar sliced pimentos
1/2 c. sliced ripe olives

Saute celery and onions in 2 tablespoons butter in large skillet until tender; remove celery and onions from skillet. Add remaining butter to skillet; heat until melted. Stir in flour; cook over low heat for 1 minute, stirring constantly. Mix concentrate with water; add to flour mixture gradually, stirring constantly. Cook, stirring, until thickened. Add noodles, ham, pimentos, olives and celery mixture; toss to mix well. Cook for several minutes longer or until heated through. Yield: 4 servings.

Mrs. Charlotte Van Arum
Greece Olympia H.S., Rochester, New York

SPICY ORANGE YAMS AND CHOPS

3 16-oz. cans Louisiana yams
1 6-oz. can frozen orange juice
concentrate, thawed
1 tbsp. lemon juice
3 tbsp. dark brown sugar
1 tsp. ginger
Dash of ground cloves
3/4 tsp. salt
6 pork chops, 1 in. thick
1 tbsp. salad oil

Drain syrup from yams into bowl; there should be about 2 cups syrup. Add orange juice concentrate, lemon juice, sugar, spices and salt to syrup; mix well. Trim excess fat from pork chops. Cook chops in oil in heavy skillet until well browned on both sides; drain off fat, if necessary. Pour syrup mixture over chops; cover. Simmer for 30 minutes, turning chops occasionally and adding water to skillet, if needed. Add yams; cook for 15 minutes longer, spooning syrup mixture over yams and chops occasionally. Garnish with orange slices and parsley, if desired. Yield: 6 servings.

MEXICAN LUNCHEON

1 lb. bulk sausage
1 c. chopped onions
1 c. chopped green pepper
1 1-lb. can tomatoes
2 c. macaroni
1 c. milk
1 c. sour cream
2 tbsp. sugar
1 tbsp. chili powder
1 tsp. salt

Cook sausage, onions and green pepper in a skillet until sausage is brown. Add tomatoes, macaroni, milk, sour cream and seasonings. Cook for 25 minutes, stirring occasionally. Yield: 6-8 servings.

Mary Nan Story
Frisco H.S., Frisco, Texas

JAMBALAYA JAMBOREE

1/2 lb. fresh mushrooms, sliced
1/4 c. butter
1 1-lb. can French-style green
  beans, drained
1/2 c. packaged precooked rice
1 1-lb. can stewed tomatoes
1/4 tsp. salt
1/2 lb. brown-and-serve sausage
1/2 c. shredded sharp Cheddar
  cheese

Saute mushrooms in butter in skillet until tender. Add green beans; sprinkle rice over beans. Cover with tomatoes; season with salt. Cover. Simmer for about 20 minutes or until rice is tender. Cook sausage in skillet until brown; drain. Place sausage on tomatoes; sprinkle cheese over sausage. Heat for 5 minutes or until cheese is melted; serve hot. Yield: 6 servings.

Susan Carothers
Franklin Reg. Sr. H.S., Murrysville, Pennsylvania

PEPPER AND PORK CHOP SUEY

1 1-lb. can chop suey vegetables
6 to 8 pork chops
1 sm. onion, chopped
1 clove of garlic, minced
3 tbsp. oil
1 env. chicken broth
2 med. green peppers, chopped
2 med. tomatoes, chopped
Small amount green beans, cut in
  1-in. diagonal slices (opt.)
3 or 4 water chestnuts,
  sliced (opt.)
3 or 4 stalks fresh asparagus, cut in
  1-inch diagonal slices (opt.)
1 tsp. salt
2 tbsp. cornstarch
3 tbsp. soy sauce

Drain and rinse vegetables. Trim fat and bone from pork chops; cut pork in julienne strips. Saute onion and garlic in oil in frypan until soft. Stir in pork; cook, stirring occasionally, for 5 minutes or until pork is brown. Stir in chicken broth, 3/4 cup water, vegetables, green peppers, tomatoes, green beans, water chestnuts, asparagus and salt. Heat to boiling point; cook until green peppers are crisp-tender. Mix cornstarch with 1/4 cup water and soy sauce until smooth. Stir into mixture in frypan; cook, stirring constantly, until thickened. Boil for 2 minutes; remove from heat. One teaspoon instant chicken bouillon may be used instead of chicken broth.

Joann Gardner
Pembroke H.S., Hampton, Virginia

SHRIMP CREOLE ORLEANS

1/4 c. butter or margarine
3/4 c. chopped onions
1 clove of garlic, minced
1 c. chopped green pepper
3 c. sliced celery
1 1-lb. 13-oz. can tomatoes
3 tbsp. brown sugar
1 1/2 tsp. salt
1/8 tsp. pepper
1 tsp. thyme
2 bay leaves, crumbled
2 lb. fresh cleaned shrimp
2 tbsp. lemon juice
3 c. hot cooked rice

Melt butter in large skillet. Add onions, garlic, green pepper and celery; cook over low heat for about 20 minutes or until vegetables are tender. Add tomatoes, brown sugar, salt, pepper, thyme and bay leaves; simmer for 15 to 20 minutes. Add shrimp and lemon juice; cover. Simmer for 6 to 8 minutes longer. Serve over rice. Yield: 6 servings.

Mrs. Caroline Bode
Robert E. Lee H.S., San Antonio, Texas

Rock Lobster Polynesian

ROCK LOBSTER POLYNESIAN

    3   8-oz. packages frozen South African
        rock lobster-tails
    1   3 1/2-oz. can flaked coconut
    3 c. milk
    1/2 c. butter
    1 sour apple, peeled and chopped
    1 sm. onion, chopped
    1/2 c. flour
    2 tbsp. curry powder
    Juice of 1 lemon
    1 tsp. ginger
    Salt to taste

Drop lobster-tails into boiling, salted water; bring to a boil again. Boil for 1 minute. Drain lobster-tails; drench with cold water. Remove underside membrane with scissors; pull out lobster meat in 1 piece. Cut into slices. Combine coconut and milk in saucepan; bring to boiling point. Strain milk, pressing out all liquid from coconut. Melt butter in saucepan. Add apple and onion; saute until soft. Sprinkle with flour and curry powder; mix well. Stir in coconut milk gradually; cook, stirring, until thickened. Stir in lemon juice and ginger. Add lobster slices; reheat until bubbly. Season with salt; garnish with quartered pineapple slices. Serve over rice. Yield: 6 servings.

SHRIMP JAMBALAYA

    3 tbsp. margarine
    1 med. onion, chopped
    1 med. bell pepper, chopped
    1/4 c. chopped celery
    2 c. shelled deveined shrimp
    1 c. rice
    1 No. 303 can whole tomatoes
    1   4-oz. can chopped mushrooms
    2 tbsp. Worcestershire sauce
    2 tsp. salt
    1/2 tsp. pepper
    1/4 tsp. red pepper

Melt margarine in skillet. Add onion, bell pepper and celery; saute until vegetables are tender. Add shrimp, rice, tomatoes, undrained mushrooms, Worcestershire sauce, salt and peppers; stir until well mixed. Reduce heat to low; simmer for 25 minutes or until rice is tender, stirring occasionally. Yield: 6 servings.

Mrs. Kathleen Hudson
River Oaks Acad. H.S., Belle Chasse, Louisiana

SALMON VEGETABLE PAELLA

    1/2 c. butter or margarine
    1 med. onion, chopped
    1 clove of garlic, minced
    2 stalks celery, chopped
    1 sm. green pepper, chopped
    2 c. sliced summer squash or
        zucchini
    3 tomatoes, quartered
    1 1/2 c. rice
    1   1-lb. can salmon
    3 c. water or chicken broth
    1 tsp. salt
    1/4 tsp. pepper
    1   1-lb. can peas

Melt butter in heavy saucepan. Add onion, garlic, celery and green pepper; saute for 5 minutes or until onion is tender, stirring frequently. Add squash and tomatoes; cover tightly. Cook over low heat for 10 minutes. Add rice; stir until well mixed. Drain salmon liquid into saucepan; stir in water, salt and pepper. Bring to a rapid boil; cover tightly. Turn heat to very low; cook for 30 minutes. Fluff rice mixture with a fork. Flake salmon; add to saucepan. Cover; simmer for 5 minutes. Heat peas and liquid in saucepan; drain peas. Place salmon mixture in serving dish; garnish with peas. Yield: 6 servings.

Mrs. Kathleen Boeckstiegel
Detroit H.S., Detroit, Oregon

TUNA MAC

1 pkg. Kraft macaroni and cheese
   dinner
1 9-oz. can tuna, drained and
   flaked
1 to 2 c. canned or cooked frozen
   peas

Prepare macaroni and cheese according to package directions; stir in tuna. Heat peas in saucepan; drain. Add to tuna mixture; mix well. Yield: 4-6 servings.

Jan Kent
Yates City Comm. Sch. No. 207
Yates City, Illinois

FIVE-DECKER DINNER

1 lb. ground meat
3 med. potatoes
2 lg. carrots
1 med. onion
4 strips bacon
Salt and pepper to taste
1/2 c. water

Shape meat into 4 patties. Peel potatoes, carrots and onion; slice each about 1/4 inch thick. Place bacon strips in skillet; top with patties. Sprinkle with salt and pepper. Cook until bacon sizzles; top with potatoes. Season with salt and pepper. Add carrots; season with salt and pepper. Add onion; season with salt and pepper. Add water; cover. Cook over low heat for 30 minutes or until vegetables are tender. Yield: 4 servings.

Mrs. Pat Willoughby
Hamlin H.S., Hamlin, Texas

HOT POTATOES AND FRANKS

1/2 lb. frankfurters
1 tbsp. butter
1/2 env. onion soup mix
1 tbsp. flour
1 tbsp. sugar
Dash of pepper
1/2 c. water
2 tbsp. vinegar
4 c. sliced cooked potatoes
1/2 c. sour cream

Cook frankfurters in butter in skillet until brown; remove from heat. Remove frankfurters from skillet. Stir soup mix, flour, sugar and pepper into pan drippings. Add water and vinegar; stir well. Add frankfurters; return to heat. Cook, stirring, until mixture comes to a boil. Reduce heat; cover. Simmer for 10 minutes. Add potatoes and sour cream; heat just to boiling point. Yield: 6 servings.

Martha Harless
Bayside Jr. H.S., Virginia Beach, Virginia

TOMATOES AND OKRA

2 tbsp. butter or bacon drippings
1/2 c. finely chopped onion
1 qt. sliced okra
2 1/2 c. canned tomatoes
1 1/2 tsp. salt
1/2 tsp. paprika
1/4 tsp. curry powder
1 tbsp. chili powder (opt.)
2 tsp. brown sugar
3 tbsp. chopped green pepper (opt.)
1/8 tsp. diced garlic (opt.)

Melt butter in skillet, then add onion and saute until brown. Add okra and cook until brown, stirring occasionally. Add tomatoes, salt, paprika, curry powder, chili powder and brown sugar. Add green pepper and garlic. Cover and simmer until okra is tender. Yield: 6 servings.

Mrs. Joe Wayne Carter
Hamlin H.S., Hamlin, Texas

CORN AND GREEN BEAN CASSEROLE

1 4 1/2-oz. can deviled ham
3/4 tsp. paprika
2 tsp. flour
1 3/4 c. light cream
1 tbsp. grated onion
3/4 tsp. salt
1/4 tsp. pepper
2 No. 2 cans green beans
1 No. 2 can whole kernel corn
1/2 c. sour cream

Place deviled ham in skillet; heat through, stirring constantly. Add paprika, flour, cream, onion, salt and pepper. Heat, stirring, until thickened. Drain beans and corn; add to sauce with sour cream. Simmer, stirring constantly, until well mixed and heated through. Yield: 6 servings.

Hilda Harman
Smithville H.S., Smithville, Mississippi

FIESTA CORN AND OKRA

6 slices bacon, diced
1/4 c. chopped onion
1 16-oz. can cut okra, drained
1 12-oz. can whole kernel corn
   with peppers, drained
1 7 1/2-oz. can tomatoes

Cook bacon and onion in medium skillet until onion is translucent. Add okra, corn and tomatoes; heat through, stirring occasionally. Yield: 6-8 servings.

Elva Sigrest
South Leake H.S., Walnut Grove, Mississippi

ARIZONA ZUCCHINI

4 c. zucchini, sliced
2 tbsp. oil
1 med. onion, chopped
1 green pepper, chopped
1 can corn, drained
1 8-oz. can tomato sauce
1/4 tsp. Italian seasoning
1 clove of garlic, minced
Salt and pepper to taste
1/2 c. sliced mushrooms

Cook zucchini in oil in large frying pan until soft. Add onion and pepper; cook until softened. Add corn, tomato sauce and seasonings; cook for about 5 minutes. Add mushrooms; cook until heated through.

Gay McLaughlin
Mayer H.S., Mayer, Arizona

ZUCCHINI OREGANO

4 strips bacon, cut up
1 clove of garlic, sliced thin
1/4 c. chopped onion
1 to 1 1/2 lb. unpeeled zucchini,
   sliced thin
Salt and pepper to taste
1 tbsp. crushed oregano
2 lg. fresh tomatoes, sliced
1/4 c. grated Parmesan cheese
1/4 lb. mozzarella cheese slices

Fry bacon until crisp; remove from pan. Saute garlic in drippings until brown; remove. Add onion and saute until tender. Add zucchini, salt and pepper; stir. Fry until just soft. Add oregano and bacon pieces; add tomatoes. Cover with Parmesan cheese. Arrange mozza-

rella cheese over all. Place under broiler until cheese is melted and bubbly. Yield: 4 servings.

Mrs. Ethel M. Poley
Narrowsburg Central Rural Sch.
Narrowsburg, New York

ZUCCHINI SUPREME

1 med. onion
1 green pepper
2 8-in. zucchini
3 med. tomatoes
3 to 4 tbsp. margarine
1 c. diced potato
1 sm. can mushrooms
1 tsp. salt
Generous dash of pepper
Dash of garlic salt

Cut onion in half lengthwise, then slice. Cut the green pepper in half and remove the seeds and membrane, then cut in strips. Cut the zucchini in half, then cut in slices. Cut the tomatoes in half lengthwise, then cut in slices. Melt the margarine in large heavy skillet over medium heat. Add the onion, green pepper, potato and mushrooms and saute until potato is lightly browned. Add zucchini and sprinkle with salt, pepper and garlic salt. Saute and stir for about 5 minutes or until zucchini is fork-tender. Add tomatoes and cover, then cook for 2 to 3 minutes longer. Serve immediately. Yield: 4 servings.

Alice Hansberger
Canton Sr. H.S., Canton, Illinois

WILD RICE DISH

1 6-oz. box Uncle Ben's long grain
   and wild rice
1 lb. hot pork sausage
1/2 c. chopped green onions
1/2 c. chopped bell pepper
1/2 c. chopped celery
1 2-oz. can sliced mushrooms,
   drained

Cook rice according to package directions. Fry sausage in skillet until brown; drain, leaving sausage drippings in skillet. Saute green onions, bell pepper and celery in sausage drippings until tender. Add sausage, vegetables, and mushrooms to rice; toss until well mixed.

Susan Dorsey
Hogg Jr. H.S., Houston, Texas

Butterscotch Pecan Meringue Pudding

Delicious Dessert Casseroles

A delicious homemade dessert is always a welcome sight, even after the heartiest of meals. The superb collection of desserts which follows is made up of luscious dessert casseroles, mouth-watering combinations of sweets, fruits, nuts and flavorings, baked till they're hot and bubbly.

Many delicious concoctions await you in the following pages, like Autumn Fruit Casserole, an irresistible combination of pineapple chunks, peach halves, apricot halves, cloves and cinnamon, and Cherry-Noodle Pudding, made with noodles, cherries, sour cream, cottage cheese and cream cheese. You'll also find the best recipes for old family favorites, such as Apple Cobbler, Peach Cobbler and Bread Pudding.

Once you prepare and serve the following Delicious Dessert Casseroles, your family will request them over and over again.

PERSIMMON PUDDING

2 c. pureed persimmons
3 eggs
2 c. flour
1/2 c. sugar
1 tsp. soda
1/2 tsp. cinnamon
1/2 tsp. nutmeg
1/2 c. raisins (opt.)
1/2 c. shredded coconut (opt.)
1/2 c. chopped pecans (opt.)
1/3 c. melted margarine

Place persimmons in bowl; beat in eggs. Combine flour, sugar, soda, spices, raisins, coconut and pecans. Add to persimmon mixture; mix well. Add margarine; stir until blended. Turn into oiled large, rectangular baking dish. Bake in preheated 300-degree oven for 1 hour. Cool, then chill. Cut into squares; serve with whipped cream, if desired.

Mrs. Barbara Crabtree
Central Jr. H.S., Melbourne, Florida

AEBLEKAGE

3 lb. apples
Sugar
1 tbsp. grated lemon peel
1 tsp. cinnamon
Fresh bread crumbs
Currant jelly
1/2 c. melted butter
Whipped cream

Peel, core and dice apples. Combine apples, 1 cup water, 1/2 cup sugar and lemon peel in a kettle; cook until apples are tender. Drain apples, reserving syrup; press apples through a coarse sieve. Combine apples, 1/4 cup reserved syrup and cinnamon in a saucepan; cook until slightly thickened, stirring frequently. Press a layer of bread crumbs in a well-buttered baking dish; spread half the apple mixture over the crumbs. Spread jelly over the apple mixture, then sprinkle with sugar. Repeat layers, then top with a layer of bread crumbs. Press cake firmly into baking dish; drizzle butter over top. Bake in a preheated 325 to 375-degree oven for 30 minutes. Let cool, then turn out onto serving plate. Top with whipped cream to serve. Yield: 6 servings.

Mrs. Cora E. Fagre
Centaurus H.S., Lafayette, Colorado

APPLE COBBLER

5 c. sliced apples
1 1/4 c. sugar
Flour
1/2 tsp. cinnamon
1/2 tsp. salt
1 tsp. vanilla
1 tbsp. butter
1/2 tsp. baking powder
2 tbsp. soft butter
1 egg, slightly beaten

Combine apples, 3/4 cup sugar, 2 tablespoons flour, cinnamon, 1/4 teaspoon salt and vanilla in mixing bowl. Add 1/4 cup water; mix well. Pour into 9-inch square baking dish; dot with butter. Combine 1/2 cup sifted flour, remaining sugar, baking powder, remaining salt, soft butter and egg in bowl; beat with wooden spoon until smooth. Drop batter in 9 portions over apples, spacing evenly. Bake in preheated 375-degree oven for 35 to 40 minutes or until apples are fork-tender and crust is golden brown. Serve warm with whipped cream or ice cream.

Mrs. Deborah Wheeler
Cabot H.S., Cabot, Vermont

EASY APPLE DISH

8 to 12 apples, pared and sliced
1/2 c. sugar
1 c. (packed) brown sugar
1/2 c. butter or margarine,
   softened
1 c. flour
1/2 c. chopped pecans

Place apples in 9 x 12-inch buttered baking dish or casserole; cover with sugar. Mix brown sugar, butter and flour; sprinkle over sugar. Bake in preheated 350-degree oven for 30 minutes. Remove from oven; sprinkle with pecans. Return to oven; reduce temperature to 300 degrees. Bake for 30 minutes longer. Serve hot with cream or ice cream. Yield: 8-10 servings.

Ardith Wakefield
Eisenhower Jr. H.S., Darien, Illinois

APPLE DANISH CASSEROLE

1 c. peeled diced apples
1 lg. egg, beaten
1/4 tsp. salt

3/4 c. sugar
1/2 c. flour
3/4 tsp. baking powder
1/2 tsp. cinnamon
2 tsp. lemon juice
1 tsp. vanilla
1/2 c. chopped walnuts

Combine apples, egg, salt, sugar, flour, baking powder, cinnamon, lemon juice, vanilla and walnuts in a large bowl; toss until well mixed. Turn into a well-greased 8-inch round casserole. Bake in preheated 350-degree oven for 30 minutes. Serve warm with ice cream or hard sauce. May be cooled and top spread with whipped cream, then cut in wedges. Yield: 6-8 servings.

Patricia Shradel Mundy
Perry Jr. H.S., Perry, Iowa

APPLE DUMPLINGS

1 10-count can refrigerator
    biscuits
2 or 3 apples
Cinnamon to taste
Nutmeg to taste
2 1/2 c. water
2 c. sugar
1 1/2 tsp. vanilla
1/2 c. margarine

Roll each biscuit out on lightly floured surface into circle. Peel and core apples; cut each into 3 or 4 pieces. Place 1 piece of apple on each biscuit. Fold over; seal edges. Place in buttered baking dish; sprinkle with cinnamon and nutmeg. Mix remaining ingredients in saucepan; bring to a boil. Pour over apples; cover. Bake in preheated 350-degree oven for 1 hour and 30 minutes; serve warm. Yield: 4-6 servings.

Mrs. Marian G. Craddock
Colorado H.S., Colorado City, Texas

QUICK APPLE CRISP

4 or 5 pared apples, sliced
1 tbsp. lemon juice
1 c. sifted flour
1 c. (packed) brown sugar
1/2 tsp. cinnamon
1/2 c. margarine

Place apple slices in baking dish; sprinkle with lemon juice. Combine, flour, brown sugar and cinnamon in mixing bowl; cut in margarine until mixture is crumbly. Spoon crumb mix-

ture over apples. Bake in preheated 350-degree oven for 30 to 35 minutes.

Linda Ann Ulrich
Benjamin Franklin Jr. H.S., Kenmore, New York

APPLE-PINEAPPLE CASSEROLE

4 or 5 med. baking apples
1 sm. can crushed pineapple
1/4 c. red cinnamon candies
Flour
3/4 c. sugar
5 tbsp. melted butter

Pare and slice apples; mix with pineapple, cinnamon candies and 2 tablespoons flour. Toss to mix. Spoon into greased 1 1/2-quart casserole. Combine 3/4 cup flour, sugar and melted butter; place over apple mixture. Bake in preheated 350-degree oven for 30 minutes or until apples are tender and top is browned.

Linda Adams
Millersburg Area Sch., Millersburg, Pennsylvania

BUTTERSCOTCH PECAN MERINGUE PUDDING

1/4 c. butter
Brown sugar
2 eggs, separated
2 1/4 c. milk
3 tbsp. quick-cooking tapioca
1/8 tsp. salt
1/2 tsp. vanilla
1/3 c. pecan halves, cut in half
    lengthwise

Melt butter in small saucepan. Add 1/3 cup firmly packed brown sugar; cook, stirring, until sugar is dissolved. Set aside. Combine beaten egg yolks with small amount of the milk in saucepan. Add tapioca, salt and remaining milk; let stand for 5 minutes. Beat egg whites in bowl until foamy. Add 1/4 cup firmly packed brown sugar, 2 tablespoons at a time, beating thoroughly after each addition. Continue beating until soft peaks form. Place tapioca mixture over medium heat; cook, stirring, until mixture comes to a boil. Remove from heat; stir in melted brown sugar and vanilla. Pour into 1-quart casserole; spoon meringue over tapioca mixture. Sprinkle with pecans. Bake in preheated 375-degree oven for 15 minutes or until meringue is golden brown. Yield: 6 servings.

Photograph for this recipe on page 184.

185

Broiled Butterscotch-Rice Puddings

BROILED BUTTERSCOTCH-RICE PUDDINGS

1/2 c. rice
1 c. water
1/4 tsp. salt
1 tsp. maple extract
1   3 1/4-oz. package butterscotch
    pudding mix
2 c. milk
1 tbsp. butter or margarine
1/3 c. maple syrup
2 tbsp. melted butter or margarine
1 c. shredded coconut

Combine rice, water, salt and maple extract in saucepan; bring to a boil over high heat. Stir once; cover. Reduce heat; simmer for 15 minutes. Blend pudding mix with milk and butter in saucepan; cook over medium heat, stirring constantly, for about 5 minutes. Fold in rice. Spoon into 6 ovenproof serving dishes; chill. Mix maple syrup, melted butter and coconut when ready to serve puddings; spread on each pudding. Broil for 2 to 3 minutes or until golden brown, watching carefully so as not to burn. Yield: 6 servings.

AUTUMN FRUIT CASSEROLE

1   1-lb. can pineapple chunks
1   1-lb. 14-oz. can peach halves
1   1-lb. 4-oz. can apricot halves
1/3 c. melted butter
2/3 c. (packed) brown sugar
1/4 tsp. ground cloves
1/4 tsp. cinnamon
1 tbsp. curry powder

Drain all fruits well; arrange in layers in medium casserole. Combine butter, sugar and spices; sprinkle over fruits. Bake in preheated 350-degree oven for 1 hour. Serve hot with vanilla ice cream or sour cream on each serving. May be transferred to chafing dish for serving at table or buffet.

Mrs. Elizabeth Peterson
Paullina Comm. Sch., Paullina, Iowa

BUTTERSCOTCH RICE

2/3 c. packaged precooked rice
2 c. milk
1/4 tsp. salt
1 tbsp. butter
1/3 c. (packed) brown sugar
1 tsp. vanilla extract
1/2 c. chopped dates

Combine rice, milk and salt in large saucepan; cover loosely. Bring to a boil; reduce heat. Simmer for 15 minutes. Melt butter in another saucepan; stir in sugar. Cook, stirring, until sugar dissolves. Add to rice; add vanilla and dates. Mix well. Serve warm or cold. Yield: 4 servings.

Lynnell Holland
Chiloquin H.S., Chiloquin, Oregon

CHERRY CRUMBLE

1 or 2 No. 303 cans tart pitted
    cherries
2 c. flour
1 1/4 tsp. salt
1 1/4 c. sugar
1 c. melted butter
Cinnamon to taste
Cloves to taste

Drain cherries; reserve juice. Combine flour, salt, sugar and melted butter to form a crumbly mixture. Place 1/2 of the crumb mixture in a 9-inch square pan. Arrange cherries over crumb mixture; sprinkle with cinnamon and cloves. Add remaining crumb mixture; pat gently. Sprinkle with cinnamon and cloves. Bake in preheated 375-degree oven for 30 to 40 minutes or until golden brown. The reserved cherry juice may be boiled, adding sugar to taste, salt and red food coloring, then thickened with cornstarch. Spoon over squares and serve warm. Yield: 6 servings.

Mrs. Karen Doerksen
Colorado Springs Christian Sch.
Colorado Springs, Colorado

CHERRY-NOODLE PUDDING

1   8-oz. package fine noodles
1/4 c. butter
1/2   8-oz. package cream cheese, softened
1   1-lb. carton cottage cheese
4 eggs
1/2 c. milk
1 c. sugar
1/3 c. sour cream
2 tsp. vanilla
1 can cherry pie filling

Cook noodles in boiling salted water until tender; drain. Add butter and stir until butter is melted. Blend cream cheese and cottage cheese together; stir into noodles. Beat eggs until light and fluffy; add to noodles. Add remaining ingredients except pie filling to noodle mixture; mix thoroughly. Turn into a buttered 11 x 8 x 2-inch pan. Bake in preheated 350-degree oven for 30 minutes. Top with pie filling; bake for 30 minutes longer.

Mrs. Ruth K. Ockman
Maplewood Jr. H.S., Maplewood, New Jersey

CARAMEL-TOPPED RICE PUDDING

3 eggs
1/2 c. sugar
3/4 tsp. salt
1/2 tsp. nutmeg
3 c. milk
1/4 c. butter
1 c. cooked rice
1 tsp. vanilla
1/2 tsp. rum extract
1/3 c. slivered almonds
1/2 c. (firmly packed) brown sugar

Place eggs in bowl; beat lightly. Add sugar, salt and nutmeg; mix well. Combine milk and 2 tablespoons butter in saucepan; place over low heat until scalded. Pour into egg mixture in fine stream, stirring constantly. Stir in rice, vanilla and rum extract; pour into shallow 1 1/2-quart casserole. Place casserole in shallow pan of hot water. Bake in preheated 350-degree oven for 30 minutes or until metal knife inserted in center comes out clean. Remove pudding from oven, then from hot water. Brown almonds lightly in remaining butter; stir in brown sugar. Sprinkle over top of pudding. Broil about 3 inches from source of heat until topping is hot and bubbly. Cool slightly; serve. May be chilled before serving, if desired. Yield: 6-8 servings.

Caramel-Topped Rice Pudding

CHOCOLATE SOUFFLE

1/4 c. butter
1/4 c. flour
1/4 tsp. salt
3/4 c. milk
2 sq. unsweetened chocolate,
    cut up
3 eggs, separated
1/2 c. sugar
1/4 tsp. cream of tartar
Whipped cream

Melt butter in saucepan; blend in flour and salt. Cook until smooth and bubbly. Remove from heat; stir in milk and chocolate. Bring to a boil; boil for 1 minute, stirring constantly, until chocolate is melted. Remove from heat. Beat egg yolks until thick and lemon colored; beat in sugar gradually, then blend in chocolate mixture. Beat egg whites with cream of tartar until stiff, then fold in egg yolk mixture carefully. Pour into greased 2-quart baking dish. Place in pan containing 1 inch of hot water. Bake in preheated 350-degree oven for about 45 minutes or until silver knife inserted in center comes out clean. Serve warm topped with whipped cream.

Louise Vrable
Ramsay Jr. H.S., Mount Pleasant, Pennsylvania

ROSY PEAR COMPOTE

6 fresh pears
2 med. oranges
1   16-oz. can whole cranberry
    sauce
1/3 c. sugar
1 tbsp. lemon juice
1/4 tsp. ground cinnamon
1/4 tsp. ground ginger

Peel, core and quarter pears. Peel and slice oranges; remove seeds. Cut slices in half. Combine cranberry sauce, sugar, lemon juice, cinnamon and ginger in saucepan; bring to boiling point. Place pears and orange pieces in 1 1/2-quart casserole or baking dish; pour cranberry mixture over pear mixture. Cover. Bake in preheated 350-degree oven for 40 minutes or until pears are tender. Spoon into sherbet glasses; serve warm. Yield: 6 servings.

Mrs. Barbara Goedicke
Lindsay Thurber Comp. H.S.
Red Deer, Alberta, Canada

ROYAL RHUBARB CRISP

4 c. rhubarb, cut in 1-in. pieces
3/4 c. sugar
2 tbsp. quick-cooking tapioca
1/2 tsp. salt
1   11-oz. can mandarin orange
    segments, drained
1 c. rolled oats
1/4 c. sifted flour
1/3 c. (firmly packed) brown
    sugar
1/4 c. melted butter
Vanilla ice cream

Combine rhubarb, sugar, tapioca and salt; toss lightly to mix. Let stand for 30 minutes, stirring occasionally. Stir in orange segments. Place in ungreased 8-inch baking pan. Combine oats, flour, brown sugar and butter; mix well. Sprinkle over rhubarb mixture. Bake in preheated 350-degree oven for 40 to 45 minutes; serve warm with ice cream.

Corinne Rasmussen
Burt Comm. Sch., Burt, Iowa

MIXED FRUIT CASSEROLE

1/4 c. melted butter
3 tbsp. flour
1/2 tsp. curry powder
1   13-oz. can peach halves,
    drained
1   1-lb. 4-oz. can pineapple spears,
    drained
1   1-lb. can pears, drained
1   1-lb. can whole apricots,
    drained
1 stick of whole ginger
1/4 c. (packed) brown sugar

Mix butter, flour and curry powder. Mix fruits; place in casserole. Add ginger; sprinkle with brown sugar. Sprinkle butter mixture over all. Bake in preheated 375-degree oven for 30 minutes; remove ginger before serving.

Mrs. James H. Bryan
Harrisonburg H.S., Harrisonburg, Virginia

DELICIOUS SCALLOPED PINEAPPLE

4 c. bread crumbs
3 eggs, beaten
1/2 c. milk
1 c. sugar

1 No. 2 can crushed pineapple
1/2 c. melted butter

Mix all ingredients; place in casserole. Bake in preheated 350-degree oven for about 1 hour. Serve hot or cold with whipped cream, if desired.

Phyllis T. Krumrine
Susquehannock H.S., Glen Rock, Pennsylvania

POTATO DESSERT CASSEROLE

2 eggs
1/2 c. milk
3/4 c. sugar
1 c. margarine
1 can sweet potatoes, drained
   and mashed
1 tsp. vanilla
1/2 c. flour
1/2 c. (packed) brown sugar
1/2 c. chopped nuts

Place eggs, milk, sugar and half the margarine in blender container; process until blended. Add potatoes gradually; blend well. Add vanilla; blend. Pour into greased casserole. Mix flour, remaining margarine and brown sugar until mixture resembles coarse meal; stir in nuts. Sprinkle over potato mixture. Bake in preheated 375-degree oven for 20 to 25 minutes; serve hot or cold. Yield: 6-8 servings.

Mrs. Ruth Jordan
Benjamin Russell H.S., Alexander City, Alabama

PUMPKIN PIE SQUARES

1 c. sifted flour
1/2 c. quick-cooking oats
1 c. (packed) brown sugar
Butter
1   1-lb. can pumpkin
1   13 1/2-oz. can evaporated milk
2 eggs, beaten
3/4 c. sugar
1/2 tsp. salt
1 tsp. ground cinnamon
1/2 tsp. ground ginger
1/4 tsp. ground cloves
1/2 c. chopped pecans

Combine flour, oats, half the brown sugar and 1/2 cup butter in mixing bowl; mix with electric mixer at low speed until consistency of crumbs. Press into ungreased 13 x 9 x 2-inch baking pan. Bake in preheated 350-degree oven for 15 minutes. Remove from oven; do not turn off heat. Combine pumpkin, milk, eggs, sugar, salt and spices in bowl; beat well. Pour onto crust. Bake for 20 minutes. Combine pecans, remaining brown sugar and 2 tablespoons butter; sprinkle over pumpkin filling. Bake for 15 to 20 minutes longer or until filling is set. Cool in pan; cut into 2-inch squares. Garnish with whipped cream and whole pecans. Yield: 2 dozen squares.

Jenny L. Curtis
Orrville H.S., Orrville, Ohio

RAISIN-NOODLE PUDDING

Raisins to taste
1   8-oz. package broad noodles,
   cooked
1/2 c. apple juice
1/2 c. melted butter
1/4 c. (packed) brown sugar
3 eggs, beaten
3 tsp. cinnamon

Soak raisins in warm water; drain. Combine all ingredients in large bowl; mix well. Spread in greased casserole; cover. Bake in preheated 350-degree oven for 45 minutes.

Mrs. Barbara Taksey
Fairview Jr. H.S., Fairview, New Jersey

SPICY BREAD PUDDING

1 c. bread crumbs
1 c. sour milk
1 c. (packed) brown sugar
1/4 c. melted shortening
3/4 c. seedless raisins
1/2 c. flour
1/2 tsp. cinnamon
1/4 tsp. cloves
1 tsp. soda
1/2 tsp. salt

Soak bread crumbs in milk until milk is absorbed. Add sugar, shortening and raisins. Sift remaining ingredients together. Add to milk mixture; mix well. Place in greased casserole. Bake in preheated 350-degree oven for 1 hour; serve with sauce or whipped cream, if desired. One tablespoon vinegar may be mixed with milk to make sour milk.

Susan J. Thomas
Mascenic Reg. Sch., New Ipswich, New Hampshire

Index

Index

Index

Index

COLOR ILLUSTRATIONS

PHOTOGRAPHY CREDITS: Standard Brands Products: Planters Peanuts, Blue Bonnet Margarine; Pie Filling Institute; International Shrimp Council; American Lamb Council; Rice Council; Seven Seas Creole French Dressing; Ocean Spray Cranberries, Inc.; Dole Company; National Broiler Council; Knox Gelatine, Inc.; Pickle Packers International, Inc.; Spanish Green Olive Commission; Louisiana Yam Commission; National Kraut Packers Association; Brussels Sprouts Marketing Program; National Macaroni Institute; The R. T. French Company; California Avocado Advisory Board; National Dairy Council; California Beef Council; Angostura-Wuppermann Corporation; South African Rock Lobster Service Corporation; United Fresh Fruit and Vegetable Association; Campbell Soup Company; Evaporated Milk Association; American Dairy Association; Best Foods, a Division of CPC International, Inc.; Pet, Inc.; American Dry Milk Institute; Western Research Kitchens; The Borden Company; General Foods Kitchens.

Favorite Recipes of Home Economics Teachers--
Please the palate, tickle the imagination
& fortify the purse!

New Casseroles Cookbook – 1974's timely cookbook offers meal-in-a-dish casseroles – a delicious and economi-cal way to present everything from hamburger and bean sprouts to Crabmeat St. Jacques with Mushrooms! **Blue Ribbon Poultry Cookbook** – This award winning cookbook focuses on the delights of chicken, pheasant, turkey, duck – making everyday's dinner Sunday dinner! **Blue Ribbon Pies and Pastries** – Fresh baked apple or fluffy chiffon pie? Turnovers, éclairs, cream and custard pies, tarts & tassies? Here are over 500 award winning recipes for a fantastic dessert every time! **Americana Cookery** – Yankee Pot Roast, Southern Pecan Pie, New England Clam Chowder . . . other favorite American dishes that best reflect our great heritage.

Quick and Easy Cookbook – The perfect answer to all those last minute meals for families on the go! Hundreds of recipes – to make delicious desserts, dinners, suppers and snacks in a snap. Sure to be a real family favorite! **Meats Cookbook** – It's hard to beat beef, lamb, pork, veal . . . or any other meat dish. Plain or fancy, here are mouth watering main dishes for every taste and occasion. **Desserts Cookbook** – Flaming crêpes to frosted cakes . . . desserts are the crowning com-plement to every meal. Here are hundreds of tempting desserts – sure to bring smiles of delight! **Holiday Cookbook** – Delicious, festive recipes not only for Christmas, Thanksgiving and New Year's . . . but Halloween, the Fourth of July and other exciting occasions! **Money-Saving Cookbook** – Prepare delicious and appealing meals – for dollars less with these nifty, budget-pleasing recipes. The perfect answer to today's rising prices!

America's Home Economics Teachers Want to Share Their All-Star Cooking Revue With You!

And where could one better begin than with the **New Casseroles Cookbook!** Give your family a welcome change from holiday fare with tasty Double-Good Manicotti! Or, how about Cheese-It-Up Beef, combining two protein-packed main meal favorites? Chicken comes to center stage as Mississippi Chicken Paprikash, and Chicken Continental — offering a wealth of ways to serve this economical meat. Or, on the vegetable scene, vary your menu with Spanish Noodles — spicy and filling — or Eggplant Casserole, which gives this practically-priced vegetable an elegant setting! Why not brighten your cooking library with all editions of the *Favorite Recipes of Home Economics Teachers* cookbooks! You'll find thousands of just-right recipes for every taste and occasion at your fingertips. And they're all so easy to prepare! Each recipe has been personally tested and tasted by Home Economics Teachers from all over the country . . . and each has the enthusiastic approval of their families. We're so proud of these recipes, and want you and your family to enjoy them as much as we do. Order the complete library of *Favorite Recipes of Home Economics Teachers* cookbooks today — including the newest star of them all, **New Casseroles!** Remember, these books make perfect gifts for birthdays, weddings, showers, anniversaries, etc. Don't miss this great opportunity to really show off your cooking talents . . . with the *Favorite Recipes of Home Economics Teachers* cookbook series!

Favorite Recipes of Home Economics Teachers Cookbooks

Use these handy order forms to order individual books for yourself and for friends.

Order Form 40190

PLEASE SEND ME THE FOLLOWING BOOKS:

Name

Address

City   State   Zip

☐ Please Bill Me — Plus Postage and Handling

☐ Enclosed is payment for full amount. No charge for postage and handling.

[1]Price subject to approval of Price Committee.
[2]Limited supply.

Quan.	Cookbook Title	Item No.	Price [1]Each	Total
	New Casseroles	101027	4.50	
	Poultry	101026	4.50	
	Pies & Pastries	101023	4.50	
	Quick & Easy	101014	4.50	
	Money-Saving	101021	4.50	
	Holiday[2]	101019	4.50	
	Meats[2]	101010	4.50	
	Desserts[2]	101013	4.50	
	Americana Cookery	101022	4.50	
	Total Order			

MAIL TO: FAVORITE RECIPES PRESS ●P.O. BOX 3396 ●MONTGOMERY, ALABAMA 36109

Order Form 40190

PLEASE SEND ME THE FOLLOWING BOOKS:

Name

Address

City   State   Zip

☐ Please Bill Me — Plus Postage and Handling

☐ Enclosed is payment for full amount. No charge for postage and handling.

[1]Price subject to approval of Price Committee.
[2]Limited supply.

Quan.	Cookbook Title	Item No.	Price [1]Each	Total
	New Casseroles	101027	4.50	
	Poultry	101026	4.50	
	Pies & Pastries	101023	4.50	
	Quick & Easy	101014	4.50	
	Money-Saving	101021	4.50	
	Holiday[2]	101019	4.50	
	Meats[2]	101010	4.50	
	Desserts[2]	101013	4.50	
	Americana Cookery	101022	4.50	
	Total Order			

MAIL TO: FAVORITE RECIPES PRESS ●P.O. BOX 3396 ●MONTGOMERY, ALABAMA 36109

Order Form 40190

PLEASE SEND ME THE FOLLOWING BOOKS:

Name

Address

City   State   Zip

☐ Please Bill Me — Plus Postage and Handling

☐ Enclosed is payment for full amount. No charge for postage and handling.

[1]Price subject to approval of Price Committee.
[2]Limited supply.

Quan.	Cookbook Title	Item No.	Price [1]Each	Total
	New Casseroles	101027	4.50	
	Poultry	101026	4.50	
	Pies & Pastries	101023	4.50	
	Quick & Easy	101014	4.50	
	Money-Saving	101021	4.50	
	Holiday[2]	101019	4.50	
	Meats[2]	101010	4.50	
	Desserts[2]	101013	4.50	
	Americana Cookery	101022	4.50	
	Total Order			

MAIL TO: FAVORITE RECIPES PRESS ●P.O. BOX 3396 ●MONTGOMERY, ALABAMA 36109